THE JEWISH NEW YEAR FESTIVAL

THE JEWISH NEW YEAR FESTIVAL

ITS ORIGINS AND DEVELOPMENT

BY

NORMAN H. SNAITH, M.A.

*Tutor in Old Testament Languages and Literature
at Wesley College, Headingley, Leeds*

WIPF & STOCK · Eugene, Oregon

Wipf and Stock Publishers
199 W 8th Ave, Suite 3
Eugene, OR 97401

The Jewish New Year Festical
Its Origins and Development
By Snaith, Norman H.
Copyright©1947 SPCK
ISBN 13: 978-1-4982-9568-0
Publication date 8/11/2016
Previously published by SPCK, 1947

This Edition reprinted by Wipf and Stock Publishers
by arrangement with SPCK, London.

CONTENTS

	PAGE
PREFACE	vii

1. THE PRE-EXILIC NEW YEAR FEAST: A.—THE END OF THE YEAR - - - - - - - - - 9

   The harvest festival as a primitive institution—Early Hebrew harvest festivals—Passover is not a harvest festival—Passover is not a new year festival—Passover is a seasonal apotropaic festival—The three Hebrew harvest festivals—The importance of the autumnal feast—Was there ever a spring new year in Palestine?—Was there a double new year in Palestine?—Autumn was the time for the annual pilgrimage—The family feast at Bethlehem—Absalom's hair—Solomon's dedication feast—Jeroboam's dedication feast—Isaiah xxix, 1—Jeremiah xli, 4 ff.—Judges xi, 40 and xxi, 21—Conclusion.

2. THE PRE-EXILIC NEW YEAR FEAST: B.—THE BEGINNING OF THE YEAR - - - - - - - - 58

   The going-out of the year'—The anxiety for the rains—The eighth century with its growing difficulties—The change of fate—The autumnal feast and the coronation of the king.

3. THE EXILE AND THE CHANGE OF CALENDAR: A.—NEW-MONTH DAYS AND SABBATHS - - - - - - 81

   The beginnings of Jewish astronomy—(i) Canaanite month names—(ii) New-month day and the full moon—Water-pouring at the full moon—New Year's Day and the harvest moon—The Passover full moon—*Chodesh* means new-month day—The meaning of 1 Samuel xx, 27—The meaning of Psalm lxxxi, 4.—(iii) The origin of the Sabbath—Harranian sacred days—Mesopotamian rest-days—The Jewish Sabbath and its taboos—Rest-days in Assyria in the tenth century—The nineteenth day—The ninth day—The seven-day week depends on the sacred 'seven'—The Sabbath is independent of 'seven'—The *shabattu* is not a rest-day—The sacred 'seven'—The 'seven' and marriage—The Sabbath in old Israel—The Jewish Sabbath and the Mesopotamian *shabattu*—The Babylonian *shabattu* and the Hebrew *shabbathon*—'The morrow of the Sabbath'—The spelling of *shabbath*.

4. THE EXILE AND THE CHANGE OF CALENDAR: B.—NEW YEAR'S DAY - - - - - - - - 131

   Tishri 10 as New Year's Day—Equality of Tishri 1 and Nisan 1—New Year's Days for tithes.

CONTENTS

5. **TISHRI 1: THE DAY OF MEMORIAL** - - - - 150

    Tishri 1 among the Samaritans—The Bene Israel—The Jews of Cochin—The Jews of Kai-fung-fu—Josephus and Tishri 1—Philo and Tishri 1—The Talmud and the trumpet-blowing—Sa'adiyah and the trumpet-blowing—Maimonides and the trumpet-blowing—Tishri 1 as a day of penitence—Tishri 1 and the Readings from the Law—The proper psalms for Tishri 1—Trumpet-blowing and the delayed rains.

6. **THE BENEDICTIONS FOR NEW YEAR'S DAY** - - - 177

    The Malkiyyoth—The Zikronoth—The Shofaroth—Earliest references to the recitation of the Benedictions—The insertion of the Malkiyyoth.

7. **THE CORONATION PSALMS** - - - - - 195

    No connexion with the new year liturgy—They are Sabbath psalms—The Sabbath and the Kingdom of God.

8. **NEW YEAR FESTIVALS IN MESOPOTAMIA AND SYRIA** - - 204

    The three 'breaks' in Hebrew religious development—Mowinckel's theory of the Coronation Feast of Jehovah—Babylonian influence in Palestine—The myth-ritual pattern—Variations in Mesopotamia—The different strata of the Babylonian New Year Festival—Akitu and the New Year—The fixing of the fate—Astral Mesopotamian cults—The king in the cultus—Parallel rites—Conclusion.

PREFACE

This study has its origin in a twenty-year-old interest in Sigmund Mowinckel's theory of an annual new year Coronation Feast of Jehovah in Israel. The first outcome of this interest was a volume entitled *Studies in the Psalter* (1934) in which I endeavoured to show that the psalms which Mowinckel associated most closely with this supposed Coronation Feast were actually post-exilic, and in any case were Sabbath psalms. It is impossible, if my thesis is sound, that these psalms could ever have been the apparatus of a pre-exilic feast of the type which Mowinckel proposed.

In this volume, I have sought to set forth the origin of the association of the Kingdom of God with the Jewish New Year Festival (Rosh hashShanah). This association I find to begin in the early years of the Christian Era, during the troubles of the Roman wars. I have sought to show the new year ideas of pre-exilic Israel, and have traced the results of the change of calendar which the exile brought. This change of calendar involved a change in the beginning of the month as well as in the beginning of the year. Before the exile the new month began with the full moon and not with the new moon. This involves the theory that the pre-exilic Sabbath was a new moon festival and not a full moon festival as has been supposed. I have set forth my reasons for this view.

The last chapter contains a discussion of the relation between Babylonian rituals and Canaanite rituals, a discussion in which we are necessarily involved because of the prevalent theories of a myth-ritual pattern common to the whole of the Near East.

I desire to place on record my thanks to Mr. Eric Powell, of Woodhouse Grove School, for help in correcting the proofs.

NORMAN SNAITH.

1
THE PRE-EXILIC NEW YEAR FEAST

A.—The End of the Year

The Harvest Festival as a Primitive Institution

AT all times and in all places, almost without exception, men have celebrated, though with diverse traditions and rites, the ingathering of the increase of field and fold. This is a natural expression of man's reaction to the circumstances in which he finds himself. He has herded and shepherded, or he has sown and reaped and garnered, and then he has turned aside to thank and to praise his gods. Sometimes he has praised the High God whom he has believed to dwell in the sky, or to live on some distant, towering mountain peak. More generally in primitive societies, he has given thanks to the 'low gods', those nearer superhuman beings, over whom, because of their lowness and their nearness, he has believed himself to have some degree of influence and power. These sometimes have been the spirits of earth and river and rock and tree. Sometimes they have been the far-off ancestors of the clan and the tribe, or even the ghosts of the recently departed. Yet again, they have sometimes been vegetation gods of the type of the ancient Dionysus, *daimones* who have become regular gods, but have never quite, as Miss Jane Harrison put it,[1] been admitted to Olympus. But whatever the gods or the spirits or the ghosts which man has worshipped, he has unfailingly remembered them at the end of the year. At the time of harvest he has praised them and thanked them, and has shared with them the good things which they have given.

Such has been the general attitude of mankind all the world over, and ever since the world was young. The exceptions are very few indeed. Apart from the modern intellectual who has no need of such hypotheses, and apart from the modern man-in-the-street who eats and drinks and is as merry as his economic circumstances will allow, the exceptions are con-

[1] *Themis* (2nd ed., 1927), pp. xii, 260 ff.

fined to the very lowest stage of culture. They belong to tribes who have no harvest in any proper or even approximate sense of the word, and who can be said to worship their gods, only by extending the meanings of the words 'worship' and 'gods' to the widest and most comprehensive extent. Such an exception is to be found in the Arunta tribe of Central Australia, now almost extinct because chiefly of its impact with the whites. This tribe is the King Charles's Head of all students of primitive religion. It is impossible to discuss the beginnings of religion without referring to them. They are the one primitive stone age people of whose customs and ideas we have anything like full and adequate knowledge.

It is doubtful indeed whether anywhere in 'black Australia' there was a true harvest festival, not even in the more fertile south-east area where the Kurnai tribe once lived between the mountains and the sea. The early isolation of Australia from the rest of the world, if perchance there was ever any connexion apart from a sporadic interchange with Melanesia, seems to have resulted in all sorts of differences of development, not only in the flora and fauna, but also in mankind. In particular, the distinctive development of totemism throughout that continent seems to have largely prevented the development of harvest festivals even remotely comparable to those which we know to have existed elsewhere. Especially is this true of the Arunta tribe and its neighbours the Ilpirra, who have ideas concerning the relationship between a man and his totem which are " in a way quite unlike that which is usually associated with the idea of a totem ".[2] Whether this reason is fully adequate or not, the ceremonies which they observe in connexion with the promotion of an adequate food supply are characterized by a most sparing consumption of the totem animal, and in some cases by a total prohibition. These ceremonies, known as *Intichiuma* ceremonies, are performed according to strict tradition by the various totemic groups, and at traditional seasons of the year. They are not, however, by any means harvest ceremonies celebrated at the end of a harvest season, for there are no harvests among them in anything like the ordinary meaning of the term. These tribes neither

[2] B. Spencer and Gillen, *The Native Tribes of Central Australia* (London, 1899), p. 211.

till the soil, nor do they keep cattle. Indeed, they are ignorant even of any association between human copulation and the birth of children. Their hunting, such as it is, is 'the lower hunting'. The *Intichiuma* ceremonies are performed at the beginning of the season when the totemic food is just beginning to be found, whether it is the witchetty-grub or the sugar-manna of the mulga tree. There is, as a matter of fact, no food which is not totemic, and which is not thereby connected with its own totemic group in the tribe. The close connexion in time between the ceremonies and the general eating of the food by the community makes it tempting at first to imagine that the *Intichiuma* ceremonies are a strange and unusual type of harvest festival rites, but this is not the case. Even a cursory examination of the details of the rites shows that they are performed to promote the food supply and to ensure its safe consumption, but not by any means to celebrate its gathering. They are primarily the native equivalent to sowing and tilling. Inasmuch as there are details in the ceremonies which guard against the dangers of general consumption of what originally is taboo food, we have an approximation to first-fruits ceremonies,[3] but these are the only elements where there is any point of contact with harvest festival rites.

Still further, it is difficult to say to what extent these Central Australian aborigine tribes may be said to worship either their totem (bird, animal, insect, water, etc.) or their *Alchera* ancestors.[4] The term 'worship' has to be extended up to, and even beyond, its utmost limits and to be emasculated of any distinctive significance, in order to include within its scope the rites and the ideas which were prevalent amongst these tribes before they were so seriously decimated by their impact with the whites.[5]

[3] *The Distinctive Ideas of the Old Testament* (London, 1944), pp. 35 f.
[4] The *Alcheringa* is the mythical period of the first days of their semi-superhuman ancestors, who freely roamed across the desert spaces of the continent.
[5] "Of the local group of Udnirringita (witchetty-grub) people at Alice Springs, that numbered forty when we knew them in 1896, not a solitary man, woman, or child remains, and this is only one of many such groups, studied by us in the early days, upon whom the same fate has fallen" (Spencer and Gillen, *The Arunta* (London, 1927), vol. i, p. ix).

We must say, therefore, that wherever men have reached the stage of regular harvests (i.e. gathering the food in order to store, to whatever limited extent), wherever they have tilled the land or kept herds of domesticated beasts or even have 'the higher hunting', wherever, that is, either as food-gatherers or as hunters, they have passed beyond the stage to which the Arunta attained, they have celebrated the end of the year with ceremonies of thankfulness and with religious feasts.

Early Hebrew Harvest Festivals

There is abundant evidence that in respect of their harvest festivals the Hebrews, from the earliest times of which we have any information, were at one with the other peoples of the world. This is part of their common heritage with the sons of men. Even in those far-off and scarce-remembered days when, as nomads of the desert, they wandered in the Fertile Crescent, they brought to their God annually an offering from the increase of their flocks and herds. This fact is embodied in those traditions of the Creation which the Hebrews inherited from their nomad ancestors. These traditions have been preserved in Gen. ii, 4b–iv, 26, part of the J-tradition, and a section which is full from beginning to end of ancient desert lore.[6] Both Cain and Abel brought their gifts "at the end of the year" (Hebrew *miqqeç yamim*: the EVV. "in process of time" is wholly inadequate), Gen. iv, 3. Abel was a desert man, "a keeper of sheep", and his offering was necessarily "of the firstlings of his flock and of the fat thereof". Cain, on the other hand, before his expulsion from Eden to be a nomad ("a fugitive and a wanderer ... in the earth"), was an agriculturalist, "a tiller of the ground", and he brought the husbandman's gift "of the fruit of the ground". As we should expect in a desert tradition, the nomad's gift is represented as being more acceptable to God than that of the man of the settled lands. God, said the ancient story, loved the shepherd-herdsman and the flesh-offer-

---

[6] E.g. the origin of the tribal mark (iv, 15), and of the blood feud. Or, again, all the world was a desert, and God made an oasis in the midst of it, etc.

ing, and would not have anything to do with the husbandman and his offering of fruits and cereals.⁷

It is generally assumed that the two brothers brought their gifts together at the same period of the year, appearing with their respective gifts at one and the same time and place. Nothing definite as to this can properly be argued from the story itself. Indeed, such preciseness is not to be found in such an ancient tradition, and ought never to be demanded. It may be that Abel brought his gifts from the fold in the spring, but there is no certain guarantee of this. Cain's gift would presumably depend for the time of its presentation upon what exactly he brought. If he brought barley, his time of bringing it might be as early as April, but for other produce the occasion might be at any time onwards from the spring, through the summer and even into the autumn. The point is immaterial, except in so far as it indicates that there is no clear evidence to be found in the Eden story as to whether or not the two brothers appeared side by side, say at a shrine, standing there together, each with his gifts in his hand or beside him. The story refers in general terms to the general and, for that part of the world, universal custom of bringing first-fruits at the end of the year.

Passover is not a Harvest Festival

The suggestion that Cain and Abel may have brought their gifts at different times of the year falls far short of any statement that they must have done so. Such an assumption is implicit in all those theories of the origin of Passover which would connect it with tithes and firstlings. Wellhausen, for instance, connected Passover "with the firstlings of Abel the shepherd", and the other three feasts of Canaan "with the fruits presented by Cain the husbandman".⁸ Robertson Smith found a parallel between the Passover and the Arab offerings of the month Rajab, which Wellhausen held were

---

⁷ Cf. Gunkel, *Genesis* (Göttingen, 1901), S. 38. It is strange that the cereal offering (post-exilic *minchah*) remains subsidiary to the meat-offering down to the very end of the Temple sacrifices in 70 A.D. Perhaps it is significant as a stubborn relic of ancient origins.

⁸ *Prolegomena to the History of Israel* (Eng. tr., Edinburgh, 1885), p. 89.

firstlings, though Ewald made them tithes.[9] All this would make Passover something in the nature of a harvest festival, for the connexion between firstlings and harvest festivals is established firmly for the Old Testament by Exod. xxiii, 16 (E), "the feast of harvest, the first-fruits of thy labours". But none of it would necessarily fix Passover in the spring. Perhaps the reason why we have been so ready in time past in Western Europe to assume that Passover, being associated both with a lamb and also with the spring, is necessarily also to be connected with firstlings or tithes, is that with us the association of springtime and frisking lambs is so strong that we can scarcely think of the one without the other. The ancient rule is that the Passover lamb must be "of the first year" (Exod. xii, 5: P), and this was interpreted to mean between eight days old and one year old.[10] Whether the restriction " of the first year " is original with the Priestly Code or not, the regulation suggests that in the spring the lambs might be of any age up to one year. That is, so far as Palestine is concerned, lambs might be born at any time of the year. The connexion of the Passover with the spring is therefore not necessarily because of the firstlings, so that if Passover is really to be thought of as being originally a nomadic-pastoral festival, then we are probably very much nearer the truth in connecting it with the desert custom of sacrificing a lamb immediately before the shepherds move to their new pasturages of fresh green grass,[11] the Hebrew *deshe'*, which springs up fresh and sweet and green after the latter rain (the spring monsoon).

But all this depends upon the assumption that the Passover lamb was an offering to God of the same type as, presumably, Abel's offering of firstlings. This equation is unwarranted. There is nowhere any direct connexion between the Passover lamb or kid[12] and firstlings. What connexion there is, is through the first-born. It arises most directly from Exod. xii, 22-27 (J),

---

[9] *The Religion of the Semites* (Edinburgh, 1889), pp. 210 (note 2), 387. See also *ibid.*, p. 445 note), and Wellhausen, *op. cit.*, p. 87.

[10] Cf. Exod. xxii, 29; Lev. xxii, 27. Also Rashi on Exod. xii, 5, expressly says that the phrase *ben-shanah* includes the whole of the first year.

[11] E. G. Hirsch, art. 'Passover', *Jewish Encyclopædia*, vol. ix (1905), p. 553b.

[12] It could be from either the sheep or the goats (Exod. xii, 5: P).

with its sprinkling of the blood on the lintel and the side-posts in order to prevent the entrance of the destroyer, combined with the statement of the smiting of the first-born of Egypt (Exod. xii, 29 (J)). If, therefore, the connexion of the Passover with the Exodus is a later association, then the connexion of the Passover lamb with the first-born may very well also be a later association. If the association with the first-born goes, then certainly the association with firstlings and such-like goes with it.

Apart from Exod. xii, 27, 29 (J), the connexions are editorial, and belong to D and P. We find the charge concerning the sanctification of the first-born in Exod. xiii, 2, which is in the Priestly Code. In the following verses 3-10, the Exodus from Egypt is connected with the eating of unleavened bread for seven days. These verses are all Deuteronomic, except for the bare statements of verses 4 and 10, which belong to J. Yet again, in the section Exod. xiii, 11-13, we find the J-charge concerning the redemption of all the first-born, whether of beast or of man. According to D (verses 14 to 16), this is to be connected with the Exodus from Egypt and the slaying of the first-born of Egypt. On the other hand, the E-charge concerning the gift of the first-born is found in a general context of first-fruits (or tithes) of fruits and liquors, oxen and sheep (Exod. xxii, 29).

It will be seen, therefore, that there is nowhere the "clear connexion with the sacrifice of the first-born" which some scholars have seen. What association there is, is through the historical events of the Exodus. The first established association which we noticed was that between the Exodus and the eating of unleavened bread for seven days (Exod. xiii, 3-10).[13] All are agreed that the Feast of Unleavened Bread (Maççoth) was beyond question a Feast to which the Hebrews were introduced at their entrance to Canaan. The explanation, therefore, of verse 8 that the eating of unleavened bread for seven days was "because of that which the Lord did for me when I came forth out of Egypt" must be a later and didactic statement. It is reasonable to suggest that the next D-statement is also a later and didactic explanation, namely the association in verses 14-16 of the Passover with the Exodus and the slay-

---

[13] See the previous paragraph.

ing of the first-born of Egypt. Particularly, it is reasonable in view of the fact that the E-association of Exod. xxii, 29, is wholly devoid of any historical association whatever. We are all accustomed to the idea that the historical explanations of the Feasts of Unleavened Bread and Tabernacles are later didactic statements. This latter is clear from Neh. viii, 17, where the dwelling in booths is said to be an innovation. Whatever exactly this statement may mean, the association of the booths of the Feast of Tabernacles (Sukkoth) with the journeyings in the wilderness belongs to the Priestly Code (Lev. xxiii, 43).

There has always been a sharp distinction between the rites of Passover and all other 'sacrificial' rites of the Jews. The regular offerings were either meals shared with the Deity (e.g. the pre-exilic *zebach*) or wholly given to God, whether consumed wholly on the altar (e.g. all *'oloth*, early and late) or partly on the altar and partly by the Temple personnel, or wholly by the Temple personnel. But in the Passover ritual the regulations as to the disposal of the victim were markedly different. What was not eaten by the participants, and that away from the Temple and in the home,[14] had to be destroyed completely before the morning. Nothing went either to the altar or to the Temple personnel. In this matter of the eating of the Passover lamb, we have what is to us a final line of demarcation between the Passover and the firstlings, and therefore a harvest festival. Firstlings were not eaten by the offerers. Nothing is more certain than this. It was only after the first-fruits had been presented at the shrine that the fruit of the vineyard was free for human use. "All the fruit belongs to Jehovah. It is *qodesh*, and no man may eat any of it. This is acknowledged in the declaration made at the presentation of first-fruits (Deut. xxvi, 5-11)." This is so *a fortiori*[15] of fruit from any tree which is newly planted. According to Lev. xix, 23-25, the fruit may not be touched at all for three years. If the Passover lamb was a substitute for 'the first-born

---

[14] The Book of Jubilees (xlix, 16) required the victim to be eaten in the Temple Court, but they also required the victim to be slain 'before it was even' (verse 1). We judge, therefore, that both statements were in the nature of proposals, and that neither had any basis in actual deed.

[15] *The Distinctive Ideas of the Old Testament*, p. 35.

of man', then how did it ever come to pass that the Passover lamb should be eaten (1) by those who offered it, (2) by people who were not *qodesh*, i.e. holy to Jehovah, or (3) away from the Temple? All three features are completely contrary to the general practice in the matter of first-fruits. All other firstlings and first-fruits were eaten by the Temple personnel, who were holy (*qodesh*) to Jehovah, and they were eaten in the Holy Place. They were never by any chance eaten by anybody else or anywhere else. These are differences, it seems to us, which are decisive against the Passover lamb having any association whatever with either first-fruits or the first-born. Customs may change with the centuries, and often do change, but never in such a way as this. Such a change as this would disturb the whole fundamental *motif* of the rite. Such fundamental customs do not change. Rather they create difficulty by not changing with advancing ideas. What happens is that age-old customs persist, and new meanings are attached to them. This is doubtless what has actually happened to the original Passover rite. It has been connected at a later date with the historical events of the Exodus, and thence with the slaying of the first-born of Egypt. What does not happen is that an age-old custom changes over completely to its contrary, whilst the meaning remains the same. This is actually what is demanded by all those who hold that Passover has to do with the first-born and the firstlings. Things just do not happen that way.

In addition to these details, there were from earliest times many other elements which make the Passover ritual entirely distinct from the rest. Professor Hooke gives seven such details. They are (1) the ritually perfect victim held in readiness till the night of the full moon, (2) the eating of the victim accompanied with unleavened bread and bitter herbs, (3) the smearing of the blood of the victim on the door-posts and the lintel, (4) the prohibition against anyone leaving the house until the morning, (5) the fact that nothing must be left over, and every remaining vestige burned, (6) the clear connexion with the sacrifice of the first-born, and (7) the continued eating of unleavened bread for seven days.[16]

[16] *The Origin of Early Semitic Ritual*, Schweich Lectures 1935, p. 48.

Passover is not a New Year Festival

Professor Hooke holds that the Passover is "first of all a New Year Feast."[17] With this we disagree. It certainly is a spring festival, but that does not by any means make it a New Year Feast. His argument is as follows: It is a spring festival. The Babylonian *akitu* festival[18] is a spring festival. It lasted for eleven days in all. The preparations for Passover began on the 10th and lasted until the 21st. Therefore the Passover is a New Year Feast.

As against this argument, a festival which began on the 10th and lasted until the 21st is a twelve-day festival, and not an eleven-day festival. Actually there was a concluding festival on the twelfth day at Babylon, but this twelfth day is comparable to the extension of Passover to the twenty-second day. In any case, the old Nisan Festival of Babylon lasted for sixteen days, and it was only during the time of Nebuchadrezzar, who destroyed the Jerusalem Temple in the eighteenth year of his reign and then reigned for another twenty-five years (604-561 B.C.), that it was reduced to eleven days.[19] Further, in old Babylonia, there was apparently no necessity that the *akitu* festival, whether New Year or not, should be held in the spring. At Ur and Adab it was in Elul, the sixth month. Also, if Nisan was always the first month, then why was the seventh month called Teshrit? For the word *teshrit* is a derivative of the root *seru*, which means 'to begin'.[20]

We must not leave out of account, however, the various restrictions of Professor Hooke's list. They are important because they bring the Passover into the general mass of magical exorcist rites which appear to have maintained themselves in a substantially identical form everywhere from Mesopotamia to the Mediterranean, i.e. from the two great rivers, across the desert, and to the Western Sea. They also have affinities with ceremonies designed the world over to protect the individual

---

[17] *The Origin of Early Semitic Ritual*, Schweich Lectures 1935, p. 48.
[18] This is the great New Year Festival which was held in Babylon in the spring.
[19] S. Langdon, *Babylonian Menologies and the Semitic Calendars*, Schweich Lectures 1933, p. 51.
[20] *Ibid.*, p. 126; also p. 29.

from the baleful influence of spirits and against all mischances of the changes of the seasons. We emphasize this matter of the changes of the seasons because, amongst primitive peoples, not only were there rites connected with the dangers which beset the individual as he passed from one stage of life to another, but equally there were ceremonies connected with the changes of the seasons. The ceremonies which mark the changes in human life are all what van Gennep called *les rites de passage*.[21] It is a fact that ceremonies of the greatest importance in human life cluster round the events of birth, adolescence, marriage and death. These are all 'passages' from one life to another, and they are every one fraught with grave dangers from supernatural powers. But it is generally forgotten that there are also *rites de passage* in connexion with Nature herself. The changes of nature, i.e. the changes which mark the passing seasons of the year, are also fraught with danger. The important results of harvest, which make all the difference between life and death, depend upon the proper behaviour of the seasons. Care must therefore be taken that the seasons actually do follow each other in proper order. These precautions involve ceremonies connected with sowing, reaping, and, indeed, with all the many tasks of the husbandman. They involve all sorts of fertility rites, each belonging to its own season of the year. They are not necessarily connected with the end or with the beginning of the year, but only with the proper season. This is why the undoubted fact that Passover is a spring rite does not necessarily make it into a new year festival. It is undoubtedly often difficult to keep them wholly separate. The Tammuz rites, for instance, which belong to the height of the summer heat, and are associated with the departure of the greenness of things, can never be kept properly distinct from harvest celebrations, but they are nevertheless quite distinct from them, both in origin and in content. It is therefore far too great an assumption to make that all ceremonies for the prevention of evil from malign spirits must necessarily belong to the new year. Some of them do, but by no means all. They may belong to any of the great and obvious seasonal changes. In Mesopotamia, before the seventh century B.C., such restrictive rites belonged

[21] A. van Gennep, *Les Rites de Passage* (Paris, 1909).

in great fulness to the time of the darkness of the new moon.[22]

On the other hand, it is quite clear, as Professor Hooke has pointed out,[23] that there is no need to assume that Passover was originally a nomad festival, known to the Hebrews and not known to the Canaanites. The Babylonian evidence shows that Passover rites belonged to Canaan, equally as to the desert. The sacrifice of kids and lambs, accompanied by all sorts of taboos, is common enough everywhere, and is by no means confined to desert or shepherd peoples. Such customs are firm and strong amongst the urbanized peoples of Mesopotamia, and are firmly supported even by the earliest evidence which we have.

Equally there is abundant evidence that in Mesopotamia lunar influence over the calendar and over the religious ritual was paramount from early times. The lunar element, therefore, in the Passover rites is no guarantee of nomadic origin,[24] as against a Canaanite origin. Actually the restrictive observances of the new-moon days were not dropped in Mesopotamia until the time of Asshur-bani-pal in the seventh century (669-626 B.C.), when he reformed the calendar and abolished the special restrictions of the 1st, the 29th, and the 30th days of the month, all three of which are the days of the darkness of the new moon when the demons were supposed to have full scope for their malignant activity.[25] It is curious that in Mesopotamia there never seems to have been any particular emphasis on the full moon day,[26] but there is plenty of evidence that in Canaan in the earliest times the importance of both full moon and new moon was recognized.[27]

[22] The belief that the new moon affects the weather still persists, especially in country districts and amongst the weather-wise. See below, pp. 107 f.

[23] *Op. cit.*, p. 50 and note.

[24] Cf. S. H. Hooke, *ibid.*, p. 50.

[25] He abolished also the strict restrictions of the 9th day; see pp. 109 f. below.

[26] We do not regard the 15th day (*shabattu*) as being connected with the full moon, so much as being the concluding day of the first half of the month; see pp. 112 f. below.

[27] Cf. the pre-exilic observance of 'sabbath' and of 'new-month day'; see pp. 117 f. below.

Passover is a Seasonal Apotropaic Festival

All the restrictions which accompany the eating of the Passover lamb find ready parallels in the restrictions with which the new-moon days of Babylonia were bound, down to the time of Asshur-bani-pal, and in such ceremonies as the Athenian spring festival of Anthesteria. This festival lasted for three days. The doors of the houses were smeared with pitch, and the Athenians chewed buckthorn.[28] The Arab custom of sprinkling every tent with blood is a similar protective rite against the power of spirits;[29] that is, it is an apotropaic rite. Robertson Smith quotes the Arab historian Waçidi, that before they went forth to the battle of Bedr the Qoraish slaughtered camels and sprinkled every tent with the blood of a victim *whose life was still in it*. There is evidence of the custom of smearing the door-post or tent-pole with other substances that are or possess *mana* (the Moroccan word is *baraka*). "If anybody enters another person's house or tent carrying honey, he must, before it is taken out again, give a trifle of it to the people there to eat, or smear a little on the door-post or tent-pole, lest some evil should befall the household."[30] There is no need whatever to assume that the similarity of the Arab custom demands a nomadic origin for the Passover. Westermarck's illustration shows that the door-post or the tent-pole is the essential factor, and the Athenian rite at the Anthesteria shows that such emphasis is by no means confined to the desert. The custom and the essence of the rite therefore belong to Canaan just as much as to the desert, and we agree with Professor Hooke[31] that the Arab custom of sprinkling the tents is probably an adaptation to nomad conditions, and not the sprinkling on door-posts an adaptation from nomad conditions.

The precaution of not leaving the slightest trace of the victim, whether flesh, bone, entrails, blood or skin, belongs definitely to the sphere of the magical exorcism of evil

---

[28] Miss J. E. Harrison, *Themis* (1912 ed.), pp. 288-293.
[29] W. Robertson Smith, *The Religion of the Semites* (London, 1889), p. 326.
[30] E. Westermarck, *Ritual and Belief in Morocco* (London, 1926), vol. i, p. 222.
[31] *Op. cit.*, p. 50 (note).

spirits.³² The prohibition against leaving the house is paralleled by the restrictions which are regularly found for the taboo-days of the Mesopotamian menologies. They are found for the new-moon days of the earlier Mesopotamian calendars, e.g. for Nisan 29th and 30th, and also for other days to which for one reason or another taboos apply, e.g. Nisan 2nd, 4th, 6th (for the king), and 28th.³³ The belief in the power of demons at the beginning and end of the month is shown in the Syriac phrase for a 'lunatic'. It is *debar 'eggara*, lit. ' of a son of the house-top'. This is because of the custom of worshipping these demons on the flat roof of the house, especially at the times of the darkness of the moon, when they were believed to have greater power than normally. Ordinary demon possession is *dayawnutha* (from the Persian *dew* and the Zend *daewa*, ' an evil spirit '), but there is also the lunacy which was supposed to be due to the activity of evil spirits under the influence of the phases of the moon.

We would not, therefore, separate the Passover so decisively from the other festivals as to say that it was non-Canaanite as against the others being Canaanite. The fact that Passover was always different from the others in that it was, as it still is, a family and home festival, whilst the others were pilgrimage festivals, does not make it non-Canaanite, even though it may well have been the only festival which the Hebrews knew before they entered Canaan. Probably all of them, Canaanites in Canaan and Hebrews both in and out of Canaan, brought their firstlings, and so had a pilgrimage ceremony distinct from the piacular and apotropaic Passover. Passover was necessarily observed indoors because of its apotropaic nature, just as the other festivals were necessarily observed at the shrine because of their nature. Anything to do with first-fruits, firstlings, or harvest festivals, is bound to involve a pilgrimage. This applies even to the offerings of Cain and Abel, and is a final reason why it is wrong to attempt to link the Passover with the gifts of Abel the husbandman.

Nevertheless, whilst we agree with Professor Hooke that the Hebrew festival of Passover is not exclusively of desert origin, we cannot agree with him in the close connexion he

---

³² Cf. S. H. Hooke, *ibid.*, pp. 49 ff.
³³ S. Langdon, *ibid.*, pp. 74 ff., 81 ff.

maintains between Passover and *Maççoth* (Unleavened Bread). Here we apply the test of the fundamental difference between the two sets of ceremonies. The Passover is an apotropaic festival, and is therefore a home and indoor rite. *Maççoth* is a harvest festival, and is therefore a pilgrimage rite. Passover, with its apotropaic rites, is essentially a spring festival. *Maççoth*, being the barley harvest festival, was conditioned by the seasons of Palestine, which brought the barley to ripeness some seven weeks before the wheat was ripe. The climate of Palestine brought the two together on to the same full moon. In view of the fundamental difference between the two sets of ceremonies, we do not accept the eating of unleavened bread on Passover night as being original to the ceremony equally with the eating of bitter herbs. Indeed, strictly speaking, the Hebrew does not say that they ate the Passover lamb with unleavened bread and bitter herbs. The passage actually reads: "and they shall eat the flesh in that night; roast with fire, and unleavened bread; with bitter herbs shall they eat it" (Exod. xii, 8). Here, though the accentuation of the Masoretes is strange, it is clear that the unleavened cakes go with the roast victim, and not with the bitter herbs. It is very tempting to suppose, from the way in which the Hebrew sentence is built up, that there was an original instruction in which the unleavened cakes were not mentioned at all. The unleavened cakes belong to *Maççoth*, just as certainly as the bitter herbs belong to Passover. Similarly, we would object to the seventh of Professor Hooke's detailed characteristics of the Passover, namely "the continued eating of unleavened bread for seven days". We do not accept this as having originally anything to do with Passover, and far from being the continuation of the Passover rites, the unleavened bread is an intrusion into the ritual of the Passover night. It is all due to the incidence of two separate rites because of the climate of Canaan.

The Three Hebrew Harvest Festivals

Passover, we have seen, was neither a pilgrimage feast nor a harvest festival. The other three festivals were both. They were pilgrimages because they were harvest festivals, just as Passover was not a pilgrimage because it was not a harvest festival. They were pilgrimages in that the custom was to go up every year to make the offering to God, to worship, and to eat the sacred meal at the local shrine. It was according to this age-old custom of his fathers that Elkanah went up to Shiloh every year, and in particular on the occasion when Hannah prayed for a man child (1 Sam. i, 3). These three pilgrimages were comparable to the Islamic pilgrimage to Mecca, and indeed the same word is used in each case, *chag(g)*, both in Hebrew and in Arabic. *Maççoth* (Unleavened Bread) was the barley harvest festival, *Qaçir* (Harvest) was the wheat harvest festival, and *'Asiph* (Ingathering) was the vintage. This latter was the great Harvest Festival, always *the* Feast, that which marked the end of one agricultural year and inaugurated its successor. The Hebrews adopted all three when they entered Palestine, though in due course they found new reasons for observing them, just as they also did, or perhaps had already done, for the observation of the Passover rites. They associated all the three agricultural festivals of Canaan and also the apotropaic Passover with the great acts of deliverance of the time of the Exodus and the Wanderings in the Wilderness. Perhaps, already before the Hebrews had entered Canaan, the Passover rites there had tended to coalesce with those of the barley harvest festival, since both were associated with the full moon, and both naturally belonged to the same full moon in Canaan. But the tendency towards identification was mostly due to the centralization policy of the later (?) Deuteronomists. The passage of Scripture which most binds together the two sets of ceremonies is Exod. xiii, 3-10, of which verses 4 and 10 are J, but the remainder is D, and probably not the earliest stratum of D. Similarly, whereas verses 11-13 are allocated to J, yet with verse 14 and its association with the Egyptian deliverance we are once more in a later stratum of D.

The centralization and the reinterpretation of all the festival rites, whether of the harvest festivals or of the Passover, tend to belong to the Deuteronomic period generally. This centralization, with the eating of the Passover lamb at Jerusalem, is perhaps what is meant in 2 Kings xxiii, 22, when it is stated that Josiah's celebration of the Passover was unique, there never having been anything like it before, neither in the time of the judges, nor in all the times of the kings. Nevertheless, the Passover still remained largely independent of the Temple, even though it was observed in Jerusalem. The fact of its independence of any shrine needs to be remembered in all discussions of the existence of sacrifice during the desert period of Hebrew history, and in all discussions of the meaning of such a phrase as " our passover also hath been sacrificed, even Christ " (1 Cor. v, 7). The discussion as to " whether Passover was a sacrifice " is not by any means " an antiquated question which belongs to dead controversies as between Protestants and Roman Catholics ". Whatever sacrificial elements may be found in the Christian Eucharist, or may be sought for in the Lord's Supper, do not come from the Jewish Paschal 'sacrifice'. This much seems to become more and more clear from a closer examination of the origins and significant features of the ancient rites.[34]

The Importance of the Autumnal Feast

We are, in these present studies, chiefly, indeed almost exclusively, concerned with the great vintage feast at the end of the year. Even though, according to the post-exilic calendar, Passover was held in the first month of the year, there was never any suggestion that it was a new year festival. Nor was it the most important feast. In pre-exilic times the autumnal vintage feast was by far the most important of all the religious festivals. This was partly because, being the vintage feast, it gave, in the nature of the case, most occasion for merrymaking, but also partly because it marked the end of one year and the beginning of the next. This vintage festival is that which was known as "*the* feast (*hachag*)". " Then gathered together to king Solomon every man of Israel in the month Ethanim *in the feast* (that is, says P, in the seventh month)" (1 Kings viii, 2). Or, again, it is stated that Jeroboam son of Nebat made a feast in the eighth month " like the feast which is in Judah " (1 Kings xii, 32). The custom of referring to the autumnal vintage feast as 'the feast' is carried right down into the New Testament, e.g. "Now the feast of the Jews, the

[34] For discussions as to the significance of Passover, its victim, its ritual, and its relation to the New Testament, see G. B. Gray, *Sacrifice in the Old Testament* (Oxford, 1925), pp. 337-397.

feast of tabernacles, was at hand" (John vii, 2). Other feasts are referred to as 'the feast of passover' or 'the feast of dedication', but 'the feast', without qualification other than the definite article, is always the Feast of Tabernacles, the great autumnal feast of the Jews. This was the feast *par excellence*.

There was a time, in the closing years of the Second Temple, in the days immediately prior to its destruction by the Romans in 70 A.D., when the Passover became outstanding in popularity. This increased popularity is reflected in the fact that the Passover is mentioned much more often in the Gospels than any other feast of the Jews. According to Josephus, whose figures, however, are not always wholly to be trusted when he is writing of the Jewish greatness of past days, the number of those who went up to Jerusalem for the Passover during the three years prior to the outbreak of the Jewish War amounted each year to over two and a half millions.[35] He gives the figure for the year 64 A.D. as being three millions.[36] This increased importance was doubtless due to the growing unrest of the Jews under the none too considerate rule of the later Roman procurators, i.e. from Valerius Gratus (15-26 A.D.) onwards, combined with an expectation that Messiah would appear at Passover. This tradition is seen in the Septuagint of Jer. xxxi, 8 (LXX: xxxviii, 8), where it is written: "Behold I will bring them from the north country, and gather them from the end of the earth *in the feast of passover*",[37] and so also for the Old Latin Version. Also, the sense of immediacy was increased by the remembrance of Mal. iii, 1: "the Lord, whom ye seek, shall suddenly come to his temple; even the messenger of the covenant, whom ye delight in, behold, he cometh, saith the Lord of Hosts". Further, it so chanced that Ps. ii, a psalm full to overflowing of Messianic ideas of the most turbulent type, was sung on the second Sabbath of Nisan, which was, as of course it still is, the Sabbath immediately preceding Passover.[38] Which was cause

---

[35] *Bell. Iud.* VI, ix, 3. [36] *Ibid.*, II, xiv, 3.
[37] Reading *bemo'ed pesach* for *bam 'iwwer uphisseach*.
[38] There is no direct evidence of this. Actual evidence of the way in which individual psalms were used by the Jews in pre-Christian times is singularly lacking, except for the psalms which were used on special occasions, and for those which, according to the Mishnah, were used for the days of the week. It is highly probable, however, that the

and which was effect it is hard to say, but it is easy to understand the intense excitement and the sense of imminent expectation which characterized the Jerusalem Passovers at the beginning of the Christian era. Especially is it easy to appreciate the ready way in which Zech. ix, 9, sprang to the lips of every Jew when, on that day of all days, he saw the Lord Jesus entering Jerusalem " lowly and riding upon an ass, even upon a colt the foal of an ass ". Certainly the Romans, who were wise in their generation, always took special precautions against the sudden outbreak of a revolt at the time of Passover. The procurator took up his residence for that period in Jerusalem instead of, as usual, remaining at Cæsarea.[39] The chief priests and the elders of the people knew very well the risks of a tumult concerning the Messiah at Passover (Matt. xxvi, 5). The absolute readiness of the Roman garrison to quell even the first elements of any disturbance at a feast is shown by the speed with which, fortunately for Paul, the chief captain, hearing of the scuffle in the Court of the Gentiles, " took soldiers and centurions, and ran down with them " to arrest Paul, who seemed to be the centre of the commotion (Acts xxi, 33). This particular feast was that of Pentecost (Acts xx, 16); but the incident shows the extreme vigilance of the Romans on every occasion when there were many Jews gathered together in the Temple Courts. All these difficulties and dangers need to be taken into account in assessing the conduct of Pontius Pilate in the extraordinarily difficult situation in which the Jewish authorities had taken care to place him. His conduct cannot be excused, but it can very easily be understood.

Psalter was once recited in Palestine according to a triennial cycle, comparable to the known ancient Palestinian cycle for the Reading of the Law, with the corresponding Readings from the Prophets (Haphtaroth). See A. Büchler, *Jewish Quarterly Review*, old series, vol. v, pp. 420 ff.; vol. vi, pp. 1 ff. If this is so, then, whatever the allocation of subsequent psalms may have been, the second psalm must have belonged to the Sabbath next before Passover, or immediately at the very opening of the Passover itself, since the 14th is obviously the latest possible date for the second Sabbath. This fact is significant in view of Our Lord's Entry into Jerusalem on the day following the Sabbath before Passover. For the relevant literature, see E. G. King, *JTS*, v, 203 ff.; J. Jacobs, *JE*, xii, 253 ff.; St. John Thackeray, *JTS*, xvi, 177 ff.; N. H. Snaith, *ZATW*, x, 302 ff.; L. Rabinowitz, *JQR*, xxvi, 349 ff.

[39] Josephus, *Ant. Iud.* XVII, ix, 3; XX, v, 3.

And yet, in spite of all the emphasis which Josephus makes on the tremendous crowds which gathered at Jerusalem for the Passover during those last days, he still insists that the autumn feast was " by far the greatest and holiest feast ".[40]

Was there ever a Spring New Year in Palestine?

The end of the year for the Hebrews in the days before the settlement in Canaan may possibly have been in the spring. In those days, that is, in the time of the patriarchs, they were essentially shepherds and keepers of cattle (Gen. xlvi, 32-34), though Joseph advised his brethren to emphasize the cattle and to omit all reference to sheep when they spoke to the Pharaoh. Evidently the Pharaoh of that period was allergic to the mention of shepherds. Perhaps succeeding Pharaohs disliked the memory of the Hyksos shepherd kings, though apparently the lapse of Gen. xlvii, 3, when, in spite of Joseph's warning, the brethren spoke the horrid truth, was not attended by the dreadful consequences which Joseph had feared. Apart from the bare[41] possibility of a spring new year because of the pastoral pursuits of the patriarchs, there is no evidence of a spring new year in Palestine in pre-exilic times. If the Hebrews did indeed keep a spring new year in the desert, either in the period between Egypt and Canaan or in the earlier days of the patriarchs, then, as has often happened, the customs of the land survived against the customs of the conquerors and the Palestinian autumnal new year survived. The necessities of the agricultural life would ensure this. William of Normandy may win at Senlac, but Harold the Saxon will always win everywhere else.

Gütesman argues[42] for the existence of a spring new year before the Exile on the basis that the Jews of Elephantine apparently had a new year in the month Nisan, the first month of the post-exilic calendar, the month of the Passover full moon. These colonists had undoubtedly been in Egypt for some considerable time prior to the conquest of Egypt by Cambyses in the year 525 B.C. One of the letters which have been

[40] *Ant. Iud.* VIII, iv, 1.
[41] The possibility is indeed remote, as we have seen (p. 18 above), for it depends largely upon the false identification of Passover as a nomadic harvest festival.
[42] *Revue des Études Juives*, Tome 53 (1907), p. 195.

found says that "when Cambyses came into Egypt he found the temple built". The temple to which reference is made is that which the colonists had built in their island fortress of Yeb, close by Assouan. The letter is dated 408 B.C., and the date is important for more reasons than one. From our present point of view it is important because it is so very post-exilic. These Jews may have entered Egypt as early as with the armies of Asshur-bani-pal in 667 B.C., and their original home may well have been Samaria,[43] but whatever the date of their settlement on this island in the Nile of Upper Egypt, the papyri on which solely we depend for our knowledge of them are all dated between 494 and 400 B.C. All, therefore, that such evidence involves, so far as the calendar is concerned, is that these Jews had in the fifth century B.C. adopted the Babylonian calendar with its spring new year. No one would argue to the contrary so far as Jews were concerned who lived in areas under Babylonian influence. Even if it should be argued that these Jews had not been subject to Mesopotamian influence from the time of the Babylonian invasion of Egypt, their subjection to Assyria from at least 722 B.C. would ensure their use of the Nisan new year. We know that the Nippurian names for the months of the year, of which Nisan is the first month, came into common use throughout Assyria in about the twelfth century. Further, in the Assyrian tenth-eleventh century copies of Cassite calendars the names of all the months are written after the Nippurian style.[44]

There is some late evidence for the full adoption of a new year in the spring, to the complete exclusion of the autumn new year in the customs of the Karaites. The Karaites are a Jewish sect, which amounted, before the present troublous times, to about twelve thousand souls, mostly in Southern Russia. Their origin is to be traced back to a certain Anan, a vigorous reformer who died towards the end of the eighth century A.D. The name itself means 'Followers (Readers) of the Bible', a name which the followers of Anan adopted when, in the next two or three generations, they emancipated themselves somewhat from the most severe of the restrictions of

[43] Oesterley and Robinson, *A History of Israel* (Oxford, 1932), vol. ii, pp. 159 ff.; A. E. Cowley, *Aramaic Papyri of the Fifth Century B.C.* (Oxford, 1923), p. xvi.
[44] S. Langdon, *ibid.*, p. 42.

Anan's own teaching. Ananism itself disappeared during the tenth century, but Karaism still survives with its traditional customs and interpretations, allegedly based strictly on the actual Bible text, though differing in many respects from orthodox Jewish beliefs and customs. The reason why their new year customs are mentioned here is that they allege that they follow the strict letter of Scripture and are truer to ancient custom than are the orthodox Jews. So far as we are here concerned with the Karaite calendar rules,[45] they consider the beginning of the year in all respects to be Nisan 1, and to them Tishri 1 (autumn) is a day of contrition and not a day of trumpet-blowing. This is a curious deviation from the clear statement of Scripture (Lev. xxiii, 23), but their omission of the trumpet-blowing may have something to do with the particular regard which Rabbi Sa'adiyah paid to this matter. What Ezra was to the Samaritans, Rabbi Sa'adiyah was to the Karaites. He was their great antagonist in the tenth century A.D., and his considered reasons for the blowing of trumpets on Tishri 1 are embodied in Jewish Prayer-books to this day.[46] Apart from such a divergence, apparently deliberate, as this, the whole of their divergences from the orthodox traditions can be explained, either on the ground that they are reverting to Scriptural authority against the (to them) unauthorized additions of the Palestinian and Babylonian Rabbis as shown in the Talmuds, or on the ground that where there is no direct word of Scripture on the matter, they are differing from the orthodox as a matter of principle. Even in the matter of Tishri 1, there is, as we shall see later,[47] a very great deal of evidence that in the matter of contrition they are very much nearer to the ancient traditions than are the orthodox Jews. They are anti-Talmudic with a thoroughness that on occasion involves them in a departure from the word of Scripture.

Their anti-Talmudic attitude is to be seen in more than one matter. For instance, the Karaites agree with the Samaritans in observing the Feast of Weeks (*Shabu'oth*) on the day after the Sabbath.[48] This is not, however, evidence that they are

---

[45] For a further discussion of their calendar, see pp. 139 f.
[46] See pp. 160 f. below.   [47] See pp. 165 f. below.
[48] See further on this point, pp. 125 f. below.

agreeing with the Samaritans in following any pre-Ezraite custom, since the Sadducees also held this view. The Karaites actually are following the Sadducees in their interpretation of Lev. xxiii, 16, as against their rivals the Pharisees. It is an anti-Talmudic attitude.

Another instance of the survival of an ancient calendar custom among the Karaites is their custom of intercalating the extra month of the leap year before the twelfth month Adar instead of after it, as the orthodox Jewish custom has always done. It is true that this was the custom of the far-away Sumerians as early as about 3000 B.C. The Sumerians inserted a month, when necessary, before the twelfth month *shegurkud* (barley harvest) in order to keep both the month-name and the harvest in the proper places. The argument that the Karaites were following an ancient pre-Ezraite tradition could never stand. If they were following any ancient custom, then it was a very old Mesopotamian custom, and not a Jewish custom at all. Although the Babylonians adopted the custom of inserting the intercalary month after Adar, the twelfth month, yet the older system persisted in the provincial areas until the whole civilization was finally broken up by the Parthians about the beginning of the Christian Era. It is possible that the Karaites were influenced by some strange survival, since the area of the controversy with Rabbi Sa'adiyah was in part also the area with which the Karaites in their earlier period had most to do.[49] It is more probable that the similarity is a coincidence, and has nothing to do with anything that transpired in orthodox circles except by way of general contrariness to the established state of affairs. The general attitude of opposition on the part of the Karaites, sometimes amounting even to opposition for opposition's sake, was carried so far that there was a tendency in Karaite circles in Babylonia and in other places far distant from Palestine to depart even from the 'orthodox' Karaite custom of fixing the calendar by noticing the state of the growing crops. This is stated, and this reason is given, in the 'Book of Precepts' attributed to Levi ha-Levi, son of Yefet ben Ali (*c.* 1007 A.D.),

[49] For details of the Karaites, see *Jewish Encyclopædia*, vol. vii, pp. 438-447. For Sumerian intercalations, see S. Langdon, *Babylonian Menologies*, etc., p. 10.

quoted by Jacob Mann.[50] Any Karaite evidence, therefore, as to the spring new year is not evidence of any ancient Palestinian or other custom, but only of the determined opposition of the Karaites to orthodoxy, and in particular to the Talmud.

Was there a Double New Year in Palestine?

L. I. Pap has held[51] that there was a double new year in old Israel, one in the autumn and the other in the spring. He bases his argument in part on the passage "the return (*teshubah*) of the year when kings go forth (i.e. campaigning in war)",[52] 2 Sam. xi, 1, of the war of David against the sons of Ammon, and 1 Kings xx, 22, 26, of the long-continued wars between Ahab of Israel and Ben-hadad of Syria-Damascus. The same argument is used by Epstein.[53]

The weakness of this argument is similar to the weakness of the argument that Passover is originally a festival of first-fruits. In the case of the Passover, the argument depends upon the supposition that lambs were born in the spring, a supposition which is due to the customs of Western Europe and cannot be assumed for a Near East background. Here again in the assumption of spring campaigns we have the same type of error. It arises from the custom, familiar from our first acquaintance with Latin prose, of going into winter quarters, and then of renewing the war with a spring campaign when the winter snows have gone. We remember how Cæsar left his winter quarters very early in the year 52 B.C., whilst the snow still lay deep on the hills of Gaul, and surprised the insurgent Gauls by the earliness and the rapidity of his movements.[54] We remember, too, the spring campaigns of the two great wars of the twentieth century. The assumption is then made that the petty kings of Palestine and of the Near East also went out to war in the spring. Therefore, the argument runs, the phrase *teshubath hashShanah* (the return, turning

---

[50] *JQR* (new series), vol. xii, pp. 270 f.
[51] *Das Israelitische Neujahrsfest* (Kampen, 1933), pp. 18-32.
[52] The root *yaça'* is the technical term for going out to battle, and is used of a hero and champion going forth to do mighty deeds (Isa. xlii, 13). See further p. 59 below.
[53] *The Origin of the Jews* (in Hebrew), p. 8; quoted by Morgenstern (see below).
[54] *De bello gall.* vii, 8.

back of the year) refers to the spring, and consequently the new year was in the spring.

But the time when these petty kings went forth to war was not the spring. It was the summer, and the late summer rather than the early summer. The time when the corn was being threshed (Judg. vi, 4, 11) was the time when the raiding Bedawi gathered themselves together, and came up " as locusts for multitude ". It was the time, after the sowing (verse 3), when they could destroy the increase of the earth (verse 4). It was when produce could be left lying in a yard over the top of a well so as to cover the top of the well, and, in so doing, excite no comment (2 Sam. xvii, 19), that ambitious princelings set out to win their fortunes and a crown. According to 1 Sam. xxiii, 1, the message which was brought to David read: " Behold the Philistines are fighting against Keilah, and they rob the threshing floors." All this makes the campaigns begin certainly no earlier than June, which was the normal time for threshing.

No war could possibly begin before the harvest was complete. It was necessary for the harvest of that year to be secure before the militia (Heb. *çaba'*, lit. ' the host ') could be called up. This ensured the food supply for the next year, both for those left at home and for those away on active service. It was, indeed, only after the harvest had been gathered and stored in reasonable security that the semi-disciplined peasant, always strong for his own rights, would be prepared to answer the call-up and join ' the host '. The work on the land had then come to a temporary standstill. Or, viewing the matter from the other point of view, it was wise for the attacker, especially if he came up from the wilderness, to attack the settled lands when the food was ripened and ready for the eating. This would be in the fulness of summer, or even in the early autumn. If they longed for the wine, as well as for the corn and the oil, it would certainly be towards the end of the summer. It would be in the highest degree unlikely for hostilities to break out in the spring. At that time not even the barley had been gathered, and the wheat was far from ripe in the ear. In addition, the needs of the winter would have eaten into supplies which could never have been very plentiful in those lands which bordered the eastern desert. There was never any wheat crop to carry over past the next harvest. Even Joseph had very soon to draw upon his reserves in fertile Egypt. The limited food supply of Canaan is sufficiently indicated by the anxiety portrayed throughout the Old Testament as to the regularity and adequacy of the two monsoon rains, the former (autumn) and the latter (spring) rain.[55] It was after the harvest that the Midianites attacked Canaan in the days of Gideon. In fact, it was the time of heavy dews (Judg. vi, 37-40), and therefore not very early in the summer. Equally it was the time of harvest when the Hebrews themselves under Joshua entered the Promised Land for Jordan was then in flood (Josh. iv, 18), and " Jordan overfloweth his banks all the time of harvest" (Josh. iii, 15). Modern times confirm the wisdom of the ancients in these matters. The outbreak of the two greatest wars of history has in each case been delayed until the harvests of that year were secure.

We thus see that the phrase *teshubath hashShanah* cannot be maintained to mean the spring, on the ground that the spring was the time when these kings went forth to war. If the phrase is to be interpreted as denoting any particular time of the year, then it cannot be earlier than the summer, and is probably late rather than early summer. Absalom's hair was very long when he revolted against his father David, and the autumn was the time for the fulfilment of vows.

Morgenstern argues[56] that the phrase *teshubath hashShanah* (the return of the year) need mean no more than an equinox, and so can refer either to the spring equinox or to the autumnal equinox. In this particular instance, he maintains, it refers to the spring equinox. He takes the word *teshubah* to be the equivalent of the word *tequphah* (coming round, circuit), and so to mean 'equinox', thus giving the word the meaning which it sometimes has in Rabbinic Hebrew. Morgenstern, both in the first volume and also in the third volume of the series of the *Hebrew Union College Annuals*, is arguing for a triple calendar in old Israel.

We do not agree that it can be argued on the basis of the

---

[55] If there was indeed a spring new year in Palestine, then why, in the oldest sources, is the former rain the October rains and the latter rain the March-April rains?

[56] *Hebrew Union College Annual*, I, pp. 16-19.

late and Rabbinic use of the word *tequphah* that the phrase *teshubath hashShanah* refers to the spring equinox, especially when that phrase is used in the Books of Samuel and Kings, and when the Chronicler is so uncertain about the meaning of the term that he has to insert "at the time of" (1 Chron. xx, 1): adding *le'eth*. The most that the phrase can mean is 'the return (turning back) of the year'. Even if it can be shown that the reference is to an equinox, then it must be decided on other grounds which of the two equinoxes is intended. The identification with the word *tequphah* is precarious at best, and in any case we are not warranted in reading back into pre-exilic times anything of the preciseness which was attached to the word in Rabbinic Hebrew, particularly when our Rabbinic sources are Babylonian rather than Palestinian.[57] Apart from the fact of there being an interval of considerably more than a thousand years between the two periods there was, as we shall see below,[58] a preciseness in matters astronomical among the Babylonian rabbis which was wholly absent from their Palestinian contemporaries. This interest and accuracy on the part of the Babylonian rabbis was due to the general interest in such matters on the part of the astronomers of Babylonia. They were the founders of this science, and were regular and systematic observers of the planets and the other heavenly bodies from a very early date. According to Diodorus Siculus, their observations extended over 470,000 years, whilst Pliny fixed the figure at 720,000 years. It used to be thought at one time that the Egyptians were the great astronomers of the ancient world, or the Chinese, but we know now that such interests were originally Mesopotamian, that the origin of the science, empirical and non-theoretical as it was, was in Mesopotamia, and that the knowledge of these matters spread east and west from there.[59]

In the Rabbinic contexts, which are in the Babylonian Talmud, the word *tequphah* is used of the turn of the sun. It can be used quite generally of the calculation of astronomical cycles (*b. Sabb.* 75a), but in its more restricted use it can refer either to the equinoxes or to the solstices. For instance, *tequ-*

---

[57] See pp. 81 f.   [58] See pp. 81 f.
[59] Sir E. A. Wallis Budge, *Babylonian Life and History* (London, 2nd ed., 1925), pp. 210-212.

phath Nisan refers to the turning of the sun in the month Nisan, i.e. the vernal equinox. Similarly the phrase *tequphath Tishri* refers to the autumnal equinox, whilst *tequphath Tammuz* and *tequphath Tebeth* are the summer and the winter solstices. So far, therefore, as the word *tequphah* is concerned, the phrase 'the turn of the year' might refer to any of the four critical points of the apparent journey of the sun through the heavens. The summer solstice is as good as the vernal equinox, and indeed much better, for starting a war which is likely to last only for a short campaign. But even all this depends upon the equation of *teshubah* and *tequphah*, an identification which we hold to be wholly illegitimate.

The time, therefore, when the kings of the Near East, i.e. of Palestine and the neighbouring states (since it is of these small wars that the phrase in question is used), went forth to war was not earlier than the summer. Since it was, as we have seen from the story of Gideon and the fleeces, the time of heavy dew, and since it was the time when Absalom's hair was reaching its maximum length, we may suppose that the time was later rather than earlier in the heat of the summer. All this points steadily towards the autumn rather than to the spring as the time of the 'return of the year'.

On the main issue, it has to be pointed out that L. I. Pap does not date his sources. This is a frequent characteristic of the work of those who advocate a new year feast in old Israel, and also a variant of it in post-exilic Israel, after the pattern of the new year festivals of Babylonia. Mowinckel himself, who has been foremost in his advocacy of such a theory,[60] made no attempt to fix the date of his 'Coronation Psalms', xciii, xcv-xcix, xlvii, with diverse others, but assumed without discussion that they could be used for any period of Israelite-Judahite history. In the case, for instance, of Ps. xcviii, 3b, it is plain from the Hebrew that we have a transcription from Isa. lii, 10; and there are many other indications of dependence upon Isa. xl-lv. The procedure of

[60] Sigmund Mowinckel, *Psalmenstudien II, Das Thronbesteigungsfest Jahwäs und der Ursprung der Eschatologie* (Kristiania, 1922). See my *Studies in the Psalter* (London, 1934), pp. 62-69, 91-94; and the comments by Prof. N. W. Porteous, *The Kingship of God in Pre-exilic Hebrew Religion*, Lectio No. 3 (London, Shapiro, Vallentine and Co., 1938), pp. 1 f.

attempting to date the evidence is always advisable, difficult as this often is in respect particularly of the psalms. But in a case like that of Mowinckel and the Coronation Psalms, or in the similar case of L. I. Pap and his double new year theory, such an attempt at dating is essential. In a case where, as here, there is even the barest possibility of a change of calendar, and particularly where, as here, the whole point at issue is the very calendar itself, any neglect of this preliminary precaution is fraught with peril. Everything depends upon it here, since we do certainly know from such explanatory notes as "this is the seventh month" (1 Kings viii, 2) that there must have been some sort of an alteration in the calendar in post-exilic times. This change comes between the times of the events and the date of our record of them.

Further, L. I. Pap rests his conclusions chiefly on the synchronization of the years of Judahite and Babylonian kings during the last days of the Kingdom of Judah. This is most treacherous ground, since his sources, as they are now extant, and especially in so far as the synchronization is concerned, must belong to the actual time of calendar change and confusion, and this at their very earliest dating.

Yet again, the discrepancies of the Hebrew Masoretic Text, the Septuagint, and Lucian's translation, in these matters of chronology, in their texts of the Books of Kings (Kingdoms), both each chronology within itself, and each with the other two, do not create any measure of confidence in any of the figures given in any of the three versions. It may be possible to choose out of all the medley of conflicting dates such figures as would establish any reasonably conceived hypothesis, but it is unsafe to the highest degree to use any one set of figures as the main basis of any theory of chronology. The general effect of such an argument is comparable to that produced by the long discussion in the first pages of the tract *Rosh hashShanah* of the Babylonian Talmud, on the statement of the Mishnah *Rosh hashShanah I*, 1a, that "on the first of Nisan is the new year for kings and for feasts". The effect of that discussion is a full acknowledgment of the skill of the rabbis, but a realization of the fact that if it were frankly acknowledged that there had been a change of calendar, then there would have been no need of the discussion. The fact that in the evidence which

38   THE JEWISH NEW YEAR FESTIVAL

Pap adduces we are no longer troubled with the complications of the relative lengths of the reigns of the kings of Israel and of Judah does not reduce the difficulties to any marked extent. The difficulties and the discrepancies are still there.

Autumn was the Time for the Annual Pilgrimage

Whatever may have been the state of affairs with respect to the calendar before the settlement of the Hebrews in the land of Canaan, it is certain that after the settlement the autumn was the time when they fulfilled their vows and made their thank-offerings. They were by this time largely agriculturalists, and especially so in the centre and in the north. Those who retained their pastoral pursuits, and with them their nomadic outlook on life, were those Hebrew elements which settled east of Jordan. These men from the Gilead country have a very great deal to do with the development of the religion of the Hebrews in the time of the two kingdoms, and at least as much to do with the political policy of the Northern kings. Especially is this the case in respect of Elijah, who came from Tishbe of Gilead, and his successor Elisha of Abel-meholah, supported by the Rechabites under Jonadab. They were responsible for the Jehovist revival, the overthrow of the House of Omri, the usurpation of the throne of Damascus-Syria by Hazael, the change of national policy from the alliance policy of the Aramæan league of the House of Omri to the isolationist policy of Jehu. All this dissipated the power of the weaker nations, while the appeasement policy of Jehu made it easier for the Assyrian conqueror to eat up first one and then another of the smaller peoples which lay between Mesopotamia and the Western Sea. But great as was Gileadite influence on the religion of the Hebrews of the North from the middle of the ninth century onwards, and equally on the national and political history, the bed-rock and basis of the religious institutions depended largely on those who had settled in Canaan and had adopted the agricultural life of the country.

In Canaan, the most outstanding feast of all was the autumnal pilgrimage. This autumnal vintage feast was a most hilarious occasion, with eating and drinking, dancing and singing, and merriment of every kind, rivalling even the joy and abandon of the Jewish Purim Festival of mediæval times. They gave themselves up to the pleasure of the sacred harvest meal with all the freedom of a people who lived close to the rich brown earth, on the best of friendly terms with an easy-going deity, and with no fears of anything beyond the horizon of their immediate environment. This was before the days of the great warring empires of the Near East. These peasants of Canaan thanked the good god of the land for all his gifts, and proceeded to eat and drink right joyfully, sharing with him that fulness which he had given and they had received. Such a scene is described in Judg. ix, 27, when the "lords of Shechem" (the masters, burgesses) "went out into the fields, gathered the vintage, trod the grapes, held a merrymaking, and entered the house of their gods". There they ate and drank and cursed Abimelech, a thing which, considering Abimelech's well-known and generally unpleasant reputation, they would scarcely have done unless they had been full of new wine. Abimelech was probably not the first adventurer, and he has certainly not proved to be the last, to talk about the advantages of rule by one man, to follow it up with talk about the importance of proper descent, and then to establish his dictatorship by gathering round him a bodyguard of "vain and light fellows" (Judg. ix, 2, 4); the Hebrew might well be translated 'irresponsible toughs'.

Equally with the masters of Shechem, the Israelites were on these occasions apt to drink somewhat freely of the heady new wine. Eli, priest of Shiloh, and guardian of the Ark as his family had been from pre-Canaan days, was quick to suspect Hannah of drunkenness, when she left the merry company to pray silently, but with moving lips (1 Sam. i, 9-13). This incident took place at the end of the year. The visit was an annual one, for Elkanah "went up out of his city annually (*miyyamin yamimah*) to bow down and to sacrifice to Jehovah Sabaoth in Shiloh" (1 Sam. i, 3). The verb translated 'to sacrifice' is *zabach*. This root originally meant 'slaughter'. In the earliest days every slaughter was regarded as a meal shared between the god and the worshipper, since the blood was "poured out unto the Lord", even if the slayer-worshipper ate the remainder. Even when the word *zebach* became a sacrificial term in pre-exilic Israel, the idea of the worshipper eating was still predominant. The translation 'to sacrifice' therefore scarcely does justice to the meaning of the original Hebrew, and this further explanation is necessary.

Every year (*shanah beshanah*) the fruitful Peninnah mocked the barren Hannah (1 Sam. i, 7), for this was a time when every type of unfruitfulness of whatever kind was a matter for reproach. In the case where rival wives were concerned, barrenness was more than a matter of reproach. It was a source of great bitterness of heart for the barren one, and of unseemly ostentation for the fruitful one, particularly if, as in the case of Hannah and Peninnah, the barren wife was the favourite wife.

What such a pilgrimage feast in the earliest times involved can be seen in the story of the Golden Calf (Ex. xxxii, 5f.) (E). "And Aaron made proclamation and said, Tomorrow shall be a feast (Heb. *chag*, cf. Arabic *chajj*) unto the Lord. And they rose up early on the morrow, and offered burnt-offerings ('*oloth*, offerings which were wholly burned on the altar), and brought peace-offerings (*shelamim*, or, to give these shared meals their full title, *zebach shelamim*); and the people sat down to eat and to drink, and rose up to play". There is no indication in the text as to the time of the year at which this feast took place,[61] though when Jeroboam son of Nebat established Bethel as a royal sanctuary (1 Kings xii, 28-33), he copied the sin of the Golden Calf in two particulars. One was that he set up the Golden Calf, and the other was that he greeted it with the selfsame cry with which the children of Israel greeted the Golden Calf in the desert: "These be (behold) thy gods, O Israel, which brought thee up out of the land of Egypt" (Exod. xxxii, 4; 1 Kings xii, 28). Jeroboam's feast was the great harvest feast at the end of the year.[62]

The noise of the people and the shouting of their 'play' must have been considerable, since Moses and Joshua heard it in the far distance, whilst they were still on the mountain-side, and before ever they came within sight of the camp. So great was the noise that Joshua the soldier thought that it was

---

[61] According to Jewish tradition (*b. Sabb.* 89a; and Rashi), the date was Tammuz 16, Moses having ascended the Mount on Siwan 7. These traditional dates depend upon the Triennial Cycle for the Reading of the Law; see A. Büchler, *JQR* (old series), vol. v, pp. 420 ff.

[62] See pp. 47 f. below.

the sound of the sudden onset of raiding Bedawin tribesmen (verses 17 f.). Moses knew better. He had not had to deal with the continued waywardness of this people, scarce redeemed from slavery, without knowing something of the ease with which they lost their faith in their Redeemer God. This apostasy at Sinai was the crowning deed of their disloyalty, that final act which at last drove Moses to desperation (Exod. xxxii, 20, 27 f.). It was the culmination of a series of disloyalties, which began before they were well out of Egypt (Exod. xiv, 10-14), and which continued with the murmuring in the Wilderness of Sin (xvi, 2 f.), and in the striving at Rephidim-Meribah-Massah (xvii, 1-7). The people needed forty years of desert wanderings to drive out their craven fears, and to give them any confidence in Jehovah as their God, or in themselves as His people. No slave-minded folk could enter the Promised Land, and actually none of those adults did enter, except Caleb and Joshua (Num. xxxii, 11 f.). The 'playing' of Exod. xxxii, 6, was doubtless general merriment and dancing of a none too orderly character, though Jewish tradition interpreted it as sexual immorality and bloodshed. This is the interpretation of Rashi (*in loc.*), who refers to Gen. xxxix, 17 (Potiphar's wife's account of Joseph's behaviour; cf. also Gen. xxvi, 8, which Rashi does not mention, presumably because the behaviour was that of Abraham and legitimate, though ill-timed), and to 2 Sam. ii, 14 (the trial by combat beside the Pool of Gibeon, ancient prototype of such a fight as that between the Clan Chattan and the Clan Quhele in *The Fair Maid of Perth*).

The occasion of Samson's last discomfiture and his final triumph (Judg. xvi, 22-31) was another harvest feast of the typically hilarious character which we have seen to belong to these occasions. The lords of the Philistines came together " to offer a great sacrifice " to Dagon their god. The Hebrew is *lizboach zebach gadhol*, which means ' to hold a great sacred feast', the *zebach* being a victim which was mostly eaten by the worshippers in Old Israel. Apart from the feast itself, the description as given in Judg. xvi bears a remarkable resemblance to the scene at the Feast of Sukkoth (Tabernacles, Booths) in the last days of the Jerusalem Temple, as described in the Mishnah *Sukkah* v, 1-4, and also in the *Tosefta*

Sukkah iv, 1. The Philistine feast took place in a central court surrounded by galleries. The space below was filled with men and women, "and all the lords of the Philistines were there". Presumably these were the Philistine aristocracy, for on the roof, watching but not taking part, were about three thousand other men and women. The maintenance of such distinctions, combined with such gracious acts of condescension on the part of the aristocracy, are common enough in all lands.[63] When the hearts of the feasters were merry with wine, they called for Samson that they might mock him in his blindness and helplessness. He was 'to make sport'[64] before them as he stood between the two massive pillars on which the chief weight of the temple building rested.

The Tosefta and the Mishnah similarly both speak of the merry-making at the autumnal feast of selected participants in the open court of the Temple. These were great men of wisdom and religion, as Maimonides describes them.[65] According to the Mishnah and the Tosefta, they were the Chasidim and 'the men of Deed'. They danced and leapt and whirled the whole night through in a strange and lurid torch dance. Edersheim gives a fragment of one of the hymns which they sang in company with a group of penitents. It is a song of great joy, both on the part of the saints that their youth brings them no shame in old age, and on the part of the penitents that old age brings the opportunity to repair the sins of foolish youth.[66] Maimonides says that the spectators were the common people, this being an inference from the Mishnah and the Tosefta traditions.

The Tosefta is confused as to where these spectators were. It speaks of men looking on from within the Temple precincts, and of women looking on from without. Then it proceeds (iv, 1), "but when the supreme court saw that they behaved in a frivolous manner, they erected three balconies in the Court,[67] facing three sides, that from them the women

---

[63] Cf. *The Surgeon's Daughter*, chap. iii.
[64] The Hebrew verb is that used in the story of the Golden Calf and elsewhere (see preceding paragraph).
[65] *Sukkah*, viii, 14.
[66] *The Temple, its Ministry and Services* (London, n.d.), p. 247.
[67] I.e., the Court of the Women, where the worshippers gathered during the Temple services.

might behold the rejoicing of the ceremony, so that, when they were rejoicing at the ceremony, the men and the women were not mixed together ". The whole passage evidently deals with a time of great and intense excitement, when serious misbehaviour between the sexes was liable to occur. It is evident, in spite of the earlier part of the passage which suggests that the men and the women were always separated, that at one time they were actually together, possibly without, but more probably within the Temple precincts. Else how could any serious misbehaviour have resulted? It is equally clear from the whole description that in every age the limits of what is seemly were liable to be overstepped at the great autumnal feast. A feast of the same general type on the part of the aristocracy was known both to Amos (ii, 8) and to Hosea (vii, 5), and, according to Hosea, not without excess.

The discrepancy in the passage from the Tosefta *Sukkah* is probably due to a remembrance of the time when the Court of the Women had not been built. Such discrepancies are due to various strata in the Mishnah and in the other traditions, such as those embodied in the Toseftas, representing various stages in the development of the traditions.[68] Compare the differences in the tractate *Middoth* concerning the position of the Gate of Nicanor. *Midd.* ii, 3, refers to the gate as being in the boundary wall of the Temple precincts proper, as though it were immediately inside the Soreg and the Chel on the eastern side. But *Midd.* i, 4, makes it the gate which led up from the Court of the Women into the Court of Israel. This is the position as it was in the last days of the Temple. The two statements can be reconciled on the basis of the supposition that the Court of the Women was built at a later date than the Gate of Nicanor. Whether this means that the Court of Israel, which in the last days was within the Gate of Nicanor and higher than the Court of the Women by fifteen steps, originally covered the whole area, or whether

[68] A modern example of lack of care in revision necessary because of changed views and circumstances is Trollope's reference in his *Autobiography* (written 1876) to his unfortunate misunderstanding with Charles Reade (see chapter xiii, p. 231 in *The World's Classics* edition). The breach between the two was healed in the next year, but Trollope never rewrote that cruel and unjust paragraph. Cf. Michael Sadleir, *Trollope: A Commentary* (London, 1927), pp. 307 f.

the Court of the Women was a later enclosure from the Court of the Gentiles, is not clear. From our present point of view, the matter is immaterial, but the discrepancies in the description of the Tosefta *Sukkah* can be resolved by supposing that before the building of the Court of the Women the ceremonies of the Feast of Tabernacles were held in a larger Court of Israel. In this case the Court of Israel may well have covered the whole area, and there would be one gate only, that which later was known as the Gate Beautiful, situated at the entrance from the Court of the Gentiles. There would not be enough room for the ceremonies to be held within the Gate of Nicanor, beyond which no woman on any account was ever allowed to pass. A larger Court of Israel would provide the necessary room, and the sexes would be together, though the women would still be outside what then would be the more sacred court of the Temple, namely the Court of the Priests.

The case for the existence at one time of a larger Court of Israel has other support. The major difficulty in reconstructing the plan of Herod's Temple is in finding adequate room for the Court of Israel. Most plans place it just inside the Gate of Nicanor, extending from wall to wall, but with a depth of only eleven cubits. Sir Conrad Schick makes it much more extensive at the expense of the Court of the Priests. He is probably right in thinking that the Court of Israel ought really to be very much bigger than it was in the last days. An original and much larger court extending as far as the site of the Gate Beautiful might well solve the whole problem.[69]

We continue with other references in the Old Testament to annual festivals, some of which, though not all, are instances of the celebration of the autumnal vintage feast.

The Family Feast at Bethlehem

According to 1 Sam. xx, 6, David and Jonathan agree that the former's absence from Saul's table is to be explained by saying that at Bethlehem there was an annual feast (*zebach hayyamim*), at which every member of Jesse's family must per-

[69] See *H.D.B.*, vol. iv, pp. 711-716, and the discussions and references there.

THE PRE-EXILIC NEW YEAR FEAST 45

force be present. Whether David did actually go to Bethlehem is not wholly clear, though verse 19 probably means that he stayed there for the full three days. In any case, Jonathan's story to his father would have to bear all the marks of credibility if a growingly suspicious and jealous Saul was to be satisfied. In order that the story might pass muster as providing the true reason for David's absence, there would have to be an annual feast at Bethlehem, and this would have to be generally and well recognized as being the normal procedure. Further, as Meinhold pointed out,[70] it could not have been a purely local and domestic affair, peculiar to that one place. It would only be on account of a 'high feast' that David would dare to absent himself from the royal court, particularly in view of the strained relations already existing between him and Saul. There is no need to assume that this feast at Bethlehem was not the annual harvest feast, on the ground that Saul did not celebrate it at the same time. Actually it was the annual feast for all Jesse's family (verse 6), and further it was the new-month day,[71] when David ought not to have failed to sit at meat with the king (verse 5). There is therefore every indication that it was the annual feast both at Saul's court and at David's home in Bethlehem. Even if it should be maintained that this was not the case, there was no necessity in those early days that the harvest feast should be held at the same date throughout the country.[72] There was no official calendar, and the seasons vary considerably from district to district.

Absalom's Hair

It is stated in 2 Sam. xiv, 25 f., that at the end of every year (*miqqeç yamim leyamim*) Absalom used to poll his hair, and offer it as a gift to Jehovah. The end of the year was the proper time for the offering of sacred gifts and for the fulfilment of vows. The Greek analogy for the dedication of the

---

[70] *Sabbat und Woche im alten Testament* (Göttingen, 1905), S. 4.
[71] For the evidence that 'new-month day' is the true and proper translation of *chodesh*, and that this date is in favour of the supposition that here we are dealing with the annual feast at Saul's court, the period being pre-exilic, see p. 96 ff. below.
[72] For this variation of the date of the annual harvest feast, see the discussion of 1 Kings viii, 2, and xii, 32, on pp. 46 f. below.

hair to a god is in Homer, *Iliad* xxiii, 135, 144, where Achilles clothes the body of his dead friend Patroklos with the hair which his own father Peleus has vowed for another purpose to the river god Spercheus. Absalom did not let his hair grow long for reasons of personal vanity, though this may well have helped towards his habit, but in connexion with his pretensions and ambitions for the throne. The hair of all sacred persons, priests, kings, Nazirites, is sacred almost the whole world over. It must not be touched by common hands, nor must it be shorn except under particular and stringent conditions. The hair must therefore be worn long, as in the case of kings (whence the fillet, and later the crown) and some priests (e.g. the Druids), or the head must be shaved, as in the case of the priests of Egypt and Tibet. The supernatural strength of Samson was in his hair. This was where his *mana* rested. When his hair was shorn, he was weak and 'like any other man' (Judg. xvi, 17, 19 f.); in the day of his triumph and death, when he received once more his supernatural strength, the hair of his head had grown again after he had been shaven (verse 22). In respect of Absalom, we have already pointed out[73] that the autumn was the time when this ambitious princeling set out to win his crown and kingdom. The fact that, at the time of his rebellion, Absalom's hair was very long and wide-flowing is indicated by the way in which "his head caught hold of the oak" (2 Sam. xviii, 9), and "he was taken up between the heaven and the earth", so that "he was hanging in the oak". It must have been close upon the time when normally his locks were shorn.

Solomon's Dedication Feast

In 1 Kings viii, 2, we read that Solomon dedicated the new Temple which he had built, at the feast in the month Ethanim. The post-exilic writer added, though not wholly accurately, as we shall see later,[74] "this is the seventh month". In pre-exilic times Ethanim was the first month. Solomon therefore dedicated the Temple on the occasion of the great annual harvest feast, that annual pilgrimage when all men gathered to the shrine of their god at the end of the year.

[73] See p. 33 above.   [74] See pp. 102 f. below.

Jeroboam's Dedication Feast

There has been considerable discussion concerning 1 Kings xii, 32. Jeroboam son of Nebat, having been instigated in the first place by Ahijah of the ancient ark priesthood of Shiloh (1 Kings xi, 29 f.), led the Israelite revolt away from the Judæan dominion of David and Solomon. Amongst other things, he instituted a feast for the Northern Kingdom at Bethel "on the fifteenth of the eighth month" (so the post-exilic writer once more), "like the feast which is in Judah". This Northern feast was thus at the full moon of Bul, the second month of the pre-exilic calendar, and the month following Ethanim. This variation between the dates of these two Feasts of Asiph (Ingathering) has always been regarded as creating a difficulty. How could the two feasts, it is asked, be rival feasts when the Northern feast was celebrated one month later than the Southern feast? The difficulty is more apparent than real. It is due to a misguided tendency to read back into earlier times the later ideas of centralization and precision and authority.

There can be no shadow of doubt that Jeroboam's motive was to wean the people away from Jerusalem. His aim was a double one, both religious and political.

Religiously, Jeroboam's aim was to restore the Northern cult which had suffered during Solomon's reign because of the expensive and attractive nature of the cultus of the new Temple. Jeroboam had the full support of the Shiloh priesthood in his revolt. As we have seen, Ahijah the Shilonite encouraged him from the first, as far back as the time when Jeroboam was in charge of the *corvée*, or forced levies, of the Joseph tribes (1 Kings xi, 28). The Shiloh priests could not be expected to view the domination and the 'establishment' of the Zadokite priests of Jerusalem with anything approaching the smallest degree of equanimity.[75] Zadok, probably of the original Jebusite priesthood of Jerusalem,[76] had been

---

[75] Compare the early rivalries of York and Canterbury, the relics of which still survive in the titles 'Primate of England' and 'Primate of all England'. See G. F. Browne, *The Church in these Islands before Augustine* (London, 1899).

[76] H. H. Rowley, 'Zadok and Nehushtan', *J.B.L.*, vol. lviii, ii (1939), pp. 113-142.

appointed sole priest by Solomon (1 Kings ii, 35), whilst Abiathar, the sole survivor of the massacre of the Shilonite priests at Nob, had been dismissed to Anathoth. Judging by what happened to the other supporters of the unsuccessful Adonijah, Abiathar owed his life solely to the fact that he was a priest and therefore a sacred person. Especially would the feeling of enmity be marked, since their own Ark, the chief cult-object of the Joseph tribes, had been enshrined in Solomon's Temple in the South, and the rites connected with it celebrated by the alien priests of the South. The Northern tribes had been temporarily weakened by the Philistine successes in the time of Saul, so that David with Southern support was able to exercise dominion over the whole country. During this period he had transported the Northern Ark to Jerusalem. When Jeremiah, himself a descendant of the old Shiloh priesthood, called the Jerusalem Temple "a den of robbers" (Jer. vii, 11), his immediate justification was the way in which the Zadokite priesthood had taken advantage of the centralization movement under Josiah, and had refused to share with the provincial priests those dues which previously had been their sole means of subsistence (2 Kings xxiii, 9). But there was a deeper reason than this, for Jeremiah was also influenced, as the following verse (Jer. vii, 12) suggests, by his love for the ancient Shiloh traditions of his fathers. Pathetic references to the ancient glory and present desolation of this ancient shrine are one of the features of Jeremiah's prophecies. These Zadokite priests of Jerusalem, having become the favourites of the king, had robbed the descendants of the House of Eli even of the very Ark itself, of which Eli and his fathers were the time-honoured guardians. Jeroboam was supported by the old Shiloh and true Josephite priesthood, just as later Jehu was supported in his revolt against the House of Omri by the Northern prophets under the leadership of Elisha (2 Kings ix, 1-10). After his success in securing the throne, Jehu kept his bargain with the strict Jehovah prophets and their Rechabite allies in the "great sacrifice" which he made to Baal (2 Kings x, 19). Jeroboam did not keep his bargain. He incurred the displeasure of his original supporters to such an extent that later, in order to obtain an oracle from Ahijah the Shilonite, his wife had to attempt a disguise (1 Kings xiv, 1-18). Apparently the counsel which Jeroboam took (1 Kings xii, 28) before he made the calves of gold was not of the Shiloh priests, but of the priests of another shrine, Bethel, whose local cult varied in favour of the ancient bull-worship of the desert, away from the purer and non-idolatrous cult of Shiloh. These Bethel priests were probably sons of Aaron, as R. H. Kennett suggested,[77] who migrated to Jerusalem during the exile, and thenceforward were in control there in spite of the fact that in post-exilic times they were outnumbered by two to one. Aaron was certainly the priest of the golden calf in the desert (Exod. xxxii, 1-5 [E]). And so Jeroboam re-instituted the calf-worship, though the fact that he called his son Abijah (Jah is father) shows that he may well have acted unwittingly so far as true and proper Jehovah worship was concerned.

Politically, Jeroboam's policy was to wean the people away from Solomon's splendid Temple, back to their local shrines, lest, influenced by the splendour of the appointments at Jerusalem, they should grow to think more highly of that city and its king than was desirable or safe for Jeroboam (1 Kings xii, 27). Lest the people should be tempted to return to their former, though temporary,[78] allegiance to the House of David,

[77] "The Origin of the Aaronite Priesthood," *J.T.S.*, vol. vi (1905), pp. 151-186.

[78] It is often forgotten how temporary the so-called United Kingdom was. It lasted for seventy-three years only, and even this period was marred by more than one rebellion against Judahite supremacy and domination. The true centre of the Northern tribes was Shechem, where Jacob bought a parcel of ground from the sons of Hamor (Gen. xxxiii, 19), just as Abraham bought a field from Ephron the Hittite at Hebron (Gen. xxiii, 16 f.). What Hebron was to the South, Shechem was to the North. It was to Shechem that Rehoboam went to be established as king of Israel (1 Kings xii, 1); and it was in Shechem that Jeroboam settled (1 Kings xii, 25). The first attempt at a kingdom had been at Shechem in Abimelech's time (Judg. ix), and in the days of Joshua it had been the central meeting place of the Ephraimites (Josh. xxiv, 1). It is not generally realized that for the seventy-three years during the time of David and Solomon, Israel was subject to, and not the willing ally of, Judah. There are no Messianic hopes of a united kingdom under a Davidic king, either from the old Israel, or from the Samaritans. All such dreams belong to the South, the dominant partner in the glory that was David's. Subsequently to the revolt under Jeroboam, Judah generally was subject to Israel. It was only the temporary weakness of the North, occasioned by the Philistine invasion of Central Palestine, that gave David his chance to gain control,

Jeroboam followed the policy of David when he brought the Ark up to Jerusalem, and that of Solomon in building the Temple there. Jeroboam took care to see to it that the religious life of the country was under his control, a policy which has been characteristic of governments since the world was young. He saw to it also that the annual feast of the North was observed with all the splendour of kings. He himself took the leading part, and thus he ensured that Bethel should be a leading shrine and a royal sanctuary as long as the Northern Kingdom lasted (Amos vii, 10-13). Indeed, if R. H. Kennett was right in his theory that the Bethel priests were Aaronites, then the effect of Jeroboam's choice of Bethel as against Shiloh was greater, more lasting and more decisive, than ever he could have dreamed.

Since this Northern feast at Bethel was intended, from both religious and political considerations, to be deliberately in opposition to the feast which was observed at Jerusalem, both of them being pilgrimage feasts when men journeyed to particular shrines, some have held that Jeroboam must have made the dates clash. It is when we argue from what we think must have taken place that confusion is liable to begin and errors to multiply. The next step in the argument has been to say that, since Solomon's Temple was actually completed in the month Bul (1 Kings vi, 38), the dedication of the new Temple at Jerusalem must have taken place in that month, that is, in the second month of the pre-exilic year, and not in Ethanim, which was the first month. It is argued that Solomon would scarcely have been likely to wait for as long as another eleven months before the great dedication ceremony. Therefore the Southern feast was actually held in the month Bul in Solomon's time, and the dates did actually clash. So runs the argument. It must be noted that all this superstructure has been built up on the initial assumption that the dates must have clashed. But there was no need whatever for Jeroboam to make the dates clash. We are not dealing here

---

he having used the time of his flight from Saul to bind together into personal loyalty to himself the various semi-desert tribes of the Southern border. This amalgamation of mixed Arab-Edomite tribes with a Hebrew nucleus was the tribe of Judah. It is nearer the truth to say that Judah was of David than to say that David was of Judah.

with post-Deuteronomic days, the time of the One Central Sanctuary. We are dealing with a period some two hundred years earlier than the time of King Hezekiah, whose reign is on any basis the earliest possible date for any move towards centralization in the Deuteronomic sense of the word. It is three hundred years before the time of King Josiah. In Jeroboam's day it was by no means *aut Jerusalem aut nihil*. Jerusalem was but one of many shrines, as even a casual reference to the Books of Samuel, the larger part of the Books of the Kings, or the writings of any pre-exilic prophet, will show. Jerusalem rose to prominence only after David took the Ark there some seventy years before Jeroboam's revolt. Previously it had been a Jebusite city, though that may not have made it as unpopular from the Hebrew point of view as the later Deuteronomists would have us believe. Most probably it was only after Solomon had completed the Temple, and had in part impoverished the country by having to pay for the Phœnician workmen and materials which he had imported, that Jerusalem was able as a shrine to overshadow other Palestinian shrines by its splendour and prestige. Not every tenth-century Hebrew by any means, even then, whether Israelite or even Judahite, would feel himself bound to make his annual harvest pilgrimage to Jerusalem. Many of them, perhaps the majority, would continue the custom of their fathers, and would continue to appear at their local shrines, as Gibeah of Saul, Hebron, Shiloh, Shechem, Bethel and the rest. This much is clear from the references to these local shrines which the eighth-century prophet Amos makes (Amos iv, 4; v, 4 f.). Further, there were still many local shrines very much alive in Josiah's time (2 Kings xxiii, 8). Men prefer to worship where they have always worshipped, and where their fathers have worshipped. Not all the enticements of more splendid churches elsewhere, whether nearer or farther away, nor all the exhortations of central authorities, can easily wean men and women away from their original spiritual homes, as modern efforts at Church union have frequently shown.

All that Jeroboam needed to do, and actually all that he could do whatever he may have been minded to do, was to create a sufficiently rich cultus, to give it all the prestige of royal 'establishment', and to provide adequate facilities in the way of ante-rooms and so forth for the proper enjoyment of the harvest meal. Such things alone, added perhaps to the excitement of an annual journey to the metropolis, would tempt any who were prepared to travel beyond their immediate environment to go to Bethel instead of to Jerusalem. Perhaps Jeroboam's choice of Bethel in preference to Shiloh was influenced by the concessions which the Bethel priests were willing to allow, against the probably less accommodating attitude which the definitely non-idolatrous Shiloh priests may well have adopted.

There is no real difficulty about the different dates. The Feast of Asiph was, in those early days, probably held in the South in the month Ethanim, and in the North one month later, in the month Bul. There may have been seasons occasionally when the two coincided, the one being late or the other early. The feast was a full-moon feast. The people went to the shrine of their choice at the first full moon after the completion of the harvests of the agricultural year. This was either the time of the Harvest Moon or the time of the Hunter's Moon. The season varies in Palestine to such an extent that we can even read of Benaiah slaying "a lion in a pit in the time of snow" (2 Sam. xxiii, 20). The corn harvest begins in the Jordan valley and in the maritime plain as early as April. It is continued in the lowlands and the plains during May, whilst in parts of the hill-country it is often as late as June. Similar differences, though perhaps not so marked, will apply to the vintage. Solomon would have no choice as to the date when the Temple should be dedicated. He was bound to wait until the next annual feast after the completion of the building operations. It was in the proper month and at the proper full moon that the people would appear with their gifts. Similarly in the North, Jeroboam held the feast, not when he would, but when he must. In both North and South the inauguration ceremonies could be held only at the first full moon after the work in field and vineyard had been completed. This, in the nature of things, was later in the North than in the lowlands between the Judæan hills and the sea.[79] The popularity of Bethel would

[79] Keil, *Archäologie*, i, pp. 33 f.; ii, pp. 113 f. Compare the difference in the time of harvest between the south of England and the

grow with the years, whatever the date of the feast, if only the prestige and the facilities warranted it. All this would be apart from local patriotic fervour.

Isaiah xxix, 1

In Isa. xxix, 1, we read, "Woe, woe, Ariel, Ariel, the city where David camped. Add year to year; let the feasts go round (*sephu shanah ' al-shanah chaggim yinqophu*)". These pilgrimage feasts (*chaggim*) to which reference is here made are not the three pilgrimage feasts of the later rigid calendar of the post-exilic ecclesiastical system, nor are they even the three pilgrimage feasts of pre-exilic times. The reference is solely to the one great pilgrimage feast which marked the end of the year, the harvest feast, that feast which did in fact mark the turn of the year and its 'going round'. The root *n-q-ph* is used in its variant form *q-w-ph* in the word *tequphah* (going round, turning) in Exod. xxxiv, 22 (J). This latter is the word which later was used in Rabbinic literature for the solstices and the equinoxes.[80]

Jeremiah xli, 4 ff.

After the destruction of the Jerusalem Temple in 586 B.C., eighty men came from Shiloh and Samaria, bringing their gifts to Jerusalem (Jer. xli, 4 ff.). They were continuing the established custom of Deuteronomic days, oblivious of the changed circumstances of the Babylonian conquest and the restlessness of the times. They came in sorrow and with gifts, and they came in the seventh month according to post-exilic reckoning, that is, in the autumn, in what before the exile was the month Ethanim. According to pre-exilic reckoning this was at the turn of the year. Here also, incidentally, we have a further case of a princeling taking steps in the autumn to establish himself as king, for Ishmael, who slaughtered seventy of these eighty men, was himself of the seed royal (Jer. xli, 1).

---

northern counties. The difference sometimes amounts to as much as two months.

[80] See pp. 34 f. above.

Judges xi, 40, and xxi, 21

There are references to annual festivals in Judg. xi, 40, and xxi, 21. The second of these was probably in the autumn, but whenever they were observed, they were both distinct from any general harvest festival of the type with which we are concerned. Both of them were celebrated by virgins only. The first of these two festivals is in connexion with the sacrifice of Jephthah's daughter. It involved a custom whereby, in the time of the judges, the daughters of Israel went into the country annually (*miyyamim yamimah*) " four days in a year" to rehearse the story of the unfortunate maiden. The second is the story of the rape of Shiloh, made possible by the well-known, at any rate locally, custom whereby the virgins of Shiloh went out each year unattended to dance in the vineyards. Similar dances are described in the Mishnah as taking place outside Jerusalem at the beginning of the Christian Era on the 15th of Ab and on the 10th of Tishri. " Rabbi Gamaliel said, Israel has no festivals like the 15th of Ab and the Day of Atonement.[81] On these days the children of Jerusalem used to go out dressed in white.... The maidens of Jerusalem used to go out and dance in the vineyards, and say thus, ' Young man, raise your eyes, and behold the maid you are going to choose. Look not on beauty, but on birth '. And he replies thus, ' Go, daughters of Zion, and look on Solomon with the crown wherewith his mother crowned him in the day of his espousals, and in the day of the joy of his heart '" (Mishnah, *Ta'anith* iv, 8). There is thus an association with the Song of Songs, and also connexions with betrothal rites, dances of virgins in vineyards, and ultimately, we believe, with the age-old fertility rites of the Tammuz-Adonis cults. For our part, we find in the Song of Songs two distinct elements, each with its own story, connected ultimately, the one with Jephthah's daughter, and the other with the rape of Shiloh. One group of passages has its setting in the autumn. The youth-king seeks the maiden-princess and

---

[81] The idea of the Day of Atonement as a festival is strange in view of modern associations, but according to ancient tradition there is considerable division of opinion as to whether the day was a festival or a fast.

carries her off to his palace. The other group has associations with the spring, but its actual setting is the height of the summer at the time of the fruits of the gardens. Here the distressed maiden seeks her shepherd lover and leads him to her mother's house. In the southern variant the youth is Solomon and the maid is the Shulamith (a feminine form of 'Solomon'), but in the northern variant the youth was probably Ahab and the maiden was Jezebel. The two incidents in the Book of Judges have been connected with the Song of Songs by T. J. Meek, and also with the Tammuz cult.[82] We believe that the more modern counterparts of the two rites are to be found in the Jerusalem dances of Mishnaic times.[83] These customs are examples from ancient Hebrew lore of a class of rites common in many lands, not always with any observable association between the different areas. They are vegetation rites, and usually involve in their more primitive forms the death of the youthful god, followed by mourning for him on the part of the women, as in the weeping for Tammuz (cf. Ezek. viii, 14), or, alternatively, the death or abduction of the maiden. Amongst the Greeks the youth is the Kouros and the maiden is the Kore. The rape of the Kore is described in the Homeric Hymn to Demeter, where the 'slender-ancled maid' is carried off by King Aidoneus by permission of Zeus. The rape and death combined are found in the myth of Persephone and Hades (Proserpina and Pluto).[84]

[82] "Canticles and the Tammuz Cult" in *A.J.S.L.*, vol. xxxiv, pp. 1-14; also *The Song of Songs: a Symposium* (Philadelphia, Pa., 1924), pp. 51, 58. For a review of the modern study of the Song of Songs, see H. H. Rowley, "The Song of Songs: An Examination of Recent Theory," in *J.R.A.S.*, April, 1938, pp. 251-276. Other studies of importance are W. Wittekindt, *Das Hohe Lied und seine Beziehungen zum Istar-kult* (Hannover, 1926); H. H. Rowley, "The Meaning of 'the Shulamite'", in *A.J.S.L.*, vol. lvi, 1 (Jan. 1939), pp. 84-91. Cf. Jer. xxxi, 4 f.

[83] For further details, see "The Song of Songs: the Dances of the Virgins," in *A.J.S.L.*, vol. l, 3 (April, 1934, pp. 129-142). The custom is still observed among the Jews of the Caucasus and of Tripolitania. On the Day of Atonement the maidens dance in the streets or in the environs of the town, singing love songs (see R. Patai, *Edoth.* i, 1, pp. 55, 59).

[84] J. E. Harrison, *Prolegomena to the Study of Greek Religion* (1903), p. 274; Sir Gilbert Murray, *Five Stages of Greek Religion* (1935), pp. 32 f.; F. B. Jevons, *Introduction to the History of Religion* (1896), p. 377.

Conclusion

In conclusion, apart from such celebrations as the dances of virgins on dates which, according to the post-exilic calendar, were the 15th of Ab and the 10th of Tishri, there was a great pilgrimage feast in Palestine in pre-exilic days. It was held in the autumn. At Jerusalem it was held in the month Ethanim, but at Bethel in the following month. At other shrines it may have been held at other times, just as there were considerable variations in the times of the New Year's festivals at the city shrines of Babylonia.[85] The variations, however, in Palestine would probably be much less in extent than those in Mesopotamia, firstly because the differences of the seasons in Palestine would not amount to more than two full moons because of the incidence of the October rains, and secondly because the wide variation in Mesopotamia is due in part to the early urbanization of that valley, with its consequent tendency to be independent of the seasons of the agricultural year, and partly to astrological influences. This autumnal feast of Palestine was known as the Feast of 'Aṣiph (Ingathering), and it was held at the 'turning' or 'going out' of the year. The phrase of the J-tradition is 'turning' (*tequphah*) (Exod. xxxiv, 22); that of the E-tradition is 'going out' (*çe'th*) (Exod. xxiii, 16). The Deuteronomists called this feast the Feast of *Sukkoth* (booths, tabernacles), but this is a post-exilic term (Deut. xxxi, 10). As we shall see later,[86] it corresponds only in part to the pre-exilic Feast of Asiph.

The dominant feature of this feast, considered as the feast of the full year, was its joyfulness. Men, women and children, whole families, journeyed together to their local or favourite shrine. The absence of Hannah, for instance, was most unusual, and was justified by the sacred writer only because of her determination to give her son, the infant Samuel, wholly to God, so that when, after having been weaned, he at last came to Shiloh, he should never leave the Holy Service (1 Sam. i, 22-28). When the pilgrims arrived at the shrines, they thanked their God for all His gifts. They praised Him for the mercies of yet another fruitful year, and they shared with Him, often riotously, but always joyfully, the good things

---

[85] See pp. 145 ff. below.   [86] See pp. 88 f. below.

which He had provided. Every shrine had its own crowd of merry-makers, but the largest, though not necessarily for that reason the merriest, crowds were at the royal sanctuaries of Jerusalem and Bethel, shrines which had all the advantages of the royal presence and patronage. The joy would begin with the preparations for leaving home. It was continued on the journey where the gradually increasing crowds beguiled the journey with traditional songs. Some of these songs of 'going-up' are preserved in the Pilgrim Psalter of Pss. cxx-cxxxiv. In their present form these pilgrim songs are mostly post-exilic, but they doubtless contain, as do many other post-exilic psalms, many early elements, still surviving through the adaptations of the centuries. The journey back was likewise made in company, a whole group of kinsfolk and neighbours travelling together. The children would spend the whole day with other families in the large company, and perhaps the night as well as the day. Compare Luke ii, 43, a passage which refers to the journey home after the Passover Feast, but is doubtless characteristic of all the pilgrimages of Palestine, early and late.

2

THE PRE-EXILIC NEW YEAR FEAST

B.—The Beginning of the Year

We have considered in the previous chapter that aspect of the pre-exilic autumnal feast which was concerned with the end of the agricultural year. This is that aspect of it which looks backwards into the year that has passed, and it is therefore concerned with thanks for benefits received. But there is another aspect of this great autumnal feast, even more important than that which we have hitherto discussed. It is never possible for any people anywhere, and particularly if they are an agricultural people whose prosperity in any measure depends upon the climate, to celebrate the joy of harvest without looking forward into the next year, and interceding for the continuance of the blessings which they have just received. The annual pre-exilic feast of Asiph was therefore not only an Old Year Feast of thanksgiving and joy, but also a New Year Feast of prayer and supplication.

'The Going-out of the Year'

It has been suggested that the idea of the new year is actually involved in the phrase which the E-tradition used in Exod. xxiii, 16, to denote the period of the year at which the feast was held. The phrase is *çe'th hashShanah*, and it is usually translated 'the going out of the year'. It was first suggested by Reidel, and later supported by G. B. Gray,[1] that the meaning of the word *çe'th* in this instance is 'entering' and not 'going out', i.e. 'beginning' and not 'ending'. We do not think that this can be maintained, and it is possible that if Gray himself had lived to complete these studies, which were published posthumously, he might have modified his judgement on this particular point. There is actually a note[2] inserted at the foot of p. 301 which seriously detracts from the

---

[1] *Sacrifice in the Old Testament*, pp. 300 f.
[2] The note is in square brackets and therefore editorial (see p. vi).

cogency of the argument. On the basis of this meaning 'beginning', Gray went on to maintain that the Feast of Ingathering "must no longer be regarded as a festival of the old year: it is a festival of the New Year".[3] This, in our judgement, is allowing the pendulum to swing right over to the other extreme. Indeed, we do not think that the evidence on which the statement is made is nearly as sound as Gray himself conceived it to be. We regret that Gray's statement has been accepted without question by Professor S. H. Hooke.[4] The fact is that the festival looks both ways. It is, so to speak, a 'January' feast. Like the Roman god Janus, it has two faces, one with which to look back into the year that is past, and the other with which to look forward into the year that is to come.

The evidence which is adduced in favour of the meaning 'beginning' is the special use of the root *y-ç-'* in connexion with the rising of the sun, and, as a development from that, of the rising of the heavenly bodies in general. The root in normal usage means 'to go out', and in this sense its use is extended to include the idea of kings going out on military expeditions (2 Sam. xi, 1), and of troops marching out of camp in order to take up their battle positions (1 Sam. xvii, 20). A still further extension is its use in Isa. xlii, 13, of a champion going out in front of the army to challenge the chosen hero of the enemy. This use is comparable to the Arabic *baraza* (he went out), with the form *ba'raza* (to go to battle), and the noun *muba'razat* (a challenge to single combat). The special use of the root with which we are immediately concerned depends upon the idea of the sun resting or sleeping during the hours of darkness, and then going out from his bedchamber in the dawn to do his day's work. Just as a man goes out to do his work for the day (Ps. civ, 22), so also the sun goes out from his chambers at sunrise (Ps. xix, 6). The east is *moça'*, which means 'the place of (the sun's) going out' (Ps. lxxv, 7). On the other hand, when the sun sets he enters (the Hebrew root is *bo'*) his chambers. One of the Hebrew phrases for 'sunset' is *mebho' hashshemesh* (lit. 'the entrance of the sun') (Ps. civ, 19). This metaphor is carried over to the

---

[3] *Sacrifice in the Old Testament*, p. 301.
[4] Article "The Myth and Ritual Pattern on the Ancient East" in *Myth and Ritual* (ed. S. H. Hooke, Oxford, 1933), p. 12.

idea of the rising of the heavenly bodies generally, so that in Isa. xl, 26, it is used of the rising of the stars. "Lift up your eyes on high, and see who hath created these, that bringeth out (*hammoçi'*, i.e. 'causeth to go out') their host by number. . . ." Where we should say 'rise' or, of the stars, that they 'come out', the Hebrew said 'go out' (*yaça'*). Similarly, in the description of the rebuilding of the walls of Jerusalem in the time of Nehemiah, we read, "So we wrought in the work: and half of them held the spears from the ascending of the dawn until the stars appeared (*çe'th*, lit. 'went out')" [Neh, iv, 21 (Hebrew, 15)]. In Isa. xiii, 10, we get what to us is a curious inversion, so curious that this passage, as it stands in the English Versions, can be easily misunderstood. The passage says "the sun shall be darkened in his *going out*". In English this is either tautology or a statement that the sun will be eclipsed at the time of the evening twilight. The true meaning of the Hebrew is that the sun will be eclipsed from dawn onwards. Another example of this special use of the root is to be seen in Gen. xix, 23 (J), and there are others. As G. B. Gray pointed out, the same idiom is found in Assyrian, where *çit shamshi* means 'the rising of the sun'.

We have already added many instances to those which Gray gives, for the idea of the sun going out from his chamber in the dawn is common and widespread. We would add that the same idiom is found also in later Hebrew, both in the earlier Midrashes and in the Talmuds. The root is used, for instance, in *Bereshith Rabba* (p. 6) of the rising not only of the sun, but of the moon also. The noun *yeçi'ah* is used of the sunrise in *jer. Ber.* I, 2c. On the other hand, contrary to Gray's assumptions, there is no evidence that the special use of the root *y-ç-'* was ever extended in Hebrew beyond this association with the heavenly bodies. The only such instance which Gray cites is from Assyrian and not from Hebrew. It is the phrase *çit archi*, which he claims to be able to translate 'the *beginning* of the month'. But is this a legitimate rendering? It is legitimate only when the Hebrew phrase *çe'th hashShanah* has been shown to mean 'the beginning of the year'. The two phrases stand and fall together. The other example which Gray quotes is with Delitzsch from the Babylonian Creation Tablets, but his rendering depends upon a text which, as the editorial note points out, is not generally accepted. He renders the passage (p. 301) "from the day when the year set forth to the day of the end", but the generally accepted reading (see footnote on p. 301) has nothing at all to do with the end of the year, and is rendered "after he had defined (?) the days of the year by signs".

When the root *y-ç-'* is used of a period of time in later Jewish writings, the meaning is invariably 'the end'. The figure of speech on which the meaning 'the beginning' depends is due entirely to the mythological background. As soon as there is no reference to the heavenly bodies, the specialized meaning ceases, and we get the ordinary meaning 'go out, end'. For instance, in *jer. Ber.* VIII, 12b, the meaning is "when the Sabbath ended (*yaçath*)". The hiphil form of the verb is used in *b. Erub.* 63a of living through to the end of the year. The matter is finally settled by *b. Sabb.* 118b, where the phrase *hoçi' shabbath* means 'to cause the Sabbath to go out (i.e. to dismiss it)' with prayer, and in the same context the contrasting phrase is used, namely *hikniş shabbath*, which means 'to collect (i.e. to bring in, usher in) the Sabbath' with prayer.

Equally there can be no shadow of doubt concerning the Mishnaic use of the word *moça'*, from the root *y-c-'*. The phrase *moça' shabbath* refers to the period at the end of the Sabbath (*Tos. Sabb.* III, 5; *b. Chull.* 15a). So also the phrase *moça' shebi'ith* refers to the period at the end of the Sabbatical year (Mishnah *Shebi.* IV, 2, and Talmud *b. RH* 9a). We find the same word used in prescribing the restrictions which are not to be relaxed until the end of the last day of the Feast of Sukkoth (*b. Beç.* 30b; *b. Sabb.* 45a). The theory, therefore, that the Hebrew phrase *çe'th hashShanah* means the 'beginning' of the year is untenable. It means the 'end' of the year, and so also does the Assyrian *çit shatti*. On the other hand, both the Hebrew *çe'th hashshemesh* and the Assyrian *çit shamshi* mean 'the rising of the sun', and so 'the beginning of the day'. The phrases for 'the beginning of the year' are, in Assyrian *resh shatti* and in Hebrew *rosh hashShanah*.

Nevertheless, in spite of the failure of Gray's contention in respect of the phrase *çe'th hashShanah*, there is evidence that the Feast of Asiph marks the beginning of the new year as well as the end of the old year. This can be seen in the so-called Gezer Calendar.[5] This is not a calendar of the official type, and the names which are given to the various months are derived from the actual farming operations which are proper to those periods of the year. Gray gives the name of the first month on the list as 'Asiph,[6] which we know to be the name of the pre-exilic autumnal feast. It is probable, however, in view of the other names in the list, that we should read the three consonants with other vowels to make 'oṣeph, i.e. 'gathering', the form now being the active qal participle of the verb '-ṣ-ph (gather). This so-called calendar is probably the work of a peasant farmer of, say, the eighth or ninth century B.C. This suggestion is usually made to account for the fact that the names given to the various periods of the year are descriptive of the various agricultural operations peculiar to those periods. The farmer evidently thought of the time of Ingathering as the beginning of the year. It was, that is, the time to think about the new agricultural year, its work and its prospects, and this in spite of the word which characterized the first few days of that period, i.e. the word 'ingathering'.

The Anxiety for the Rains

The attitude of looking forward anxiously at the time of the New Year to the possible fortunes of the year that is coming is common to all peoples the whole world over. "What is done on New Year's Day will be done all the year", according to popular superstition. "There was an instance in 1926 in the West Country (i.e. of England) of refusal to work on that day lest it should result in hard work all the year long". According to an old Devonshire custom "soup is made (on New Year's Day) with whole peas, as split peas would split the luck" for all the year.[7] Such ideas are common even in England with all its modern ideas, where largely even still, and especially towards the West, as J. B. Priestley[8] puts it,

---

[5] R. A. S. Macalister, *Excavations from Gezer* (1912), vol. ii, pp. 24-28.
[6] *Ibid.*, p. 301. For details of the months, see p. 84 below.
[7] A. R. Wright, *English Folklore* (Benn's Sixpenny Library, No. 33, 1928), p. 40.
[8] *The Good Companions* (1929), chap. ii, 1.

"man ... has settled himself modestly and snugly in the valleys and along the hillsides ... and has been content. Yes, these two (i.e. Nature and man) signed a peace here, and it has lasted a thousand years". But in a land like Palestine, hardly won from the desert, where there can never be any quiet peace with Nature, the inhabitants must naturally be nervous of drought and its almost certain consequence of famine, particularly in days when transport is limited and the central government not able to control such scanty supplies as are available in a time of scarcity. For five months of the year, from May onwards, rain rarely falls. A thunderstorm during harvest is sufficiently unusual as to call for marked comment (1 Sam. xii, 17 f.). Indeed, this incident is responsible to a greater extent than any other for Samuel's reputation in Israel as the great man of prayer. In Ps. xcix, 6, he is equated with Moses, who again and again "called upon the Lord, and he answered him". And of Samuel it is said, "and also when his enemies pressed him about, he called upon the Lord, the Mighty One, with the offering of the sucking lamb. And the Lord thundered from heaven, and with a mighty sound made his voice to be heard" (Ecclus. xlvi, 16 f.).

During the five months from May onwards the heat increases more and more, and it is intensified by the sirocco in September. The long drought is not brought to an end until an occasional shower falls towards the end of the month. Then, after a short period of bright weather, the 'former rains' begin. The parched ground soaks up the welcome storm-rain with a thirst as of the very desert itself, the dry rocky gulleys are turned into rushing torrents, and the land becomes soft enough for ploughing. If, however, these monsoon rains are delayed, then it is impossible to begin ploughing. Even if the rains are not delayed, but are inadequate, the harvest of the next year is imperilled. The fact that these very necessary rains are due so soon after harvest increases the natural anxiety of the worshippers at the autumnal harvest feast. The short period between the harvest feast at the end of the year and the coming of the rains is indicated in Ezra x, 9, and Zech. xiv, 16 f.

The parching sun of the months ending with Ethanim has increased the anxiety of the Palestinian husbandmen beyond that of small-holders in a country like England, for here their welfare is less dependent upon particular rains falling at particular times. There is therefore need beyond the ordinary, and certainly more than is easily realized in this country, that in Palestine the prayers for rain should be answered effectively and without undue delay. There can be no greater anxiety than that which was caused in Palestine in the ancient days by the delay in the coming of the Former Rain. The worst wish that David could express for Mount Gilboa, the site of the rout of the Israelites by the Philistines and the scene of the death of Saul and Jonathan, was that there should be neither rain nor dew upon it (2 Sam. i, 21). A prolonged drought meant nothing less than disaster, for where there is no rain the people perish (Deut. xi, 17; Jer. viii, 20; xiv, 2-4). The dew is the sole means by which anything at all survives during the period of intense heat. The necessity of the heavy night dew of the Near East is woven into the ancient desert story of Creation. There can be no plant of the field, nor herb of the earth, unless there is dew (Gen. ii, 5 f.). See also the Mishnah (*Ta'anith* I, 1-III, 8), where there is a description of the special ceremonies which were observed in the hope of securing the immediate onset of the delayed rains in the period immediately following the Feast of Tabernacles of post-exilic times.[9]

Prayers for rain, therefore, have always occupied a prominent place in the ritual of the autumnal feast of Palestine. This applies both to pre-exilic times and to post-exilic times. From such circumstances as this need for good rains in the almost immediate future there arose a most insistent urgency on the part of the Hebrews of Palestine for the necessity of securing at this period of the year ' a good fate ' for the coming year. The decision as to the likelihood of a good year was apparent so very soon. It was a matter of three weeks or so at the outside. The very closeness of the final test increased the sense of immediate urgency, so much so that Jeremiah could cry, "The harvest is past, the summer fruit season is ended, and we are not saved" (Jer. viii, 20).

There is thus no need to assume that in this urgency there is necessarily any copying of the Babylonian custom of decid-

[9] See pp. 174 f. below.

THE PRE-EXILIC NEW YEAR FEAST

ing the fate of the coming year. There is no doubt that there was the association of a common need, but there is no justification for feeling bound to look to the great procession of gods to the judgement hall of Marduk as the origin of the Hebrew emphasis. For one thing, the dates do not fit in with such a theory of origin. This custom, often quoted in this connexion, whereby all the idol gods were carried in procession to the judgement hall of Marduk in Babylon, belongs necessarily to the period of Babylonian supremacy. This began with the revolt by Nabopolassar (626-604) from Assyrian domination at the death of Asshur-bani-pal in 626 B.C., and it reached its full development in the time of Nabopolassar's son, the great Nebuchadrezzar (604-562), the victor of the battle of Carchemish (605 B.C.), that decisive battle in the history of the Near East, when the rival power of Egypt under the Pharaoh Necho was eliminated, and Babylon became mistress of the world for nearly seventy years. Further, it is precisely in countries like Palestine, where the need for rain is urgent, and especially where the effectiveness of prayers for rain must be speedy, that we may expect ideas of insistent urgency to be found. Indeed, we know definitely that this urgency was most marked long before Hebrew ideas could ever have been influenced by the Marduk ceremony, a ceremony which in anything like its sixth-century form could scarcely have existed earlier. Still further, such ideas are much more likely to be emphasized in a land like Palestine than in a land like Mesopotamia, which depends largely upon irrigation for its fertility. In Mesopotamia the emphasis must be not so much on prayers to the Deity for good rains as on the practical duty of keeping the canals clear. Far away back in the time of Hammurabi (? *c.* 2000 B.C.), the proper upkeep of the irrigation channels was a matter of prime importance. In the Code of Hammurabi there are four sections which deal with the penalties to be imposed for various instances of neglect in the upkeep of the banks and of the proper regulation of the runnels (sections 53-56). There are also fines laid down for the theft of watering machines and watering buckets (sections 259, 260). In addition, Hammurabi's letters frequently deal with canal matters. There was evidently need for constant attention to these matters, not least because of the dangers of silting up and the consequent rapid growth of water weeds in the very slowly moving waters of the great flat plain.[10] All this increases the contrast between the immediate needs of Palestine and the more humanly controlled measures necessary in Mesopotamia.

It is reasonably safe, then, to assume that in Palestine prayers for rain were associated with the autumnal harvest feast from the earliest times. They must have taken a prominent place in the ritual of the feast. We do not expect them to take such an outstandingly important position as the fertility rites of the Central Australian aborigines,[11] where the need for rain can very easily become desperate beyond words. The importance will nevertheless be quite pronounced, because of the nearness of the desert and the dependence for the most part upon monsoon rains which may vary both in time and in intensity. These prayers originally take the form of water-pouring rites, sometimes with pouring and sometimes with sprinkling, when the rain is secured by sympathetic or mimetic magic, but they are prayers none the less, though never a word be spoken.

Paul Volz explains[12] many of the details of the sacrifice on Mount Carmel (1 Kings xviii) on these lines. There can be little doubt of the general correctness of the explanation which he offers. He is followed in this explanation by Mowinckel.[13] The object of the contest is to decide which God, Jehovah or Baal (Melkart or ? Hadad), can end the long drought, give the rain, and so bring fertility to the wasted land. The pouring-out of the water from the barrels at the behest of Elijah was not to make the burning of the offering more spectacular and miraculous, though something of this is to be found in the

---

[10] C. H. W. Johns, "The Code of Hammurabi," *H.D.B.*, vol. v, pp. 601, 607; L. W. King, *The Letters and Inscriptions of Hammurabi* (London, 1898), pp. 15, 16, 18, 64 and xxxvi f., lxiv f.

[11] In addition to B. Spencer and Gillen, *The Native Tribes of Central Australia*, mentioned on p. 10 note, see also, by the same authors, *Across Australia* (London, 1912); *The Arunta* (London, 1927); and Sir Baldwin Spencer, *Wanderings in Wild Australia* (London, 1928). An estimate differing in some details is to be found in C. Strehlow, *Die Aranda- und Loritja-Stämme in Zentral-Australien* (Frankfurt-am-Main, 1907-20).

[12] *Das Neujahrsfest Jahwes* (Tübingen, 1912), S. 31.

[13] *Psalmenstudien II* (1912), SS. 102 ff.

telling of the story. It was primarily the water-pouring rite, that acted prayer which, according to primitive ideas, ensured the coming of the long delayed rains. Actually the acted prayer was thrice repeated, three being one of the two really effective numbers in such cases.[14] All this is borne out in the sequel. Having dealt faithfully with the defeated prophets of the Tyrian Baal according to the summary and effective fashion of those rough times, Elijah warns Ahab of the "sound of abundance of rain" (1 Kings xviii, 41). The Hebrew word is *geshem*. This word does not refer to a shower of ordinary rain, nor even to a heavy rainstorm such as might occur, and often does occur, at any time of the year in a country like England. It refers to the heavy downpour of the winter rains, in this case doubtless the Former Rain, the monsoon rain of October, which followed so soon after the autumnal harvest feast. The opening of the former rain, delayed for three years (1 Kings xviii, 1), is coming immediately and torrentially. Elijah goes up with his servant to the top of Mount Carmel, there to wait the appearance of the rain-clouds from the west and south. At last, at the seventh looking (seven being, as we have seen, the other really effective magic number in addition to three), a cloud appears no larger than a man's hand. Such a cloud is not much to see, and signifies nothing for our cloudy skies, but it is enough in a sky which for month after month has been like iron over an earth of brass (Lev. xxvi, 19). The water-pouring prayer, thrice repeated, Elijah's spoken prayers, and the seventh looking, have proved efficacious. Jehovah, having accepted the sacrifice, has forthwith given the needed rains. Ahab must gallop his horses hard if his chariot is to reach the pass of Jezreel before the deluge turns the Plain of Esdraelon into such a quagmire as that which had discomfited Sisera and his hosts in olden time.

A further reference to water-pouring is found in Isa. xii, 3: "Ye shall draw water from the wells of salvation." According to the Mishnah *Sukkah* iv, 9, the drawing of water from the Pool of Shiloah (the modern *'Ain sitti Maryam*) was one of the leading features of the post-exilic Feast of Sukkoth

---

[14] The other effective number in suprahuman affairs is seven. Cf. the seven locks of Samson's hair; cf. also pp. 115 f.

(Booths, Tabernacles). The rite is explained in the Midrashes and the Talmud as being due to Isa. xii, 3 (See *Bereshith Rabba* lxx, 8; *Ruth Rabba* iv, 10; *jer. Sukk.* v, 1.) It is more likely that the passage in question is in reference to a well-known rite, established from time immemorial. The prophet is referring to a custom with which both he and his hearers are thoroughly well acquainted. The Midrashes and the Talmud are seeking Scriptural warrant for a custom which the authors knew to have been observed in the old days before Herod's Temple had been destroyed. People do not invent such customs as these, particularly urban populations. Things are done because they always have been done. Men continually invent new reasons for persisting in old-established ways. The invention of pseudo-archaic rites is a modern phenomenon of recent years.

We may assume, then, that there were always these elements of hopefulness and anxiety forming a basis for the ritual of this great feast at the turn of the year. Always there were prayers, acted and recited, for future well-being in general, and for good rains in particular. Especially was this the case when the immediate response to such prayers was the actual foundation of any prosperity at all in such a country. This was the time, when the harvest was past and the summer ended, that they drew water from ' wells of salvation '.

Such we have seen to be the state of affairs from the earliest times, and certainly during the earlier days of the two kingdoms. What other ceremonies were observed at the feast of the turn of the year in Old Israel we do not know for certain. We can but guess. They are not indicated for pre-exilic times with any degree of preciseness in the Old Testament. We know only of such rites as seem to be very ancient, and were retained in the Second Temple, being recorded in the Priestly Code, and later in the Mishnah, the Toseftas, and the Talmuds. It is most probable that the primitive and heathen element varied in the times of the kingdoms from shrine to shrine, and even at the same shrine from generation to generation. There may well have been a basis of cultus at every shrine common to the whole Canaanite environment, depending upon pre-Israelite custom rather than upon any true Jehovist associations. The number of primitive customs

THE PRE-EXILIC NEW YEAR FEAST

and ideas still surviving in the Priestly Code, as shown chiefly in Leviticus, is sufficient guarantee of this. The Temple which Solomon built was full of heathen symbolism. There were the pomegranates and the date palms of the fertility cults (1 Kings vii, 18, 20, 42; also Exod. xxviii, 23 f.; xxxix, 24-26), the twin pillars Jachin and Boaz which Solomon set up at the door (1 Kings vii, 21), common in heathen temples and originally sun obelisks, probably representative of the double-peaked mountain which flanked the road to the abode of the sun-god[15]; and, amongst other elements, the representation of the great primeval ocean, supported by four times three oxen, bulls being a fertility symbol from ancient times, and the primeval ocean being the site and occasion of the great first victory of the Creator God (1 Kings vii, 23-26). It is probable that the parallels to whatever cult-rites may have existed throughout pre-exilic Israel, at each shrine in its own degree, were more after the pattern of what has recently been found at Ras Shamra than after the pattern of what we have hitherto known from Babylonia.[16] What we do know for certain is that for many generations in Old Israel happiness and carefree festivities prevailed as the dominant *motif* of the autumnal feast. This is the conclusion to be drawn from such stories as that of Abimelech at Shechem and of Hannah at Shiloh.

These were the days when Israel had little thought of any peoples other than those with whom she was immediately in contact. In those days of petty states, Aramæan, Philistine, Moabite, and the rest, there was little fear of invasion beyond occasional small-scale raids. For the rest, they could "sit every man under his vine and under his fig-tree; and none shall make them afraid" (Mic. iv, 4). Even the organized wars (*justa bella*) were of comparatively small account. Just as in the days of which Amos speaks, the people were confident that the Day of the Lord[17] would be brightness and not darkness

---

[15] S. A. Cook, *The Religion of Ancient Palestine in the Light of Archæology*, Schweich Lectures 1925 (London, 1930), pp. 167, 134.

[16] See article "Worship" in *Record and Revelation* (ed. H. Wheeler Robinson, Oxford, 1938), pp. 251-258. For a fuller discussion of the dependence upon Ras Shamra as against Babylonia, see pp. 204 ff. below.

[17] This was the great Day of Days when God would bring final and complete good fortune to His people.

(Amos v, 18-20). Equally naturally the people expected a continuance of God's favour in their ordinary business of fold and field. Their part in the matter was to do their duty as good husbandmen or shepherds, and, so far as the God of the land was concerned, to continue to perform those ritual acts which time and custom sanctioned, and had apparently proved to be effective. Occasionally the rains were delayed. Sometimes there was a serious and prolonged drought, as in the days of Ahab. But generally things went very well, and there was little loss or disturbance. Raids such as that which carried the little Israelitish maid into the boudoir of Naaman's wife were not too common, and for the most part, even then, the loss and the damage were localized. The times were comparable to Victorian England and its petty wars. The masses of the people were not directly affected. They were busy about their own affairs, and the great world passed them by.

The Eighth Century with its Growing Difficulties

There came a time towards the end of the latter part of the eighth century when matters became critical. Amos and Hosea had already seen the distant danger looming steadily nearer. They knew that there were hard and desperate times ahead. Gradually the old brightness and joy faded from the Palestinian skies, and with the darkening shadows the need for a change of fate became increasingly more insistent. The march to the Mediterranean of the first of the great war-lords of the neo-Assyrian Empire, Shalmaneser III (860-823), had been stopped at Karkar in 854 B.C. by Ahab and his allies of the Aramæan confederacy. Thus the waves of this first onward rush had ebbed before they even approached the Palestinian shore. The attack of the second of these war-lords, Adad-nirari III (805-782), had come nearer, and seemed, to the optimistic adherents of the appeasement policy, to have given relief rather than to have increased the gathering gloom. But the relief was more seeming than real. Thanks to the isolationist policy of Jehu and the prophets, the Assyrian had been able to deal with the smaller Aramæan kingdoms one by one, so that with the fall of Damascus in 803 B.C. and the crippling of its power, there was now no serious obstacle between Assyria and the Western Sea. The result was that when the usurper Tiglath-pileser III (745-727) marched west, he was able to crush Damascus finally as an independent power in 734 B.C., to reach the Mediterranean, and to seal Israel's doom.

This time of the great warring empires of the Near East bore the same relation to the comparatively petty wars of the previous generation that the great world wars of the twentieth century bear to the small colonial wars of the nineteenth century. Now wholesale devastation is the rule, and great armies and air armadas sweep to and fro, leaving death, ruin and devastation in their wake. So it was in Palestine, with the chariotry of Assyria taking the place of the tanks and the bombers. From this time onwards, disaster after disaster harried the two Hebrew kingdoms, as the great Assyrian menace grew greater and greater, and as later the threats increased from both Egypt and Babylon. Again and again these little states were overrun, just as has happened time and again in recent generations to the smaller states of Europe. Sometimes, then as now, even great and powerful states fell crashing into ruin. Palestine was stripped bare by contending and marching armies. Not only did the kingdoms of Israel and Judah become pawns in the hands of the great military powers, to be pushed forward to absorb the first attacks of the enemy, but the ordinary husbandman saw the hard-earned fruits of his toil disappear time after time (cf. Deut. xxviii, 30; Isa. lxv, 21 f.). Meanwhile the nobility and the merchant princes, created in the first instance by the foreign policy of Ahab of Israel, gathered field to field into their estates, enclosing the common lands and possessing the small farms, until there was no place left, and the small man had ever less and less chance of recovering from his staggering losses, or even of making a bare living.

From these times onwards the phrase 'the Day of the Lord' changed from meaning a day of anticipation of delights to a day of darkness and disaster, until in course of time it came to mean a time when, after much tribulation and sorrow, God would exert His mighty power in order once and for all to change the current of the world's history, and set His chosen Israel on high never more to fall. This need of redemption from on high became more and more desperate as the years passed by. "Let us", said Israel, "when that day comes at last to end all our sorrow and servitude, let us break their bonds asunder, and cast away their cords from us". "Then shall he speak to them (the kings of the earth and the rulers) in his wrath, and have them in derision" (Ps. ii, 3-5). The phrase 'the Day of the Lord' came ultimately to involve the changing of the very heavens and earth themselves. Our concern with the phrase here is in the fact that the emphasis on the coming Day of the Lord, and the longing for it, march parallel with the growing seriousness of the political situation and with the increased anxiety in connexion with the need for the change of fate at the end of the years.

Mowinckel,[18] once again following Volz,[19] maintains that the phrase 'the Day of the Lord' had its origin in the autumn feast with its anxieties and its rites and fervent prayers for new and better days. The suggestion is that whereas the Baals had their days (Hos. ii, 15; ix, 5), this was Jehovah's day. This suggestion is another indication of the extraordinary influence which Babylonian religion has had upon some Old Testament scholars in their judgements concerning Israelitish religion. In the form in which it is made, this suggestion is dependent upon the Babylonian religious system, in which each deity had its own special day. These days are indicated in the Babylonian menologies.[20] But in Israel the days, whether of Jehovah or of the Baalim, were probably all of them the great day (or days) of the autumnal harvest feast. Hosea calls them 'the days of the Baalim' because of the extent to which the celebrations were intermingled with the rites of the Baalim-worship. It is a much sounder policy to explain what Hosea means by this phrase from what he says elsewhere than it is to seek to explain it from Mesopotamian ideas and customs. There is no trace of separate days for separate deities in Syria, according to the pattern with which we are familiar from Mesopotamia. It was the astral cult, with its dominating astrological ideas, which caused the development of these special Mesopotamian characteristics in the Mesopotamian cities. Where the special Mesopotamian conditions are

---

[18] *Psalmenstudien II*, S. 230. [19] *Das Neujahrsfest Jahwes*, S. 15.
[20] S. Langdon, *Babylonian Menologies and the Semitic Calendars*, pp. 73-82, 92-97.

absent, in respect both of astral cults and city conditions, it is unwise to assume similarities unless it is known definitely that there has been clear and deliberate borrowing. Our conclusion, therefore, in this matter, is that Volz and Mowinckel are most likely to be right in their suggestion, so far as it means that the phrase 'the Day of the Lord' arose out of the celebration of the autumnal harvest feast and the ideas of the change of fate which were connected with it. This does not by any manner of means involve us in accepting Mowinckel's theory of a Coronation Feast of Jehovah celebrated annually after the fashion of the Mesopotamian city temples.[21] There is no necessary connexion at all with Mesopotamian customs.

The Change of Fate

We have seen that more and more as the years passed by, each with its increasing threat of doom, the need for a change of fate became increasingly apparent, until it became the dominant factor in the celebrations at the autumnal Old Year-New Year feast. The Hebrew phrase for 'change of fate, fortune' is *shub shebuth*, lit. 'to turn a turning', or, better, 'to restore a restoration' (i.e. to restore to a former condition of prosperity). This phrase has been exhaustively analysed by E. L. Dietrich of Mainz.[22] The phrase primarily means 'to restore to a former condition'. It is composed of a transitivized *shub* which has taken the place of the hiphil (causative and transitive) form, plus a noun derived from the same root, but probably, though not certainly, originally pronounced *shabuth*. Later this noun was wrongly pronounced, and was understood to refer to 'captivity'. It was confused, or indeed was deliberately equated, with the noun *shebi(th)*, from the root *sh-b-h* (to take captive). There is complete confusion in the Masoretic Text as to whether the word should be spelled and/or pronounced *shebuth* or *shebith*. Every possible variation is found. Sometimes one is written and read; sometimes the other is written and read; and sometimes one is written and the other read. The misinterpretation 'to turn the cap-

[21] For further discussion of this theory, see pp. 195-220.
[22] *Shub Shebuth: Die endzeitliche Wiederherstellung bie den Propheten* (Giessen, 1925).

tivity' is perhaps clearest of all in Job xlii, 10. Here the English Versions, both Authorized and Revised, have translated "and the Lord turned the captivity of Job", thus following what is written in the Masoretic Text. But Job was never in captivity, except by a figure of speech, unless perchance the whole book was taken to be an elaborate allegory on the undeserved sufferings of captive Israel. According to the modern Jewish translation into English,[23] the meaning is "and the Lord changed the fortunes of Job", which is following what is read in the Masoretic Text, and is undoubtedly right. Septuagint has preserved something of the original meaning by translating the whole phrase by *euxesen* (increased). Perhaps this is due to the remainder of the verse, "and the Lord gave Job twice as much as he had before", and perhaps both the Septuagint translation and the verse itself are influenced by Isa. xl, 2: "that she hath received of the Lord double for all her sins".

In Job xlii, 10, the Roman Douai Version has "the Lord also was turned at the penance of Job, when he prayed for his friends", this being a rendering of the Vulgate *Dominus quoque conversus est ad pœnitentiam Iob*. This is an interesting example of the effect of dogma upon the versions. Incidentally, it shows that even if the Roman Church were to base its doctrines solely upon Scripture there would still be no common ground for discussion between Protestant and Roman. We do not accept the same Scriptures. It is as well that this should be fully recognized by both sections of Christendom. The Scriptures of the Protestant Church are the Hebrew Masoretic Text plus the Greek New Testament. The Scriptures of the Roman Church are the Latin Bible, namely the sixteenth-century edition of Jerome's early fifth-century Latin translation.[24] This is one reason why it is folly to think that any agreed syllabus of Scripture study would ever be acceptable to all Christians. There is a disagreement not only concerning the syllabus, but even concerning what is Scripture.

[23] *The Holy Scriptures according to the Masoretic Text: A New Translation*, issued first in America in 1916 for the Council of the Jewish War Memorial. This translation deserves to be much more widely known amongst Christians in this country.

[24] Council of Trent (1546), and Papal Bull of 1592.

THE PRE-EXILIC NEW YEAR FEAST

There is a striking confusion in the Septuagint of Jer. xxxi, 19 (LXX, xxxviii, 18). The previous verse in both versions, i.e. in both Hebrew and Greek, concludes: "turn thou me, and I shall be turned; for thou art the Lord my God". Then the Hebrew follows with "surely after that I was turned (*shubi*: the construct infinitive qal of *shub* with suffix), I repented", but Septuagint has "for after my captivity (reading *shibyi*: i.e. the noun *shebi*, captivity, with suffix), I repented".

There is a number of instances where the versions have preserved the original meaning of 'turn a turning', the translation proposed as the original meaning by Ewald[25] in 1853. Examples are, thrice by the Septuagint in Ezek. xvi, 53, and by both Symmachus and Aquila in Job xlii, 10. There are five cases in the Vulgate, four[26] of them in Jeremiah, and one in Ezek. xvi, 53. In Joel iii, 7 (EVV iv, 1), the Vulgate has added "upon your heads", and understands the Hebrew to mean 'retribution'. But the most important of all the renderings of the Versions, from the point of view of the New Year feast and its significance, is that of Septuagint in Deut. xxx, 3, where the reading is *kai iasetai Kurios tas hamartias sou*, i.e. "and the Lord will heal thy sins". The importance of this rendering will be seen later when we discuss those ideas of penitence which came to be associated with the New Year festival in increasing measure. It is evident that the same factor has been at work, and can be detected, in Lam. ii, 14: *ut te ad pœnitentiam provocarent*, which the Douai Version characteristically interprets "to excite thee to penance". With this we must associate the Vulgate rendering of Job xlii, 10, which we have previously mentioned, and its similar Douai interpretation 'penance'.

The Autumnal Feast and the Coronation of the King

There remain two important references to what may well be associations of the annual feast with the coronation of the

[25] *Jahrb. f. d. Wissenschaft*, V, SS. 126 ff.
[26] xxx, 18; xxxiii, 7, 11, 26. In these four cases, although the Vulgate is *conversionem*, the Douai Version has 'captivity'. The statement, therefore, that the Douai Version is a rendering of the Vulgate needs a certain amount of qualification. In Ezek. xvi, 53, it is made quite clear in the Douai Version that the conversion of Gentile and Jew "to the Church of Christ" is to be understood.

new king. Both instances are concerned with the two attempts to secure the throne during David's lifetime. One is the unsuccessful attempt by Absalom. The other is the successful *coup d'état* on behalf of Solomon in David's extreme old age and senility. Their chief importance lies in their possible association with the suggestions which have been made in recent years as to the existence of the myth ritual pattern of the Near East as a basis of religious customs and ideas in pre-exilic Israel, combined with the theory of the existence of the Divine King in Israel. This latter must be discussed later.[27] Here our interest in the two incidents is the probability of their connexion and even coincidence with the autumnal harvest feast.

Absalom obtained permission to go to Hebron in order, as he said, to fulfil a vow which he had made during his period of exile from the court (2 Sam. xv, 7). He may have been lying over the whole matter of the vow and the necessity of fulfilling it, for it is strange that he should have delayed so long. He said that the vow was connected with his return to Jerusalem, but he had already dwelt two full years in the city (2 Sam. xiv, 28) before he managed to persuade Joab to intercede with David on his behalf. If the vow was concerned with Absalom's restoration to the favour of his father David, then the fulfilment of the vow would come most naturally during the third year, especially since the time when Joab interceded with the king was evidently not far distant from the time of the barley harvest (2 Sam. xiv, 30). There was nothing to prevent him from fulfilling his vow at the end of the third year, i.e. in the autumn following the time of his restoration to favour, which had taken place in the spring, some six months previously. As it was, the time when Absalom went to Hebron to fulfil this vow was "at the end of four years" (so Septuagint, rightly). Mention is made of the sacred meal (*zebachim*, 2 Sam. xv, 12). Absalom evidently intended to be crowned king on this occasion, and to be crowned at Hebron, where his father David had first been crowned. Does the time reference in verse 7 mean that Absalom went to Hebron at the actual end of the year, i.e. at the precise time of the great autumnal feast? Probably so. The word *miqqeç* (at the end

[27] See pp. 211 f.

of) is precisely the word which is used in 2 Sam. xiv, 25 f., of Absalom's annual custom of shearing his hair at the end of the year. This was the proper time for the fulfilment of vows. We have seen also that the word *miqqeç* elsewhere[28] is used of the actual end of the year. We must therefore assume that Absalom saw in the incidence of this particular autumnal feast, coupled with the convenient remembrance of a vow made long before and hitherto neglected, an opportunity to establish himself as king. The earlier verses of the chapter tell how he had been preparing the ground, partly by riding out in semi-royal state in his chariot with fifty outrunners before him, and partly by currying favour with every man[29] who came up to seek justice at the king's hand. Absalom is certainly proclaimed king at Hebron with the traditional cry *malak 'Abshalom* (Absalom has become king, 2 Sam. xv, 10).

There are two possible explanations. One is that all kings were proclaimed and crowned at the harvest feast, and therefore Absalom at this particular feast. The other is that when men are full of new wine, then is the time for sedition to ripen into action and open revolt. In support of the second explanation there is the story of Abimelech and Gaal, which we know to have belonged to the story of an autumnal vintage feast at Shechem (Judg. ix, 27-29). But this story may support the first explanation also, though, if so, it is strange that there should be such emphasis on the feast itself. With respect to the first explanation, it may be urged that the proclamation of Absalom as king at the end of the year was accidental, and that the proper day for acclaiming a king is the most convenient day. For example, there may be said to be some evidence that Joash was proclaimed king at the autumnal feast. The evidence is slight, and depends upon interpreting " in the seventh year " (2 Kings xi, 4) as meaning ' in the beginning of the seventh

---

[28] See pp. 49 f. above.
[29] In 2 Sam. xv, 2, these men are described as ' of the tribes of Israel '. Does this mean of Israel as against of Judah? This question is always hard to answer, but if it does mean ' of Israel, the Northern Kingdom ' in this particular case, then Absalom was making use of the steady disaffection of the North against the domination of the South, that bitterness and rivalry which never ceased.

year'. This evidence is still slighter according to 2 Chron. xxiii, 2, which makes the gathering a specially called assembly of the Levites and "the heads of fathers' houses" of Israel.³⁰ The fact that the Chronicler turns this occasion into a specially called gathering counts heavily against Mowinckel's theory of a Coronation Feast of Jehovah on the lines of the coronations of the kings of Israel and Judah. Assuming that the coronation of Joash did actually take place at the autumnal harvest feast, it may be said that the case of Joash was unusual, since there the king was established on his throne by a bold *coup d'état* on the part of the High Priest with the help of the foreign mercenaries. The answer is that this is exactly what Absalom intended, so far as the sudden onset was concerned, though unsuccessfully. Further, we have no account of coronations in the Old Testament except those which, from the very nature of the case, were unusual and of this exact type. Solomon's successful seizure of the throne was very similar to the accession of Joash. The fact that these things happened at the harvest feast at the end-beginning of the year, if indeed this can be said of the Joash incident, may mean only that it was a matter of convenience. Yet again, necessity and custom and convenience may easily all three coincide, especially in a community which is much more primitive than we moderns can easily realize. In any case the Man of Destiny is he who can make the occasion fit the need. The question is not resolved, as the Rabbis used to say.

A closer analogy is the story of 1 Kings i, with its account of the failure of Adonijah and of the success of Solomon. This case is particularly important in view of the ideas of the fertility of the king and suchlike associations. It provides the more clear-cut of the two instances where the right to the throne in Old Israel is made to depend upon the physical vigour of the king. In this case King David himself is involved, the greatest of all the kings, and the very type of Messiah himself. It is because the aged David remains im-

---

³⁰ This probably means Judah; cf. 2 Chron. xxi, 2: "Jehoshaphat king of Israel", though in this latter instance both Septuagint and Peshitta have 'Judah', and so also about forty of Kennicott's MSS. The fact that 'Judah' is a *sebir* here is against it being the correct Masoretic Text, but probably in favour of it being right according to actual fact.

potent even in the arms of the ravishing[31] Shunammite that there is need for a new and vigorous king. The reference to the king getting no heat is not a reference to the weather, nor has it anything to do with the condition of his circulation. The question which arises is: had the test as to impotence to be made before the annual feast, and, if so, did it take place every year, or only if there seemed to be some doubt about the matter? Adonijah was certainly acclaimed on the occasion of a sacred feast which was held by the sacred stone near En-rogel (1 Kings i, 9, 25). Solomon was crowned on the selfsame day (verse 41). All the circumstances point to an annual feast, for it is stated in the sequel that there were tremendous crowds filled with ecstatic joy (verse 40). Of course, " they say such things in books ". Again, it is not mentioned specifically that it was the annual feast, but this argument from silence can be used with equal force either way. There is no doubt about this type of argument being a sharp sword, but the sword is double-edged. No line of argument can be more treacherous. If it was the established custom that all this should take place at the harvest feast, then we could scarcely expect the fact to be mentioned in any particular or outstanding fashion. Anyone who has any sense or knowledge would know without being told. We might very easily in our time, as indeed often we do, tell a story concerning the hanging up of stockings without specifically mentioning the Christmas association. Everybody knows that nobody ever hung up a stocking at any other time, and there is no need to say anything about it being Christmas Eve. Equally, if it did not matter whether Solomon's accession took place at the annual feast or not, we would expect precisely the amount of attention which is actually given.[32] The matter belongs to the general problem of pre-exilic ritual, and must be decided on

[31] Cf. the attempts to identify her with the love-maiden of the Song of Songs. These attempts began very early in the history of the interpretation of the Song.
[32] For example, in Job ii, 8, the Hebrew Text says that Job sat ' in the midst of the ashes '. Septuagint adds ' without the city '. There was no need for this to be expressed in the Hebrew, because every native of Palestine would know that the ashes were without the city. On the other hand, Septuagint did well to insert the phrase, because what was obvious and well known to the Palestinian was not obvious and not known at all to the Alexandrian.

more general grounds. There is evidence that the king must be vigorous and fertile, but there is nothing in this story which is decisive either way in respect of the incidence of the annual autumnal feast. What we have here in 1 Kings i, 1, is, as we have said, one of the two instances of the association of fertility ideas and the kingship in Old Israel. The other (probable) example is 2 Sam. xvi, 21, where, on the advice of Ahitophel, Absalom goes in to his father's concubines in the sight of all the people. The association of the annual feast is in each case probable, though whether or not it was necessary is not proven in either case.

3

THE EXILE AND THE CHANGE OF CALENDAR

A.—NEW-MONTH DAYS AND SABBATHS

It is an error to assume that in early times the Hebrews had a calendar with any pretensions whatever to scientific accuracy in anything like our modern meaning of the term 'scientific'. Such precise calculations depend upon the exact observation of the heavenly bodies. This was unknown in Palestine until long after the beginning of the Christian Era, and was indeed actively discouraged by the religious authorities, partly because of traditional conservatism, but partly also because of a real fear of idolatry. Such observations began in Palestine, so far as the Jews are concerned, as late as the tenth century A.D. The occasion was the triumph of the Babylonian schools of Rabbis under the vigorous leadership of Rabbi Sa'adiyah in the year 921 A.D.

The Beginnings of Jewish Astronomy

The story of the exact observation by Jews of the movements of the moon goes back in Babylonia as far as Mar Samuel, otherwise known as Samuel Yarchinai (c. 165- c. 257 A.D.). Just as Rabbi Sa'adiyah later established the general supremacy of the Babylonian schools, so Mar Samuel established in his day the intellectual independence of the school at Nehardea at the same time that Rab established the independence of the school at Sura. His surname Yarchinai was given him because of his fame as an astronomer, especially in the study of the movements of the moon, his fame in this respect equalling his fame as a master of the Law and as a physician. He compiled a calendar for sixty years, based on the movements of the moon. The attention to the formation of proper calendars received a considerable impulse owing to the work of the Muslim astronomers Al-Battani and Al-Khwarizmi in the ninth century, and this, as much as anything else, probably contributed to the success of Rabbi

Sa'adiyah in the next century in establishing a scientific calendar for Palestinian as well as for Babylonian Jewry. Certainly the twelfth-century Jewish calendars were based on the tables of Al-Battani, as is shown by the tables[1] of *Abraham bar Chiyya hanNasi*.

(i) Canaanite Month-Names

It is many years since Dillmann maintained[2] that months like Abib cannot be regarded as having been originally a fixed month in the calendar according to the rigid pattern to which we have long been accustomed. The months were doubtless distinguished from each other by the phase of the moon, but the names themselves represent rather certain periods of the agricultural year.

These pre-exilic month-names such as Abib are Canaanite in origin. We know only four of them from the Old Testament. These are the first, Ethanim; the second, Bul; the seventh, Abib; and the eighth, Ziv. Ethanim is the month of 'steady flowings', the month of the perennial streams. The singular form of the word is used of 'rivers of steady flow' (Ps. lxxiv, 15), i.e. true rivers (*nahar*) which never cease to flow. It is used also of permanent wady streams as against those wadies (*nachal*) which are torrents in the rainy season and little more than dry rocky beds for the rest of the year (Amos v, 24).[3] This makes Ethanim to be the month when only the most stubborn streams continue to flow. It is the last period of the summer drought, before the former rains begin.

The meaning of the word Bul, the name of the second of these lunar periods, is uncertain. There is a Hebrew word *bul*, which occurs twice, namely in Isa. xliv, 19, and in Job xl, 20. The word means 'produce,' and may be either an error or a deliberately shortened form for the more usual *yebul*. Another possible explanation is that it is the name of the Palmyrene god Bol or Bul. The Septuagint of 1 Kings vi, 38 (LXX, 3 Kgdms. vi, 5), reads *baad*, which needs only the

---

[1] *Luchoth hanNasi*, cf *JE*, vol. i, p. 109.
[2] 'Über des Kalenderwesen der Israel vor dem babylonische Exil' in *Monatschrift d. Berl. Akad.*, 1882, SS. 914 ff.
[3] The history of the word, including the loss of its true meaning and the subsequent recovery of it, is given by S. R. Driver, *Deuteronomy* (ICC), pp. 241 f.

omission of a horizontal line in the base of the last letter to be
'Baal'. Yet again, there may be a connexion with the Akkadian word *bulu*, which means 'cattle'.

We are on much safer ground when we come to the name
Abib. Here the reference is to 'freshness' and 'green shoots'.
Compare the Hebrew *'eb* (Job viii, 12, and Cant. vi, 11), and
also the similar Aramaic *'abb*. The meaning of the word Ziv
is somewhat similar. It is a good Aramaic word for 'freshness'
(cf. Dan. ii, 31, etc.). According to the Targum, this is the
month of the fragrance of flowers.

It is noticeable that the two names Abib and Ziv are both
descriptive of the freshness and greenness of the produce of
the earth. The explanation we would give of this is that the
seasons are spread over a two-month period when the whole of
the country is taken into account. On these lines we would
tentatively hold to the meaning 'produce' for the monthname Bul, especially since this was actually the produce-month
for the Northern part of the country.

There is a possibility that seven more of these Canaanite
months can be reclaimed from the Phœnician remains, but
there is no guide as to their order in the calendar, nor is there
any guarantee of their antiquity. The names are *Zabachshashim, Chiyar, Mapha', Karar, Pe'ullat, Marzeach,* and
Marpa' (Marpa'im). Yet another old Aramaic month-name is
Kinun (hearth-fire).[4] The doubt as to the antiquity of these
names is real, for the name *Marzeach* is from a Sidonian inscription found at Athens and dated as late as 96 B.C. The
word may mean 'lamentations', and *Marpa'* may mean
'ghosts'.

The four ancient Hebrew month-names of which we can be
sure are similar to the names in the so-called Gezer Calendar,
in that they have reference to agricultural matters. This
calendar, as we have said,[5] is most likely to be a list of agricultural operations which are proper to the various periods of
the year, and written down by some peasant farmer. The
suggestion that the peasant farmer might be able to write
down such a list is not so wild as might appear. To work with
the hands was never regarded in Palestine as being a degrad-

[4] S. Langdon, *Babylonian Menologies*, etc., p. 25.
[5] See p. 62 above.

ing task only for the unintelligent, as so often has been the case in this Western civilization. Even in the time of the Lord Jesus the Rabbis largely earned their own living by the work of their own hands. Gideon could find a youth, apparently by a chance meeting, who wrote down for him the names of the seventy princes and elders of the city (Judg. viii, 14). Neither Amos nor Micah was by any means a country bumpkin.

The names of the periods of the Gezer Calendar are *'oṣeph* (ingathering), *zera'* (sowing), *leqesh* (late grass), *'açad peshet* (flax harvest), *qaçar se'orim* (barley harvest), *qaçar kol* (harvest of everything), *zamar* (pruning), and *qeç* (fruit harvest). Langdon finds[6] difficulty in the word *zamar*, on the ground that in Palestine the pruning falls in February. The reference, however, is not to the first pruning, but to the second or summer pruning, as H. H. Rowley has made clear in another connexion.[7]

The names of the Gezer Calendar amount to eight in all. If *leqesh* is 'late grass', i.e. the grass that grows strongly after the latter rain (*malqosh*), then that period is not earlier than February at the very earliest. This would be what is called, in Amos vii, 1, 'the beginning of the growing up of the *leqesh*'. In that case, perhaps the period before this was *gizzey hammelek* (the king's shearings), since it says in Amos vii, 1, that "*leqesh* is after *gizzey hammelek*". The use of the phrase *qeçir (has)se'orim* (barley harvest) in 2 Sam. xxi, 9; Ruth i, 22; ii, 23, may well refer to a month-period in just the same way as does the similar phrase in the Gezer Calendar. Further speculation suggests that *qeçir (hach)chiṭṭim* (wheat harvest) in Ruth ii, 23, may be the equivalent of the *qaçar kol* of the Gezer Calendar, this latter phrase actually meaning the harvest which completes the gathering of all cereal crops. There may be two other names of the same type in Lev. xxvi, 5: which we can render " and *dayish* (threshing)[8] shall reach to *baçir* (vintage), and *baçir* shall reach to *zera'* (sowing: the exact word of the Gezer Calendar)." This would provide us with *dayish* for June and *baçir* for September. Thus the pas-

---

[6] S. Langdon, *Babylonian Menologies*, p. 25, note 1.
[7] "The Song of Songs: An Examination of Recent Theory," in *J.R.A.S.*, April, 1938, p. 269.
[8] There is no 'your', as in R.V.

sage would mean that the threshing period would last from June to September, and the vintage from September to December, three months each. There is one period remaining, and for this we would suggest *charish* (ploughing), on the basis of Gen. xlv, 6 (E). Our supplemented Gezer list would then be:

1. *'oṣeph*, ingathering, October (roughly).
2. *charish*, ploughing, November.
3. *zera'*, sowing, December.
4. *gizzey hammelek*, the king's shearings, January.
5. *leqesh*, 'late' grass, February.
6. *'aṣad peshet*, flax harvest, March.
7. *qaçar se'orim*, barley harvest, April.
8. *qaçar chiṭṭim* (wheat harvest) or *qaçar kol* (harvest of the rest of cereals), May.
9. *dayish*, threshing, June.
10. *zamar*, summer pruning, July.
11. *qeç*, summer fruit, August.
12. *baçir*, vintage, September.

We recognize that these additions to the Gezer list are almost wholly speculative, but we put them down as an adventure in prophecy, in the hope that further material will one day be brought to light to show them accurate.

(ii) New-Month Day and the Full Moon

We have said that these periods of time were probably distinguished from each other by the phase of the moon. But which phase was the divider? Was it indeed the new moon, as has generally been assumed? Or was it perchance the full moon? We believe that there is a certain amount of evidence which suggests that in pre-exilic Israel the moon-phase which divided the month-periods was the full moon, and not the new moon, as has generally been assumed.

Water Pouring at the Full Moon

We have seen that the early Hebrews of Canaan of pre-exilic times considered their year to end at the Feast of Asiph (Ingathering). After the exile, the opening day of the great vintage feast, now called the Feast of Sukkoth (Booths, Tabernacles), was the day of the full moon of Tishri. This post-exilic Feast of Tishri corresponds in part with the pre-exilic Feast of Asiph. The leading features of this post-exilic Feast of Sukkoth were the water-pouring and the all-night illuminations of the first night of the Feast, 'the House of Water-pouring', as it was called (Mishnah, *Sukkah* v, 1-4). These two ceremonies are not only outstanding features of the feast; they are essential to it; they make it what it is. In each case we have what, from the very nature of the ceremonies themselves, must be beyond question survivals of essentially primitive rites. Men do not invent such rites as these; they continue to observe them. If the study of anthropology, with its long lists from all the world of ancient rites stubbornly preserved, teaches anything, it certainly teaches this.

The water-pouring rite is the primitive ritual for rain. Elijah commanded it to be performed on Mount Carmel with the sacred-magic three. It is common all the world over among primitive communities for the rain-makers to make rain by imitating the falling rain, either by sprinkling water or by throwing pieces of down, by mimicking clouds, and by simulating thunder. Frazer[9] gives numerous instances "from sultry lands like Central Australia and some parts of Eastern and Southern Africa, where often for months together the pitiless sun beats down out of a blue and cloudless sky on the parched and gaping earth". Such customs "are, or used to be, common enough among outwardly civilized folk in the moister climate of Europe". We read of naked women and girls of the Russian village of Ploska who poured water on the ground by night at the boundaries of their village; of wizards in New Guinea and in New Britain; of Omaha Indians, the Dieri tribe of Central Australia, Greeks of Thessaly and Macedonia, and so on, almost interminably, all of them seeking, by simulating the falling rain, to promote that rainfall of which they are in such dire need. There is therefore every encouragement from anthropology to see in the water-pouring rite of the Feast of Sukkoth a survival from very early times. It is the primitive ritual for ensuring a good 'former rain'.

Ordinarily, in the Jerusalem Temple of post-exilic days, the water for the drink-offering which accompanied the morning sacrifice was brought into the Temple overnight. The water was taken when it was wanted from a golden vessel in the

[9] *The Golden Bough* (ed. in one vol., London, 1923), pp. 63-83.

Temple. This custom pertained to Sabbaths even during the Feast of Booths, the water having been brought up the previous day. On normal days throughout the year the Temple personnel, apart from those who kept the night-watch, began to stir with the first streak of dawn. Lots were cast as to which of the priests should perform the various duties involved in the offering of the morning sacrifice. At the three great feasts, Passover, Pentecost and Tabernacles, the day's work began much earlier. During the first watch of the night the altar of burnt-offering was cleansed. In the first hours after midnight the Temple doors were opened. There was much to be done, because of all the extra offerings and so forth, before the dawn had lit up "the whole sky as far as Hebron", the time, just before the sun appeared over the top of the Mount of Olives, when the morning sacrifice was slain. Already whilst the preparations for the morning sacrifice at the Feast of Tabernacles were being made in the Temple, a priest appointed by lot had gone down the long flight of steps to the Pool of Siloam. He was accompanied by a procession of worshippers, and with great joy and music. At the pool he filled his golden pitcher, holding a little more than two pints, and began his journey back, heading the joyful procession. They drew water with joy out of the wells of salvation (Isa. xii, 3). And so they returned back up the steps to the Temple precincts. It was the priest's duty so to regulate his pace that he returned just as the other priests placed the pieces of the morning sacrifice on the altar. He proceeded through the Water-gate towards the inclined plane which led up to the altar. As he entered this gate, so called because of this very ceremony, he was greeted with a triple blast from the trumpets of the priests. He went to the left of the altar, and picking up the vessel which contained the wine, waiting for him there, he poured the water and the wine into the two silver funnels beside the altar. The eastern funnel was for the wine, and was a little wider than the western funnel, which was for the water. This was arranged so that the two should empty simultaneously. Such a ceremony doubtless received accretions during the years. One such addition was the shout which the people gave as the priest poured the water. They cried, "Lift up thy hand." This was to ensure that he really did pour the water properly into the silver funnel-basin. It dates from about the year 95 B.C., when Alexander Jannæus, priest-king from 102/1 to 76/5 B.C., showed his contempt for the preciseness which the Pharisees had imposed upon the Saducean priesthood in the strict observance of ritual in the Temple. His action occasioned a riot. The people pelted him with their ethrogs, the citrous fruit which they carried at this feast, and he was saved from being assassinated by the intervention of his guard. As it was, six thousand Jews were killed in the Temple before the disturbance was quelled. Apart from such accretions, some of them due doubtless to much less serious causes, the essential features of the rite belong to primitive times.

New Year's Day and the Harvest Moon

The other characteristic ceremony of the post-exilic Feast of Sukkoth was the all-night illuminations, 'the House of Water-pouring'. In latitudes away from the equator the night of the full moon of Tishri, that is, the night of the Harvest Full Moon, is of peculiar importance. Always the full moon rises at sunset, but always when the moon is near the first point of Aries she rises at approximately the same time for two or three nights together. This is due to the variation, as the latitude gets higher, between the inclination of the ecliptic and the horizon at different points of the horizon. At the time of the Harvest Full Moon the sun is in Libra and the moon is at the first point of Aries. Thus this particular full moon rises at approximately the same time for several nights together. The two or three nights of the moon's 'stationary' rising seem to be extended on the occasion when the full moon itself is at the first point of Aries. Further, there are, for whatever reason, the well-known distinctive features of the apparent size and the colour of this particular full moon. Whilst, of course, every full moon makes the night light from dusk to dawn, the Harvest Full Moon does this in its own peculiar and distinctive fashion. On the basis of all these special features, we can safely assume that there is very good reason for the all-night celebrations of the Feast of Tabernacles being peculiar to this particular night, namely the night of the Harvest Full Moon. This means that both before the Exile and after the Exile the Hebrews held this ceremony on this particular night. The

THE EXILE AND THE CHANGE OF CALENDAR 89

night was independent of the calendar. It depended solely on the moon. They therefore regarded their year always as ending with the fulness of the Harvest Moon. The necessity of some such situation as this has already been foreseen by such a careful and conservative scholar as G. B. Gray.[10] He said, " If the inference is legitimate that it fell of old, as it fell later, on the full moon, it seems a fortnight after the year ended, *unless we could believe that the year began not with the new but with the full moon*" (the italics are ours). We believe that there is a certain amount of evidence, and a considerable amount of probability, that the Hebrews in pre-exilic times did actually believe their year to end with the Harvest Full Moon.

Whatever old year and new year customs may have gravitated in post-exilic days to Tishri 1 and Tishri 10, consequent upon the change of calendar and the break-up of the pre-exilic Feast of Asiph into the three festivals of Tishri[11], the illumination perforce maintained its original connexion with the full moon. Why should any post-exilic new year ceremonies be associated with the middle of the seventh month, unless that month, and especially the middle of it, had always been the right time for them? It is easy to account for some of the ancient new year ceremonies being diverted to the first of the month, even though it was the seventh month. We can also account, as we shall see, for some of the ceremonies being moved to the tenth of the seventh month, but it is not easy to account for any ceremonies on the fifteenth of the seventh month, unless for some reason the fifteenth of the seventh month was the right and proper time for them.

The importance attached to these illuminations on the first night of the Feast of Tabernacles, the repeated reference to them in the traditions, and the great care evidently taken to ensure that they were thoroughly effective and satisfactory—all these things show how truly fundamental they were to the proper observance of the Feast. " There were there (in the Court of the Women) three golden candlesticks, and on the top of them four golden basins; and four ladders were placed near each; and four novices mounted the ladders, having in their hands jugs of oil containing one hundred and twenty

[10] *Sacrifice in the Old Testament*, p. 301.
[11] Volz, *Das Neujahrsfest Jahwes*, S. 18. See also p. 148 below.

logs of oil,[12] with which they replenished each basin."[13] The worn-out undergarments of the priests and their belts were torn into strips and used for wicks, and the Mishnah says that "there was not a court in Jerusalem which was not made bright by the light of the water-drawing". One tradition says that a woman could pick wheat by the light of it, anywhere in Jerusalem. Meanwhile "pious men and saints danced before the people with lighted torches in their hands, singing hymns and praises before them".[14] The *Tosefta* tells us what they sang. They all said, "Happy is he who has not sinned, and whoever has sinned shall be forgiven". Then the pious men said, "Happy am I whose youth has not shamed my age," and the penitents said, "Happy am I whose old age can atone for my youth." It is told of Rabbi Simeon ben Gamaliel that once he was dancing with eight lighted torches, tossing them high in the air, and catching them as they fell, and as he did so not one of them fell to the ground. As he prostrated himself in the *Qidah* (a dance which includes falling on the face, *b. Meg.* 22b), he put his finger on the pavement of the court, bent down and kissed it, and then stood upright again.[15]

An additional reason for supposing that all this illumination, both the lights of the giant candelabra and those from the flaring torches, belonged to the night of this full moon, and to no other night than this particular full moon, is that the whole ceremony seems to be connected with the sun. It closed with a definite and deliberate denial of sun-worship. Why should the ceremony close with this denial unless there was some reason for the denial? *Qui s'excuse s'accuse.* And what other night should it so close except the night of a full moon, when the ending of the illumination coincided exactly with the rising of the sun? No night other than that of the full moon has the setting of the moon coinciding with the

---

[12] I.e. about fifteen gallons. The Jerusalem Talmud says that the candlesticks were a hundred cubits high, but the Babylonian Talmud halves this figure. If the figures are trustworthy, even the lower figure involves a man mounting a ladder some sixty-odd feet high with a jug large enough to contain fifteen gallons of oil. Possibly fifteen gallons per lamp was the total amount consumed during the whole night.

[13] Mishnah, *Sukkah* v, 2. The translation is from "Translations from Early Documents Series" (S.P.C.K.). *Sukkah, Mishna and Tosefta*, by A. W. Greenup.

[14] Mishnah, *Sukkah*, v, 4.   [15] *Tosefta Sukkah*, v, 2, 4.

rising of the sun. And of all the full moons, there is none so "bright and beautiful as the harvest moon".[16]

During the night of the House of Water-pouring, the Levites had been standing on the fifteen steps which led down from the Court of Israel to the Court of the Women, that is, on the steps which led up to the Gate of Nicanor. They formed the orchestra, and they were playing on every kind of instrument. It is stated that these fifteen steps corresponded to the fifteen Songs of Degrees (Goings-up ? Steps ?) in the Psalter (Pss. cxx-cxxxiv). Whether they actually sang these psalms on these occasions is not stated. Towards dawn two priests took up their stand in the Gate of Nicanor at the head of the fifteen steps, and at cock-crow they sounded a plain note, a tremolo, and a plain note with their trumpets. They did so as they stood on the top step, again on the tenth step, and yet again when they reached the level of the Court below. They continued in this fashion, blowing as they went, straight across the Court of the Women until they came to the East Gate of the Temple, the Beautiful Gate of the Temple, that gate which was between the Court of the Women and the Court of the Gentiles. There they turned right about. They thus faced the Holy Place, and had their backs turned towards the sun, now rising over the top of the Mount of Olives. This action thus coincided with the exact moment of the offering of the Morning Sacrifice. Then they recited, "Our fathers, who were in this place, turned their backs to the Temple and their faces towards the east, and they prostrated themselves to the east. But we lift our eyes to God". According to Rabbi Jehudah, they used to repeat, "We belong to God, and we lift our eyes to God".

Here, beyond question, is an anti-sun-worship ritual. The fact that it comes at the end of the night's observances, and thus marks the close of them, fixes the whole set of ceremonies on the night of the full moon. They could not have done what they did on any other day than that of the full moon. The reason for the ceremony may be because of what happened in the closing days of the first Temple (Ezek. viii, 16). On the other hand, it may have reference to a cult far older

[16] Anthony Trollope, *The Vicar of Bullhampton*, chapter v, of Carry Brattle before her fall.

than the times immediately prior to the Exile, some ancient cult of sun-worship on this site to which the happenings of Ezek. viii, 16, may have been a reversion. We know that these last days of Solomon's Temple were days of dreadful apostasy, when men in their desperation reverted to age-old cults. The Jews who took refuge in Egypt defended their action in burning incense to the queen of heaven on the ground that they all did this years ago, kings and princes and people, and that it was only when this worship ceased that troubles came upon them (Jer. xliv, 15-23). F. J. Hollis holds[17] that "the fundamental reason why Sun-worship persisted so tenaciously in Jahweh's sacred precincts in Jerusalem is to be found in the fact that those precincts from a remote antiquity had been a leading centre of such worship". We doubt whether all the evidence which he adduces will bear the full weight of the conclusions which he builds upon it. For instance, whilst the orientation of Solomon's Temple varied by five degrees from the orientation of the post-exilic Temples, so that both were correctly facing, when first built, the rising sun at the proper period of the year, yet this does not necessarily prove that they were built as sun-temples. It shows that all such orientated temples were built on the pattern of an original sun-temple, but not necessarily any more than that. In the buildings of the Established Church of England we get this same orientation, and devout Anglicans turn to the east when they recite the Creed. Both customs go back beyond any shadow of doubt to sun-worship, but this does not mean that Anglicans worship the sun. What it does signify, is that they have taken over and adapted an old pagan pre-Christian custom, but have provided it with a new meaning, conformable to their Christian beliefs. Nevertheless, it is clear from Mr. Hollis's essay that there is abundant evidence of an early sun-cult on the site of the Temple at Jerusalem. There also, as in much of modern Christian ritual, old pagan customs were continued, with the ancient meanings either sublimated or deliberately denied. But all this fixes the ceremony more securely to the full moon which is close to the autumnal equinox.

[17] Essay V, "The Sun-cult and the Temple at Jerusalem", in *Myth and Ritual* (ed. S. H. Hooke, Oxford, 1933), pp. 87-110. Our quotation is from p. 89.

Mr. Hollis has seen that the autumnal festival fell at the full moon. He thinks that "this more exact dating (i.e. on the fifteenth of the seventh month) may reflect an ancient practice of holding the festival at the time of a full moon, even though in early times the month was not fixed exactly, but was determined by the ripening of the crops".[18] Here he adds a footnote to the effect that "in this case the full moon to be selected was the one falling nearest to the equinox". It is interesting, and we think significant, that he should have come to the same conclusion as that to which we have come, though working from a completely different point of view. He finds, however, a difficulty in the fact that the position of the sun must have constantly varied at each equinoctial season. He says that owing to the level surface of the summit of the Mount of Olives, the variation would amount to about eleven degrees. Whilst, as he says, this difference would have been inappreciable from year to year, yet there would be difficulty "owing to the ever increasing variation in the course of the years". The difficulty is of his own making. If they kept to the full moon which was nearest to the first point of Aries, which incidentally is the full moon nearest to the autumnal equinox, then they would keep to the Harvest Full Moon. This we hold is exactly what they did. They did not deliberately intercalate a month. They simply kept to the full moon which was next after the completion of their harvests, i.e. to the Harvest Full Moon, and the intercalation looked after itself. As Mr. Hollis says, it would all come right every three years with reasonable approximation, because the difference between twelve lunar months and one solar year is eleven degrees, and a whole month amounts to approximately twenty-nine degrees. The variation would therefore amount to no more than about fifteen degrees either side of the mean.

Before the Exile the year ended with the full moon after the vintage, which in Jerusalem was the Harvest Moon. This much we regard as being fixed in pre-exilic days. The other periods of the year looked after themselves, and were separated from each other by the phase of the moon. The

---

[18] Essay V, "The Sun-cult and the Temple at Jerusalem", in *Myth and Ritual*, p. 103.

season could never vary more than a fortnight from the phase of the moon. At most it would mean what we should call an extra month every three years or so. They would intercalate the month without being particularly aware of doing it. Indeed, it would matter very little if they were aware of it, for those days were not days of any great interchange between peoples, and there was no need for that strict accuracy of date and hour to which we have become accustomed in our extensively mechanized civilization with its swift transport. The need, for instance, of establishing Eastern Time, Central Time, and Western Time in the United States of America arose only when transport became so speedy that a man could travel from one area to another at a rate not materially different from the apparent movement of the sun. When he travelled by ox-waggon, he took his noon from the sun as he went along, altered his watch, if he had one, by a few minutes a day, and all was well. For us, even to-day, we have only to be away from our urban centres, buried in the country without the daily newspaper, to realize how very little it matters what the day is, or even what the hour is. Life goes on much the same from day to day and from week to week, whatever happens elsewhere.

The Passover Full Moon

Six months away from the Harvest Full Moon is the Passover Moon. In pre-exilic times the Hebrews had no fixed point from which they counted the years. They were in no way different in this respect from other peoples. Although the Julian period is dated back to January 1, 4713 B.C., no one supposes that there were men alive then who began on that particular day to reckon the years, saying, "We will start to-day and call to-day January 1, Year 1"; any more than anyone supposes that the Greeks at one time began to count from September 1, 5598 B.C. These were datum lines fixed long afterwards, thousands of years afterwards. Such is the normal procedure. Until such fixed points are established every nation fixes its dates by such outstanding events as are memorable, either by good fortune or by their disastrous effects. Amos, or his editor, fixes the opening of his prophetic ministry by the great earthquake which took place in the time of King

Uzziah (Amos i, 1). This must have been a particularly dreadful calamity, since the echoes of it are still heard centuries afterwards, as late as in the time of Zechariah (Zech. xiv, 5). The compilers of the Books of the Kings had no better way of fixing the year of a king's accession than by reference to the year of the reign of the king in the other kingdom. Apart from the doubtful and difficult 1 Kings vi, 1, all calculations from a far-away fixed point are to be found in the Priestly Code. In Exod. xii, 40, that fixed point is the beginning of the sojourn in Egypt, but usually the fixed point is the Exodus itself (Exod. xvi, 1; xix, 1; Num. i, 1; ix, 1; Deut. i, 3). From the calendar point of view, this is a curious way to date the beginning of an era, for, according to the post-exilic calendar of the Priestly Code (Exod. xii, 6), the Exodus took place on the night of the fourteenth of the month, that is, at the full moon, or immediately prior to it. But even before the systematic dating of the Priestly Code, Passover was already fixed as immediately preceding the Palestinian, or Canaanite Feast of Maççoth (Unleavened Bread). This means that Passover must always have been associated with the full moon. There is a possibility that it may have been moved one night earlier after the settlement in Canaan, in order that it might be observed before they all trooped off to the local shrine. Passover was always a home and family feast as against a pilgrimage feast, such as the Canaanite Feast of Maççoth. But it is unlikely that it was attracted to this phase of the moon after the settlement in Canaan. Even when the custom developed of sacrificing the Passover at Jerusalem, the lamb that was slain was always eaten away from the Temple in the family circle or in a hired room by a group of friends. It was thus inconvenient rather than convenient to bring the Passover celebration into such close contact with the pilgrimage feast. On both counts, therefore, in spite of the post-exilic Nisan 1 as the beginning of the year, and in spite of the inconvenience of the Feast of Maççoth, they had to observe the Passover at the full moon, or as near to it as possible, because it always had been so observed. If, therefore, the Hebrews of pre-exilic times regarded their era of nationhood as beginning with the Exodus from Egypt, then they counted their era, in so far as they ever thought about such things, from the full moon which is six months away from the Harvest Moon. Once again, it is the full moon which counts.

We are thus faced with two alternatives. Either the pre-exilic months were independent of the years, that is, the beginning of the year did not coincide with the beginning of the month, or the pre-exilic Hebrews thought of their months as beginning with the full moon, and not with the new moon, as has generally been supposed. This latter we believe to have been the case, with the proviso that when they talked of months, they talked about them in a looser and less accurate way than we do with our modern scientific calendar. This means that when they changed the beginning of the year from the autumn to the spring, they also changed their new-month day from the full moon to the new moon. In this case the word *chodesh* should be translated 'new-month day' instead of 'new moon'.

'Chodesh' means New-Month Day

Why should the word *chodesh*, when it is clearly used of a particular day, be sometimes translated 'month' and sometimes 'new moon'? Whether the phrase *bechodesh 'abib* (Exod. xiii, 4: J) should be translated 'in the month Abib' or 'on the new-month day of Abib', if there is one thing more certain than another, it is that the actual day was the full moon day of Abib. It is not, of course, necessary that the word should here be translated 'new-month day', for the whole sentence reads well enough as it stands in the English Versions. There are, however, instances in pre-exilic writings where the word *chodesh* is used of a particular day, namely Exod. xxiii, 15; xxxiv, 18 (E); and especially 1 Sam. xx, 27; also Amos viii, 5; 2 Kings iv, 23. In Phœnician the phrase *b-ch-d-sh y-r-ch* is found,[19] and here the word *ch-d-sh* must undoubtedly refer to a particular day. That the word should come to be used for 'month' is perhaps inevitable, but the true Hebrew word for 'month' is *yerach*, and this word cannot by any means be used of a particular day. It is at least as natural that the word *chodesh* should come to be used for 'month', if it originally meant 'new-month day', as if it meant 'new moon'.

[19] *CIS*, I, i.

THE EXILE AND THE CHANGE OF CALENDAR

The Hebrew word for 'new moon' is *helal*, as in Isa. xiv, 12: "How art thou fallen, New-moon-god,[20] son of the Moon-god". Compare the Arabic *hala'l* (new moon). The root *ch-d-sh* signifies 'renew', as in the Hebrew text of Ecclus. xliii, 8: *chodesh bechodesh hu' mithchaddesh*, 'new month (moon) by new month (moon) he renews himself'.[21] We hold that originally, in pre-exilic times, the reference was to the renewing of the month, and not to the renewing of the moon. The pre-exilic equation was thus:

chodesh = new-month day = full moon,

whereas the post-exilic equation was:

chodesh = new-month day = new moon.

We do not suppose that anyone is likely to dispute the post-exilic equation. With respect to the pre-exilic equation, we have to say that in the strict factual sense there is no more evidence against it than in favour of it. All that we claim to have demonstrated hitherto is, firstly, that the word *chodesh* does sometimes refer to a particular day of the month, and, secondly, that it might just as easily be interpreted for pre-exilic times as the full-moon day as the new-moon day. Whatever be the true state of affairs in pre-exilic days in respect of the beginning of the month, it is assumed, and not definitely stated. The reason why it is generally assumed that *chodesh* always meant new-moon day, when it meant any particular day, is solely because no one ever thought of it being any other. It has always been assumed unquestioningly that there was never any change in the day from which the month was reckoned. If we hold to Bul being the second month of the pre-exilic year against such statements as 1 Kings vi, 38, there is no reason why we should not allow at least the possibility that there was a change-over in the beginning of the month, equally with a change-over in the beginning of the year.

[20] Reading *sahar* instead of *shachar* (dawn) after Winckler, *Geschichte Israels*, ii, 24. Compare the Arabic *shahr*. The word is found in Aramaic and South Arabic inscriptions of a moon god. See also *saharonim* of the crescent ornaments of camels, princes, and women (Judg. viii, 21, 26; Isa. iii, 18).

[21] Text published by H. L. Sträck, in *Schriften des Inst. iud.* (Berlin, 1903), No. 31.

There are two passages where we believe our thesis finds ready illustration. Indeed, in the second case, we do not see how the passage can be explained on the basis of any other supposition than that there was a time when the day of the Great Feast was both a full-moon day and a new-month day.

The Meaning of 1 Samuel xx, 27

The first instance is 1 Sam. xx, 27. As the verse stands it reads: "and it came to pass on the morrow of the second *chodesh*..." It is clear that *chodesh* is intended to refer to a particular day, and it is equally clear from the end of the verse that Saul noticed David's absence and remarked on it on the second day, the day after the *chodesh*. There seems to be no doubt that there has been some alteration in the Masoretic Text. We must either omit 'the second' or insert the word '*hayyom*' ('the day'), as R.V. has done, following the lead of the Septuagint. The Vulgate has "and when the second day dawned after the Kalends", whilst the Targum speaks of an intercalary month, evidently taking *chodesh* to mean 'month', and thinking of a second, and intercalary, month. It is clear that the Vulgate is right, and that *chodesh* means the *Kalends*, the first day of the month. This is the substance of A.V. But was this first day of the month the new moon? The feast was the annual feast (*zebach hayyamim*, xx, 6), and we have every encouragement to suppose that this annual feast was celebrated at the full moon. On this basis, we should translate *chodesh* as 'new-month day', understanding this also to be the day of full moon in this pre-exilic context. Then in verse 34 we should read, "and did eat no bread on the second new-month day". Here the Vulgate has *in die calendarum secunda*, which we must translate 'on the second day of the month', for the Latin *calends*, or more usually *kalends*, came to be used to mean 'month',[22] just as *chodesh*, properly 'new-month day', also came to mean 'month'.

It is true that the actual text of 1 Sam. xx, 27, could be explained equally well whatever particular day was originally meant by the word *chodesh*. The presumption that the day mentioned was actually the day of the full moon depends rather upon what we have suggested elsewhere concerning the

---

[22] Ovid, *Fasti*, 3, 99; etc.

observance of the annual feast on the day (night) of the Harvest Full Moon.

The Meaning of Psalm lxxxi, 4

When we turn to Ps. lxxxi, 4, we claim that the age-old difficulty of this verse can definitely be resolved on the basis of our pre-exilic equation. The natural interpretation of this verse is that the psalmist is speaking of one day only. All the couplets in the psalm are synthetic couplets, and it would be very unusual to find one antithetical couplet in the midst of a host of all these other synthetic couplets. If the verse were what is called a climbing parallelism, we would expect at least the copula, but the two phrases are in apposition—*bechodesh . . . bekeṣeh leyom chaggenu*, i.e. " in the *chodesh* . . . in the *keṣeh* for the day of our feast ". If one day only is intended, namely ' the day of our feast ', then either *chodesh* must mean the same as *keṣeh*, or *keṣeh* must mean the same as *chodesh*. That is, using the generally accepted meanings of the two words, both words must mean ' full moon ' or both words must mean ' new moon '.

The evidence in comparative Semitic languages that *keṣeh* means ' full moon ' is strong and certain. The Assyrian *kuṣeu* means ' tiara, head-dress ', and can be used of the full moon. Gesenius[23] was puzzled as to the way in which a root which apparently meant ' cover ' could be used of the full moon, though he did find some encouragement in Ps. civ, 2: " Who coverest thyself with light as with a garment ". The explanation is probably to be found in the Assyrian idea of the moon having his[24] head-dress when he was at the full. The reformed Assyrian calendar of Asshur-bani-pal, for instance, says: " Sin (i.e. the moon-god) wears a full crown " on the thirteenth of the month.[25] In Syriac the meaning ' full moon ' admits of no shadow of doubt whatever. The evidence for this meaning of the Syriac *keṣa'* is given in full by Gesenius. According to Isa bar Ali, the word means ' the full moon, the fourteenth night, when the full moon rises ', and the plural means ' the feasts which are celebrated in the middle of the month '. The

---

[23] *Thesaurus*, pp. 698 f.
[24] We say ' his ' because the moon is masculine in Semitic languages, he being always the moon god, and not the chaste and virgin huntress.
[25] S. Langdon, *op. cit.*, p. 76.

word is used in the Peshiṭta in 1 Kings xii, 32, of the fifteenth day of the month, and in 2 Chron. vii, 10, of the twenty-third day of the month. These two cases may well be the basis of Isa bar Ali's explanations, since the twenty-third of Tishri is the closing day of the great Feast. In *Act. Mart.* 1, 175, the plural *keṣe'* is actually contrasted with *berish yarche* (in the beginning of the months). This may be due largely to a presumed contrast between *chodesh* and *keṣeh* in Ps. lxxxi, 4, but it makes it all the more certain that *keṣeh* means 'full moon'. Whatever the basis of all these explanations, the meaning 'full moon' is supported and is in regular use by Bar Hebræus and Ephraem Syrus. Further, if *keṣa* in Syriac can stand for the full period of the great feast, as the Peshiṭta of 1 Kings xii, 32, and 2 Chron. vii, 10, suggests, then it may be right after all to leave the Masoretic Text of 1 Sam. xx, 34, as it is, and to translate it (as we have translated it) as 'the second new-month day'.

The word *keṣeh*, then, undoubtedly means 'full moon'. This is how the Revised Version translates it in its only other occurrence (in the form *keṣe'*) in the Old Testament at Prov. vii, 20. Vulgate and Aquila have 'the full moon' at Prov. vii, 20, and both Vulgate and Jerome have 'in the middle[26] of the month' in Ps. lxxxi, 4.

Ancient Jewish tradition, except in so far as Jerome may be embodying it in the Latin Versions,[27] is clear that *chodesh* and *keṣeh* refer to the same day. They have therefore forced *keṣeh* to refer to the new moon. They were evidently certain that the verse was a synonymous couplet, and they therefore went to great pains to show that *keṣeh* did not carry the meaning 'full moon'. Ibn Ezra says boldly that it means 'new moon' in Prov. vii, 20, but the difficulty of the earlier Jewish authorities is clear. The Targum of Prov. vii, 20, has *yoma' de'eda'* (the appointed day), which Rashi says means the time

---

[26] A scholia which Martianay found in the margin of one of his most trustworthy MSS. has *throno* for *medio*. The scholiast was evidently dissatisfied with the Latin rendering, and so took the word to be the equivalent of *kese'* (throne), thus leaving the verse in worse confusion than before. See Martianay, *Opera Ieronymi* I, pp. 837 f., and the Latin text *in loco*.

[27] Though here he apparently is departing wholly from Jewish tradition.

THE EXILE AND THE CHANGE OF CALENDAR 101

fixed for the feast. In Ps. lxxxi, 4, the Targum has *yarcha demithkaṣṣe'*. What this means is hard to say, unless they intended the verb to be a denominative, and to mean the month to which the *keseh*-feast belongs. All this leaves us largely where we were. The Rabbis found evidently the greatest difficulty in the interpretation of Ps. lxxxi, 4. This is not surprising, for it is likely to be a difficult matter to explain how a passage must mean something different from what it clearly does mean. They found no help from the Targum. The Talmud takes the verb of the Targum to be *kaṣah*-II, and to mean 'cover,' as in Hebrew. The two references are *b. Rosh hashShanah* 7b, 8a, and *b. Beça* 16a: "what is the feast (*chag*) on which the new moon (*chodesh*) is covered?" Similarly *Pirqe de Rabbi Eliezer* VII (end) refers to "the day when the moon is entirely covered". Such explanations as these puzzled Gesenius, as we have seen, for he knew very well that *keseh* meant 'full moon'. Further, there is no feast (*chag*) in the Jewish calendar at any period at a time when the moon was covered. Other Rabbinic authorities are equally insistent that the reference is to the new moon, but they take the verb of the Targum to be *kaṣah-I* (make incisions, mark). For instance, *Peṣiqta Rabbathi* (p. 39) says that *bekeseh* means 'in the month that is marked'. But *Wayyiqra Rabbah* (p. 29), referring to Ps. lxxxi, 4, asks, "are all other new-moon days (*chodashim*) not marked?" It then points out that the *chodesh* in question is defined by 'the day of our feast'. "And is not Nisan a marked month with a feast in it?" But the difficulty here is that in Nisan the new-month day is separate from the feast, and it is therefore necessary to think of a *chodesh* that is marked and has a festival, and that on the same day. *Peṣiqta Bachodesh* (p. 153a) takes *bekeseh* as defining the *chodesh* (new moon), and as meaning that it is the new moon of the marked (distinguished) month. All the Rabbinic authorities are clear about two things, in spite of all their confusion. Only one feast is involved, and *keseh* is defining *chodesh*. They are all sure that in some way *keseh* means the same as *chodesh*.

The usual alternative is to refuse to admit a synthetic parallelism in this one verse, and to argue that the psalmist was thinking of two occasions. Since *keseh* undoubtedly means 'full moon' and since 'the day of our feast (*chag*)' is undoubtedly the full moon of Tishri, then this line refers to the full moon of Tishri and to the Feast of Sukkoth (Tabernacles). Of this, on any basis, we do not admit the slightest shadow of doubt. The first line is then taken to refer to a new-moon festival, probably the first of Tishri. This is the position taken by Christian scholars generally, and apparently it is that taken by Rabbi Sa'adiyah when he reads 'day of sacrifice' in Prov. vii, 20, thus following the Targum, and being followed in his turn by Rashi with 'the time fixed for the feast'. These renderings certainly cut the knot. Similarly, the Septuagint avoids the difficulty in both cases,[28] and the Peshiṭta Syriac follows the Septuagint in Prov. vii, 20.

Our solution is that *chodesh*[29] means 'new-month day', and that the couplet is a survival from pre-exilic times, when the new-month day was the day of the full moon. The earlier[30] Jewish authorities were right in assuming that *keseh* and *chodesh* refer to the same day, but wrong in making that day the new-moon day. Other authorities are also right in making *keseh* refer to the same day as 'the day of our feast'. All three phrases refer to the full moon of Ethanim. We therefore translate:

"Blow ye the shofar on the new-month day,
On the full moon, for the day of our feast".

It will be seen that it is therefore inaccurate to say that after the Exile the beginning of the year was altered from Tishri to Nisan. The post-exilic months are not at all equivalent to the pre-exilic months. By this we mean that Tishri is not equivalent to Ethanim, nor Nisan to Abib. In pre-exilic days the year began on the full-moon day of Ethanim. This was the day which later was known as the 14th-15th of Tishri. In post-exilic times the civil new year began with the new moon of Nisan. This day was fourteen or fifteen days before that full moon which previously had been known as the full moon

[28] Unless Lagarde is right in suggesting that the *di' hemeron* of Prov. vii, 20, is a 'correction' of an original *dichomene* (the full moon, which divides the month into two parts).
[29] This is the only occurrence of the word in the Psalter.
[30] Later Jewish authorities tend to interpret *keseh* as 'full moon'. So the modern Jewish (American) translation, but Singer's Prayer-book (p. 253) follows the ancient Jewish tradition.

of Abib, and which at all periods has been the Passover moon. It is necessary to give an alternative of fourteen or fifteen days, because the day of the new moon in post-exilic times was decided by actual amateurish observation of the sickle of the new moon. Sometimes this would be seen on the actual day of the new moon, and sometimes not until the next day. Ethanim 1, therefore, is equivalent to Tishri 14 or 15.

(iii) The Origin of the Sabbath

This identification of *chodesh* as being, so far as pre-exilic times are concerned, the full-moon day involves a discussion of the origin of the Sabbath. This is necessary because some have held that the Sabbath was originally the full-moon day. If *chodesh* was, as we hold, originally the full-moon day, then the Sabbath cannot have been that day. We hold that the Sabbath was originally the new-moon day, and in the rest of this chapter we propose to give our reasons for this statement.

An examination of the arguments in favour of the Sabbath being originally full-moon day shows that ultimately they rest on the assumption that *chodesh* means 'new-moon day'.[31] The argument is: *chodesh* and *shabbath* are evidently in some sense corresponding and 'opposite' days of the month: one of them is the new-moon day and the other is the full-moon day: *chodesh* is the new-moon day: therefore *shabbath* is the full-moon day. That is, whichever of the two was the new-moon day, the other was the full-moon day. Meinhold's assumption was that at all periods, both before and after the Exile, *chodesh* was the new-moon day. If, therefore, it be assumed that before the Exile *chodesh* was the full-moon day, then his argument leads with equal insistence to the conclusion that *shabbath* was the new-moon day. His assumption was that A was X; his conclusion that B was Y. Our assumption is that A was Y; equally soundly, therefore, our conclusion is that B was X. Is there any justification for the suggestion that the Sabbath was originally the new-moon day? We have seen some justification for the suggestion that *chodesh* was the full-moon day in pre-exilic times, but we acknowledge freely that our case concerning *chodesh* depends also upon the justi-

[31] J. Meinhold, *Sabbat und Woche im Alten Testament* (Göttingen, 1905), SS. 3-13.

fication which we can show for the Sabbath being originally the new-moon day. The two stand or fall together.

Harranian Sacred Days

In the composite article on 'Sabbath' in the *Encyclopædia Biblica* (col. 4179) reference is made to the custom of the Harranians, who had four sacred days in the month.[32] These were at the conjunction of the moon (i.e. new moon), the opposition of the moon (i.e. full moon), the 17th of the month, and the 28th of the month. This evidence proves nothing to our purpose, except that it confirms the evidence of the Old Testament that the new moon and the full moon stand together as sacrificial days. The 17th and the 28th increase the difficulty. It may be that the 28th has something to do with the new-moon period, the new-month day being the day of the new moon under Mesopotamian influence.[33] It is scarcely likely that the 28th day has anything to do with a seven-day period. We would expect either more sevens, especially a more natural seven than the fourth seven, since seven is of great account in these matters, or we would expect no seven at all. It is difficult to see what relation the 17th bears to any scheme. The only suggestion we can make is that it is connected with the 17th day in the old pre-reformation Assyrian calendar, where the 17th is marked as an unlucky day, and offerings are due to be made to Gula, the goddess of the Underworld.[34] The significance of the mention of this dread goddess will appear when we discuss the significance of the 19th day of the month in Mesopotamian religious rites, this black day of the menologies, the Day of the Wrath of Gula. In the revised menologies the 17th is not an unlucky day. It has become the festival of Nabu and Marduk, and there is no mention at all of Gula. There is a distinct possibility of the early Harranian calendar having been influenced by Mesopotamia, since there is the ancient tradition that the ancestors of the Hebrews travelled through Harran on their

---

[32] *Fihrist*, 319, 14.
[33] The importance of the new-moon period and also of the seven-day period will appear below when we discuss the tabu-days of Mesopotamia.
[34] S. Langdon, *Babylonian Menologies and the Semitic Calendars*, p. 78.

THE EXILE AND THE CHANGE OF CALENDAR

way from Ur of the Chaldees to the land of Canaan (Gen. xi, 28-xii, 5: J, P).

Mesopotamian Rest-Days

The Sabbath of the post-exilic Jews certainly bears some relation, so far at least as the regulations are concerned, to the 'rest-days' of the Babylonian system. In the tenth-century menologies of Babylonia-Assyria there is a regular formula for the nine rest days of Nisan, with a note to the effect that these rules apply to the same days in other months also.[35] The formula is: "a physician shall not lay his hand on the sick; the prophets shall declare no word. It is not suitable for executing any affair". One tablet says that all work is forbidden throughout the whole month of Teshrit.[36] There are no oracles dated as given on any of the nine rest-days among the oracles given by Klauber in *Politisch-Religiöse Texte* and by Knudtzon in *Gebete an den Sonnengott*. In the reformed calendar and menologies of Asshur-bani-pal the same rules apply, and the same formula is given, but it is preceded by additional restrictions laid upon the king, who is described as "the shepherd of the peoples". He may not eat cooked fish or baked bread. He may not change his garments, nor put on clean garments. He may not sacrifice, nor ride in a chariot, nor speak as a lord. On the 19th day, which is the 'blackest' day of all in both the tenth-century calendars and the reformed calendar of Asshur-bani-pal, no one "may sweep his house, nor wash his feet, nor complete the construction of his house".[37] The prohibitions as to the sweeping of the house and the washing of the feet are found in the old calendar also for the 21st of the month. They were probably in the later calendar also, but this part of it is missing. On the 28th, according to the old calendar, no man may go out into the street except to approach a shrine. No man was allowed to go out of his gate during the whole of the 29th and the 30th, and this restriction was especially enjoined for the 29th, probably because there would always be a 29th in the month, but not always a 30th day. There is no record of any business being done, for instance, on the 29th of Tebit, except

[35] S. Langdon, *ibid.*, pp. 86 ff.
[36] K.3769, 16, from the Kouyunjik Collection, British Museum.
[37] *Ibid.*, pp. 78 ff.

for one contract of the time of Nabonidus, and this may well be an error for the 28th.[38]

The Jewish Sabbath and its Taboos

These rules of Mesopotamia are clearly similar in many respects to the rules concerning the Sabbath which we know to have existed in post-exilic Judaism, and were enforced by those who had returned from Exile. The prohibition against gathering sticks on the Sabbath is found in Num. xv, 32-6, which is P, and the penalty was death by stoning. There is a rule against a man "going out from his place on the seventh day" in Exod. xvi, 29, where the next verse reads "so the people rested on the seventh day". The context is a mixed one of J and P. The specific identification of the seventh day is made in verse 26, and this is P, as is the whole section from verse 16, and also the section from verse 31 to verse 36. It is probable that the first part of verse 29 is P also. This would mean that there may have been seventh-day restrictions in the J-tradition which are linked up with the Sabbath in the P-tradition.

The list of works which are prohibited on the Sabbath in Mishnaic times is given in the tract *Shabbath* vii, 1. There are 'forty lacking one', and the Rabbis held that every type of work was reducible to one of these thirty-nine works. But the whole tract is concerned with what may or may not be done on the Sabbath. In the New Testament we have the well-known case of the plucking of the ears of corn on the Sabbath (Mark ii, 23; Matt. xii, 1; Luke vi, 1), which was the third prohibited work of the Mishnah (reaping) and the fifth (threshing); and the scene in the synagogue which is related immediately following in Mark iii, 1-6: "They watched him whether he would heal him on the Sabbath day, that they might accuse him". This statement is as strict as that of the Babylonian menologies, but the Rabbinic rules allowed medical attention if it were to save life, and it is probable that the rule was interpreted liberally.[39] Still other Jewish restric-

---

[38] Langdon, *ibid.*, p. 84, note 3. See Doughty, *Yale Oriental Series*, VI, No. 27, 5.

[39] Where the Lord Jesus broke the Rabbinic rule was not in healing a man on the Sabbath, but in healing this particular man, who was in no danger of dying.

THE EXILE AND THE CHANGE OF CALENDAR 107

tions are concerned with going out on the Sabbath. There are precise details in the Mishnah as to what can and cannot be done in this respect on the Sabbath. Josephus makes the general statement that "it is not lawful for us (i.e. the Jews), neither on the Sabbath, nor at the Feast, to go on a journey".[40] There is another statement in Philo, when he speaks of Tishri as being the 'holy month',[41] thus making a parallel to the statement of tablet K.3769 that all work was forbidden throughout the whole of the month of Teshrit.

Rest-Days in Assyria in the Tenth Century

In the tenth century in Assyria the rest-days were 1, 7, 9, 14, 19, 21, 28, 29, and 30, making nine rest-days in each month. These include three which may fairly be called new-moon days, namely 1, 29, 30, for there is no suggestion that in Mesopotamia the new-month day was ever any other day than the day of the new moon. These three days are the times when the nights are dark. There is no moon, and there are supposed to be demons about. On other nights of the month it can be dark before the moon rises, or after the moon has set, but on these nights there is no moon at all, and the demons of darkness have the whole of the night in which to accomplish their nefarious designs. There is extant a menology which, for Tebit 29, prohibits the king from going out of his gate, because "he will meet with witchcraft in the wind of the street".[42] Virolleaud gives a list of the dire penalties which will follow going out of the gate on the 29th of various months. If a man goes out on Nisan 29, then he will die; if on Ayar 29, his house will be filled with gloom; if on Sivan 29, his house will be destroyed; if on Tammuz 29, his wife will die.[43] According to another text given by Ebeling (392, Rev. 21), fire will fall on the house of the man who goes out on the 29th of the month. All these prohibitions apply to the time when the moon is invisible and the nights are wholly dark. This is the period when sacrifice was made to the gods of hell. Then it was that

[40] *Ant. Iud.* xiii, 8, 4.
[41] *Hieromenia (de spec. leg.* II, 41), the name given by the Greeks to the time when the great festivals were held at Olympia, Nemæa, etc.
[42] E. Ebeling, *Keilschrifttexte aus Assur Religiösen Inhalts*, 178, Rev. II. 73-74.
[43] Langdon, *ibid.*, p. 85.

the moon-god crossed the river of death and kept company with Nergal, the lord of the dead. The 28th of the month in the reformed calendar, and the 29th in both the reformed calendar and in the earlier tenth-century menologies, are 'days of the ravishment of the moon-god'. They are the days which belong to Nergal, the lord of the dead. The association of the three days, 1st, 28th, 29th, with the darkness of the period when no moon is visible is made quite clear and certain by what is said of the 1st day of the month of the reformed calendar. This day is a 'black' day, but, according to the reformed calendar, if the new moon appears that night, then the fortune of the day changes, the king offers a white kid, bathes, and in the morning he makes sacrifices to Shamash, the sun-god, Sin, the moon-god, and Mach, the great mother-goddess, the queen of the gods, and the goddess of child-birth.

So much for the three days of the new moon. They are black days of great and severe restrictions. This is partly, as we have seen, because the darkness of the moonless sky gave the demons freedom for their active malignity, and partly also because of the association with the world of the dead. But in the reforms of the seventh century Asshur-bani-pal dropped these three new-moon days as days of restriction, and with them the 9th day also as a black day. Thus the days which were retained were the 7th, the 14th, the 21st, the 28th, and the 19th.

The Nineteenth Day

Langdon says[44] that no one has ever explained the retention by Asshur-bani-pal of the 19th day as a day of restriction. He himself begins his attempt at explanation with the *quinquatrus* (the 19th of March) as the day when the weapons of the Roman soldiers were purified, and with Ovid's statement that Minerva was born on that day. This gives him two statements, one concerning the use of arms, and the other concerning Minerva. He then adds the statement of the menologies that on this day the king offers sacrifice to Sibzianna, 'the faithful shepherd of the heavens', who is identified with the constellation Orion. Sibzianna was slain with weapons, and so was Orion in the Greek myth. Tammuz is identified with

[41] Langdon, *ibid.*, p. 87.

THE EXILE AND THE CHANGE OF CALENDAR 109

Sibzianna, and Gula is the mother of Tammuz, according to one identification. Minerva and Gula are both goddesses of medicine. And so through all this medley Langdon works to the 19th day as a day of restrictions. But there was no need for all this. An explanation of the 19th day as a day of restrictions had already been given both in *Hastings' Bible Dictionary* (iv, 319 note) and in the *Jewish Encyclopædia* (x, 591). The explanation is that it is the 49th day from the beginning of the previous month, that is, seven times seven. The days, therefore, which Asshur-bani-pal retained were the first seven, the second seven, the third seven, the fourth seven, and, the month proper being now ended, the seventh seven. This seventh-seven day is " the day of the wrath of Gula ", and it is the blackest day of all. In addition to the usual restrictions common to all the seven-days, the assembly is commanded to institute prayer and weeping. The reason for all this is because of the seven times seven. This is why the day has such a dreadful reputation from earliest times right down to the end of the Mesopotamian civilization. The number seven is a magic number, and it tends to belong to black magic rather than to white magic, though in ancient times the distinction between black and white in matters of magic can sometimes be very hard to draw. The emphasis on the seven times seven of the Mesopotamian menologies is comparable to the development among the Jews of the Year of Jubilee, that great Sabbatic year which marked the end of the seven-sevens of years. The post-exilic records say ' seven sabbaths of years ', for whatever the word *shabbath* meant in pre-exilic Israel, it was scarcely separable from ' seven ' in post-exilic times.

The Ninth Day

The reason for the existence in the original tenth-century list of black days of the 9th day is not at first apparent. Langdon offers no explanation of its inclusion. We suggest that the reason for its earlier existence as a black day is to be found in its connexion with the 19th day. The 19th is a black day primarily, as we have seen, because it is the seventh seven. Even more importantly from our present point of view, it is " the day of the wrath of Gula ". This goddess is generally equated with Aquarius the Water-pourer, though once she appears as connected with the Southern Fish.[45] The explanation of this latter variation is probably that there is no star of the first magnitude in Aquarius, and that the nearest such bright star is Fomalhaut, in the Southern Fish, the constellation next below Aquarius. But the connexion between the 9th day and the 19th day depends rather upon Gula as the Goddess of the Underworld, the "Mistress of the Palace of Aralu". She is also a storm-goddess, but her main function is to act as the consort of Nidib, the Lord of the Dead.[46]

Just as the 19th is the Day of the Wrath of Gula, so the 9th is Gula's day. There are restrictions of one kind and another for every day which belongs to one of these star gods of Babylon, but they are of no great account except for this 9th day. It is probable that the somewhat severe restrictions of the 9th day are due to the transference to it of some of the restrictions of the 19th day, the Day of the Wrath of Gula. Actually the restrictions of Gula's day (the 9th) are as great as those for any other of the rest-days, except only, of course, the 19th itself. Nevertheless, in the reforms of the seventh century the 9th as a day of restrictions was dropped in company with all other days which were not true 'seven-days'. That is, only the 7th, the 14th, the 21st, the 28th, and the 49th (19th) were retained. The 9th becomes a lucky day.

To recapitulate: the rest-days in the earlier calendars of Mesopotamia were, firstly, those connected with the darkness of the nights of the new moon, namely the 1st, the 29th, and the 30th; secondly, the 'seven' days, the 7th, the 14th, the 21st, the 28th, and the 19th; thirdly, the 9th, because of its connexion with the 19th. The connexion between the three sets is that the dark nights are the dangerous nights because of the demons; the seven-days are the dangerous days because of the holy-unholy seven; the 9th day is dangerous because it is the day of the dread goddess who most of all has to do with the occult and the darkness. By the seventh century the seven-days alone remained in the official calendar as the days of restriction.

[45] Langdon, *ibid.*, pp. 8 f.
[46] M. Jastrow, *Die Religion Babyloniens und Assyriens*, I. Band (Giessen, 1905), SS. 156 f.

THE EXILE AND THE CHANGE OF CALENDAR   111

The Seven-Day Week depends on the Sacred 'Seven'

Another factor emerges, and this we regard as being of the utmost importance. The seven-day week is not connected with the phases of the moon, but with the magic number seven. This also is the conclusion of J. Meinhold.[47] After all, the phases of the moon correspond to 7, 14, 21, 28 with only moderate accuracy. There are roughly $29\frac{1}{2}$ days in the lunar month, so the moon-god never really adapted himself to the seven-day system. The only way to make the two systems fit is to regard the 29th and the 30th, if also necessary, as intercalary days. It is tempting to suggest that this is the real reason why the 29th and the 30th were actually days of restrictions in the old calendars of Mesopotamia, and that the rigid and official seven-day week was an early institution. The difficulty of this is that we cannot then account for the restrictions of the 1st day of the month, which in the early calendars has the same restrictions as the 29th and the 30th days. Further, it is clear, as we have seen, that the restrictions of the first do actually depend upon the invisibility of the moon.[48] The 1st, the 29th, and the 30th must be considered together, and the same reasons for restrictions must apply to all. These are the dark nights and the demons.

The Sabbath is Independent of 'Seven'

There is therefore a very real alternative in the question, Was the Sabbath originally connected with the seven-day week, or was it connected with the phases of the moon? Putting this alternative in another way, Was the Sabbath originally a seven-day-week festival, or was it a lunar festival? It must be one or the other, but it cannot be both. In the Old Testament there is a close connexion between *chodesh* and *shabbath*. The two occur regularly in the same context. The inference is that both were lunar festivals in the Old Testament.

There is no mention of the days 7, 14, 21, and 28 in connexion with the division of the month. In early times, e.g. the times of Homer and Hesiod, the Greeks divided the month

---

[47] *Sabbat und Woche im Alten Testament*, SS. 13 ff.
[48] See p. 107 above.

into two parts. One was 'the waxing month', and it comprised the days 1 to 15; the other was 'the waning month', and it comprised days 16 to 30. They divided the month, that is, into two parts of fifteen days each, since each lunar month has to be made to consist of thirty days approximately as often as of twenty-nine days. Later the Greeks had three periods, the waxing month (*histamenos*), the middle month (*meson*), and the waning month (*phthinon*). There is no mention of the number seven in any of these divisions. This means that there is no inherent necessity for using the number seven in connexion with the moon. Indeed, we would go so far as to say that the number seven would never have cropped up at all in the calendar if astronomical considerations only had been taken into account.

When we come to consider the Babylonian system of dividing the month, we find once more that there is an independence of the number seven. The Babylonians divided the month into two parts. Their name for the 15th of the month is *shabattu* or *shapattu*. The root is explained as meaning *gamaru* (to be complete) or as *qatu* (end).[49] The phrase "on the day of the *shabattu*" is explained by Assyrian scribes to mean "in the middle of the month".[50] This use of the word in the sense of the middle of the month goes back to Sumerian times. When the *shabattu* is called 'the day of the resting of the heart', the association with the Hebrew *shabbath* is more apparent than real. It depends solely on the fact that the English word 'rest' has been used. The Babylonian phrase is *um nu-uch lib-bi*, which means 'the day of appeasement of the heart', and it has nothing at all to do with the meaning 'rest' in any ordinary sense of the word. The Babylonian word *nu-uch* is the same root as that which appears in the Hebrew phrase *reach hannichoach* (sweet savour, lit. 'appeasing smell'). The reference is to the causing of the heart of the god to be appeased, and has nothing at all to do with the idea of rest in the sense of cessation from labour. Whether Langdon is right in holding that the Babylonians spoke of the first half of the month as the 'former *shabattu*' and of the

---

[49] Langdon, *ibid.*, pp. 90 ff.; Meinhold, *Sabbat und Woche*, S. 11; Jensen, *Zeitschrift f. Assyriol.*, SS. 272 ff., etc.

[50] Virolleaud, *Shamash*, XIII, 17. See also *Epic of Creation*, 160, 18.

second half of the month as the 'latter *shabattu*' is debatable, but there is plenty of evidence to show that the word *shabattu* means the end of a series of days.⁵¹ The Egyptians called the 15th day of the month *samadt*. Perhaps this word has etymological associations with the Babylonian *shabattu*, though equations between Egyptian and Babylonian (or even Hebrew) words are dangerous ground, and much is left to the imagination. But the Greeks interpreted the Egyptian word as *dichomenia* (the division of the month), and it certainly was the full moon: e.g. "and I am filled as the *dichomenia*"⁵² (Ecclus. xxxix, 12).

The 'Shabattu' is not a Rest-Day

It is important to realize that there is no trace of the 15th as such being a rest-day or a taboo day after the manner of the new-moon days and the seven-days. Langdon gives a list of all the items of information which he has been able to collect as to the character of the 15th day of the month, whatever the month. The only case where there are restrictions approaching to any degree those of the black days is in the tenth-century calendar, and then solely in respect of the 15th of Nisan. Here it is clear that the restrictions for the day, wholly removed in the later calendar of Asshur-bani-pal and in the later Babylonian calendars, are due to the general restrictions of the month of Nisan. This month was the first and holy month of the Babylonian year according to the Nippurian calendar, which ultimately became the official Mesopotamian calendar. In this character of holy month, the Babylonian month Nisan is comparable to the month Tishri of the post-exilic Jews, which, according to Philo, was the 'holy month' (*hieromenia*).⁵³

The only other suggestions of restrictions on any 15th day are two. The first is in connexion with the 15th of Elul, when, according to a tablet from Uruk (Erech), "a man may

---

⁵¹ Langdon, *ibid.*, p. 91.
⁵² The reading of Codex Alexandrinus is *dichotomenia*, but the variation is of no account. Syriac and Hebrew have a curious reference to the twelfth, the former reading "as the full moon on the day of the twelfths", and the latter "as the full moon on the twelfth".
⁵³ *De spec. leg.* II, 41. See p. 107 above.

not speak ".[54] In all other calendars this day is a lucky day. Uruk (Erech) was the religious centre of the earlier times, just as Nippur was in later times. Many of the books and especially the religious hymns of Asshur-bani-pal's library were copied from the originals at Uruk. This ancient restriction, therefore, for the 15th of Elul may well be a reflexion of the observance of the New Year Feast in Elul at Ur, which is close to Erech, and also belongs to ancient rather than to later times. Another instance of the similarity between Nisan and Elul is that there was a system of intercalating after the sixth month, Elul, instead of what became the final Babylonian system of intercalating after the twelfth month, Adar, with its own variation of intercalating after the first month, Nisan.[55] The second reference to a restriction for the 15th day is given by Rawlinson in respect of the 15th of Kislev. It is that "one may not go out into a street ".[56] All other calendars say that the day is a good one for a journey.

On the other side of the picture, the 15th of Tammuz and the 15th of Teshrit are spoken of as being very lucky days. The 15th is twice spoken of as a good day to take a wife, Teshrit for any man, and Arachsamna for a king. This period, " when the lucky circle of the moon shall come ",[57] was recognized by the Greeks as being fortunate for marriages. On the 15th of Adar the king may wash his garments, and will obtain his desire. There are variations for many of these 15th days, but the general aspect of them, beyond question, is that they are lucky and favourable.

These 15th days of the month are called *shabattu*, and not one of them has any point of contact with the seven-days. The two are quite separate. The day called *shabattu* has everything to do with the lunar month. The seven-days have nothing to do with the lunar month. The distinction is complete, both in respect of the lunar month and in respect of restrictions. This distinction was fully realized, as we have said,[58] by Meinhold, whose references to the *shabattu* are extremely limited. On the other hand, Meinhold has much to say,[59] and

[54] Falkenstein, *Uruk*, 53, III, 9.   [55] Langdon, *ibid.*, p. 10, note 6.
[56] *Cuneiform Inscriptions of Western Asia* (from copies by George Smith, Edwin Norris, and T. G. Pinches), V, 49, IX.
[57] Euripides, *Iphigenia in Aulis*, 717.
[58] See p. 111 above.   [59] *Op. cit.*, SS. 13-18.

THE EXILE AND THE CHANGE OF CALENDAR 115

we believe rightly, concerning the holy 'seven' in Babylonian thought and custom. Again and again the figure crops up in lustration rites and in Temple ritual. Babylonia is the area where most of all 'the seven stars', i.e. the sun, the moon, and the five planets, were worshipped. There were seven evil spirits, and seven walls surrounded Aralu, the underworld of the dead.

The Sacred 'Seven'

Similarly the sacredness of the number 'seven' is plain at all stages of Hebrew development. We find it as early as in the fourteenth-century Tell-el-Amarna letters: "seven and seven times fell I at the feet of my lord the king".[60] The Cain vengeance was sevenfold (Gen. iv, 15); and Lamech's was seventy and sevenfold (Gen. iv, 23). In the J-story of the Flood the beasts enter by sevens so far as the clean beasts were concerned, but only a pair of each for the unclean beasts (Gen. vii, 2 f.). The number 'seven' is thus closely connected with the idea of 'clean', which here has to do with the 'holy'. There is every reason, considering the solemnity of the occasion and the issues of life and death which depended upon it, for Jacob to bow himself to the earth seven times, no more, no less, when he met Esau (Gen. xxxiii, 3), just as the writer in the Tell-el-Amarna letter bowed by sevens before the king. According to 2 Kings iv, 35, "the child sneezed until seven times", and then was fully restored to life. Elijah sends his servant to watch for the rain cloud, and at the seventh looking this appears (1 Kings xviii, 43 f.). There were seven locks on Samson's head (Judg. xvi, 19); and he spoke of "seven green withes (margin, 'bowstrings')" as having power to bind him into weakness (Judg. xvi, 7). This kind of reference appears again and again. Not every case in the Old Testament is of this special magic, holy type, but the great majority of them are. The sacredness of the number seven appears in its connexion with the swearing of oaths. The roots are the same, so that 'to swear' means 'to seven oneself' (what we would call the passive or the middle voice) or 'to bind oneself by seven things'. The association of the number seven with every kind

[60] *Berlin, VA. Th.* 1642; No. 102 in Abel und Winckler, *Der Thontafelfund von El-Amarna*; No. 286 in Knudtzon, *Die El-Amarna Tafeln.*

of dealing with the supernatural world is frequent and unmistakable. Abraham sets aside seven ewe-lambs at Beersheba (well of oath, seven) as his witnesses to Abimelech. Everything is done by sevens in Pharaoh's dreams (Gen. xli). Joseph's mourning for his father lasts for seven days (Gen. l, 10). The number seven repeatedly recurs in the sacrificial and cleansing instructions in Exodus, Leviticus and Numbers, here marching parallel with similar rites in Mesopotamian rituals. The pilgrimage feasts of Unleavened Bread, Weeks, Tabernacles, are all connected with the number seven. The first of them, Maççoth (Unleavened Bread), lasted for seven days (Exod. xii, 15). Then seven times seven days were counted (*shib'ah shabu'oth*) until the Feast of Weeks, *shabu'oth* (Deut. xvi, 10). Lastly, the Feast of Ingathering-Tabernacles lasted for seven days according to Deut. xvi, 13. Even when the Feasts of Maççoth and Sukkoth were extended to eight days, it was always made clear that the eighth day was an addition, a closing festival, *'açereth* (Lev. xxiii, 36: P); or, according to the Talmud (*b RH* 4b), an independent festival.

The 'Seven' and Marriage

The seven-day period also appears in ancient Hebrew custom in connexion with marriage festivities. These are seven-day periods, and it is misleading to refer to them as 'weeks'. A week properly means a seven-day week of a particular system of reckoning the days. The marriage period is a seven-day period, but not a week. This distinction is not as pedantic as it may at first appear, because we hold that there were seven-day periods long before there were weeks. The word used of the marriage period is *sheba'* (seven). It has nothing at all to do with the Sabbath, and only accidentally anything to do with the seven-day week. When Jacob married one of the daughters of Laban, and later discovered that he had married the other one, Laban answered his complaints by saying "fulfil the *sheba'* (seven) of this" (Gen. xxix, 27). There is no proper justification for translating 'week', except that we have grown used to thinking of any seven-day period as being a week. Such a translation assumes the existence of a seven-day week in Palestine in early times, and that is why we object to it. We do not deny the existence of seven-day

THE EXILE AND THE CHANGE OF CALENDAR

periods in ancient Palestine, especially in connexion with what van Gennep called *les rites de passage*, i.e. rites connected with the progression from one stage of life to another, such as birth, adolescence, marriage, death. The period from birth to circumcision is seven days, for circumcision must take place on the eighth day (Gen. xvii, 12); and there are seven days for mourning (Gen. l, 10). The 'seven' in the Jacob-Laban-Leah story refers to the seven days of marriage festivities mentioned in Judg. xiv, 12, and in Tob. xi, 19. These are the seven days of the modern Syrian peasant celebrations, the "King's Week", which Wetzstein brought to light during his term as consul at Damascus in recent times.[61] These celebrations lasted for seven days, during which the bridegroom played the part of the king and the bride that of his consort, their throne being improvised on the threshing floor of common use.

The Sabbath in Old Israel

It is equally clear that there were Sabbaths before the Exile in old Israel. According to the story of Elisha and the great woman of Shunem (2 Kings iv, 8-37), new-month days (*chodesh*) and Sabbaths were days when a visit could properly be made to the man of God (verse 23). Whether the journey was allowable on these days because it was to a man of God, or whether it was convenient because these were days when the ass and its driver could be released from ordinary farm duties, is not clear. Probably the latter is the explanation. It is evident that in pre-exilic Israel both new-month days and Sabbaths were special days of some kind, but they were certainly not taboo-rest days, when it was "not permissible to go out into the street", as the Babylonians put it, or "to go on a journey", as Josephus put it. In pre-exilic Israel both the new-month day and the Sabbath were days of cessation from normal business such as selling of corn or the exhibition of wheat for sale (Amos viii, 5). Rightly or wrongly, they were both days of mirth in the eighth century (Hos. ii, 11); and days of special assemblies (Isa. i, 12). Both were days of licentiousness and debauchery in the eighth century, and were con-

---

[61] There is a transcription of Wetzstein's account in Delitzsch, *Commentary on Canticles and Ecclesiastes* (Eng. tr.), p. 171.

demned as such by the prophets. Such degeneration would have come to pass only because in these early days both new-month days and Sabbaths were days of joy. This association of the Sabbath with joyfulness has never ceased among the Jews whatever the restrictions of the Sabbath may have come to be. It is the day when the Jew has dressed in his best clothes, and it is characterized by joy. The Inauguration of the Sabbath in the Ashkenazic rite opens with " O come let us exult before the Lord ", and after the recital of six Sabbath psalms there follows the famous Bridal Song of the Sabbath: " Come, my friend, to meet the bride; let us welcome the presence of the Sabbath ". The Sabbath can never be a fast-day, and if the date of a regular fast-day chances to fall on the Sabbath, then the fast-day is postponed until the following day. For instance, the great Fast of Ab is properly to be observed on the 9th of Ab, but in the years 5701 and 5704 (August 2nd, 1941, and July 29th, 1944) it was observed on the 10th of Ab because in each of these years the 9th of Ab fell on the Sabbath. Numerous passages in the Talmud testify to the joy of the Sabbath. When the Rabbis wished to say that the 1st of Tishri and the 10th of Tishri were not like ordinary fast-days in respect of mourning, they said that they were like Sabbaths.[62] The fact is that the original joyfulness of the Sabbath has never been obscured by stricter and later taboos in post-exilic days. Christians have not always realized the extent to which the Sabbath is primarily a day of joy.

The Jewish Sabbath and the Mesopotamian ' Shabattu '

The problem therefore is: How should the Jews have come to use the word *shabbath* of the seventh day, and so to make it a day of restrictions like the seven-days of the Babylonian menologies? Allied to this problem is the question: Has the Hebrew *shabbath* anything at all to do with the Mesopotamian *shabattu*?

It has always been a difficulty to bridge the gap between the Hebrew *shabbath* and the Mesopotamian *shabattu*. Mein-

---

[62] *b. Mo‘ed Qat.* 19a. Rabbi Gamaliel said they were like festivals (*b. Mo‘ed Qat.* 20a) in that the period of mourning must be suspended during the festival and continued afterwards. The Karaites followed Anan in holding that both were fast-days, and this more serious view ultimately prevailed in respect of Yom Kippur.

THE EXILE AND THE CHANGE OF CALENDAR 119

hold[63] makes no attempt to do so. Jastrow[64] realized the difficulty, but says that Gunkel failed in his attempt.[65] Jastrow built the bridge by making the *shabattu* of Mesopotamia a day of propitiation equally with the 7th, the 14th, the 21st and the 28th days. He thus creates his bridge by inventing a support on one side. It cannot be emphasized too strongly that the *shabattu* was definitely not a penitential day. There is no connexion in the menologies either between the *shabattu* and propitiation or between the *shabattu* and the seven-days which were really penitential days. Jastrow further suggests that the pre-exilic Hebrew Sabbath was marked by atoning rites. This also is pure supposition. It agrees neither with what we know of pre-exilic religion, nor with what we know of the joyfulness of the Sabbath at all times. With respect to Gunkel, we do not find that he made any attempt to deal with the question of the Babylonian *shabattu*. All he was concerned with in the passage which Jastrow mentions was to establish an ancient association between the seven-day period and the work of Creation. Then, on the strength of the P creation story of Gen. i, 1-ii, 4a, he associated this period with the Sabbath. He did well, and we agree with him, but he is speaking of an equation of the Sabbath with the seven-day week as being found in the P-story, that is, in post-exilic times. That is exactly what did happen, and if Gunkel has to look to post-exilic times for the identification, then we enlist him in support of our thesis. It is one of our main contentions that the Sabbath became identified with the closing day of the seven-day week in post-exilic times.

We would build the bridge between the Hebrew Sabbath and the Mesopotamian *shabattu* by means of our suggestion that the pre-exilic month began with the full moon. We would hold that originally the Hebrew word *shabbath* meant 'closing day'[66] equally with the Mesopotamian *shabattu*. It was the day which marked the end of the first half of the lunar month. Thus the *shabbath* of the Hebrews coincided with the new-month day of the Mesopotamians. It would there-

[63] *Sabbat und Woche im Alten Testament* (1905).
[64] *American Journal of Theology* (1898), pp. 315-52.
[65] *Schöpfung und Chaos* (Göttingen, 2nd ed., 1921), SS. 13 f.
[66] Not 'divider-day', like the Egyptian *samadt*.

fore be a taboo-rest day, since the Sabbath was bound to be either the 29th, the 30th, or the 1st day of the Mesopotamian menologies. The time when the Hebrews became acquainted with the restrictive new-month days of the Mesopotamians was also the time when they were introduced to the severe restrictions of the seven-days. The result was that they all became Sabbaths in the restrictive sense, since they were all the same type of day. There is no difficulty in the fact that Asshurbani-pal abolished the restrictive rites of the new-moon days in the seventh century, since Assyrian influence on Palestine was already strong even before that date. The evidence for this in the time of Ahaz is strong (2 Kings xvi, 9-16). We are apt to think that all the Mesopotamian influence upon the cults and life generally of the Hebrews was Babylonian influence during the Babylonian Exile. We forget the period of Assyrian domination of Palestine, which lasted for much longer, and such direct testimony as that Ahaz copied Assyrian custom even in the matter of the main altar of the Temple. Such an overlapping between the time of Ahaz and the time of the reforms in Assyria gives time for the ideas to be transferred from one set of days to the other. In any case, it is not to be supposed that the reforms of Asshur-bani-pal were instituted in far-away Palestine immediately. They may never have reached as far as that, and very probably never did, for at his death the whole Empire collapsed.

So far our position is that the *shabbath* of the pre-exilic Hebrews, being the new-moon day, coincided with the new-month days of Mesopotamia with all their severe restrictions. This was in the period of the Assyrian domination of Palestine, when we know that vassal kings like Ahaz took great pains to copy and to follow Assyrian custom. They thus copied both the new-moon restrictions and the seven-day restrictions of Assyrian custom. In this way the Sabbath suffered a double change. It gradually became overlaid with restrictions, and it gradually became classed with the seven-days.

Some time between his accession in 662 B.C. and his death in 626 B.C. Asshur-bani-pal abolished the restrictions of the new-moon days, and with them the restrictions of Gula's day, the 9th, also. This left only the five ' seven '-days as days of restrictions, namely the 7th, the 14th, the 21st, the 28th, and

THE EXILE AND THE CHANGE OF CALENDAR 121

the 49th (19th). Assyrian influence in Palestine ceased abruptly with the death of the greatest of the Assyrian warlords in 626 B.C. We believe that we are safe in assuming that his reforms did not reach Palestine before his death. In any case we do not judge Josiah to have been the sort of king to be very favourable to Assyrian cults. He soon took advantage, in 621 B.C., of the removal of Assyrian influence to institute wide and far-reaching reforms, many of which were concerned with sweeping away the Assyrian innovations of his fathers. This means that for well over a hundred years the Hebrews in Palestine may have grown used to both new-month days and seven-days as days of restrictions, i.e. the *shabbath* and the *sheba'*(seven)-days. With the Babylonian Exile they came into contact with the reformed Mesopotamian calendar which we know to have been adopted in Babylon as well as in Assyria, for both Babylon and Assyria took their cult instructions from Nippur. By this time the word *shabbath* had come to signify a day of restrictions, a day of rest. This, we hold, is why the word *shabbath*, meaning now a day of rest, came to be applied to all days of rest, the seven-days equally with the new-moon days. When, therefore, the exiled Hebrews followed the Babylonian custom, and observed only the seven-days as days of restrictions, then the word *shabbath* came to refer to the seven-days only. This, we suggest, is why the identification of the Sabbath with the seventh day belongs to the Priestly Code.

The Babylonian 'Shabattu' and the Hebrew 'Shabbathon'

The Babylonian *shabattu* as a special day distinct from the Hebrew Sabbath is preserved in the post-exilic Jewish *shabbathon*. The days which are thus designated in the Priestly Code are not necessarily full-moon days, nor new-moon days, but they do include the weekly Sabbaths. All of them are days of religious observances. The days called *shabbathon* are Tishri 1 (Lev. xxiii, 24), which happens to be a new-moon day; the first and eighth days of the Feast of Sukkoth, namely Tishri 15 and 22 (Lev. xxiii, 24), the first of which is a full-moon day, but the second of which belongs to no particular phase of the moon and is no multiple of seven by any method of computation; the Day of Atonement, Tishri 10 (Lev. xxiii, 32; xvi, 31), which again corresponds to no phase of the moon and is no multiple of seven; the whole of the Sabbatic year (Lev. xxv, 4), which is the seventh year. The references to the Sabbaths as *shabbathon* are Exod. xxxi, 15; xxxv, 2; Lev. xxiii, 3; Exod. xvi, 23. Every reference to any period of time, long or short, as *shabbathon* is in the Priestly Code, and therefore, in its present form at any rate, is post-exilic.

The explanation of the use of the word *shabbathon* in connexion with this curiously mixed collection of days, and including even the whole of the Sabbatic year, is, we believe, to be found in the first place in the fact that the word is applied to Tishri 22. This day is the eighth day of the Feast of Sukkoth (Tabernacles). It was added as a closing feast (see R.V. margin of Lev. xxiii, 36), an ʿaçereth. It was added after the Exile, and, according to the Talmud (*b. RH* 4b), it is independent of the seven days of the festival itself. This eighth day is not known in Deuteronomy (see Deut. xvi, 13-5). We find the last day of Maççoth (Unleavened Bread) called an ʿaçereth in Deut. xvi, 8, and the word is used in Amos v, 21; Isa. i, 13; and 2 Kings x, 20, without reference to any specific day, but elsewhere, where the exact day is specified, it is the day after the end of the Feast of Tabernacles: Lev. xxiii, 36; Num. xxix, 35 (both P); Neh. viii, 18. Just, therefore, as the Mesopotamian *shabattu* marks the end of the first half of the month, and is so explained in the tablets,[67] so also the Hebrew *shabbathon* here marks the end of the Feast of Tabernacles. Similarly, the seventh year is *shabbathon* because it marks the end of the seven years. We would explain the fact that the weekly Sabbath is called *shabbathon* in exactly the same way. In the Priestly Code the Sabbath is the day which concludes the six days of Creation (Exod. xxxi, 17; xxxv, 2; xx, 11; Lev. xxiii, 3). In each of these four cases the Sabbath is mentioned as concluding the six working days. We are thus left with three days, Tishri 1, Tishri 10, and Tishri 15. These are all New Year's Day in one way or another.[68] As New Year's Day, each of them is the day which concludes the Old Year, that is, it is the day next following the last day of the old year. It concludes the old year in precisely the same way in which

[67] It equals *gamaru* and *qatu* (see p. 112 above).
[68] See p. 148 below.

the other *shabbathon* days conclude the period of time which precedes them.

Our conclusion, therefore, is that the Babylonian *shabattu* is closely allied to the Hebrew *shabbathon* in that both words are used to mark the end of a period of time. We have seen that the Jewish post-exilic Sabbath is a *shabbathon* in the sense that it marks the close of the six-day working week.

The Sabbath as the day which marks the close of the working week of six days is one of the two main functions of the day. The other is that it is a day of restrictions, i.e. a day of rest in the sense that in it " ye shall do no servile work ".

We find the double aspect of the Jewish Sabbath shown in the double statement of Gen. ii, 2. The verse opens with one statement—" And on the seventh day God finished his work which he had made ", and it concludes with the statement— " and he rested on the seventh day from all his work which he had made ". Here, in both statements, the equation of the Sabbath with the seventh day occurs. This we hold to be derivative, partly because of the survival of the ' seven-days ' of Babylonia as rest-days, and partly also because of the two statements, one that it is the day which marks the end of the six working days, and the other that it is a rest-day.

The first statement of Gen. ii, 2, is that the seventh day marks the end of the six days of the Work of Creation. This statement has occasioned a certain amount of difficulty from early times. The difficulty is that the Scripture says that God finished His Work of Creation *on* the seventh day, and not *before* it. Rashi seeks to remove the difficulty occasioned by the words of Gen. ii, 2, by quoting from Rabbi Simeon, who said, " Flesh and blood (i.e. mortal man), who cannot know his times and his moments, must add from the profane to the holy, but the Holy One, blessed be He, who knows His times and His moments, began it (i.e. the Sabbath) to a hair's breadth, and so it appeared as if He had made an ending on that day ". That is, man is not able to distinguish precisely the moment which separates one period of time from another. God alone can be so precise in the matter as to be able to work right up to the last fraction of the last second of the sixth day.

The second statement of Gen. ii, 2, is that the seventh day is a rest-day: " he rested on the seventh day from all his work which he had made". Once again, as in the previous statement, the phrase 'the seventh day' is used to signify the Sabbath. The Sabbath, as we have maintained, became a rest-day, not directly because it was the seventh day, but because, by the time the Hebrews came into close and renewed contact with the Mesopotamian civilization in the time of the Exile, these seventh days were the only rest-days which were observed.

'The Morrow of the Sabbath'

In support of our contention that the Sabbath day is only incidentally the seventh day, we believe that there is a case where the term Sabbath is used of a rest-day which is not a seventh day. The case is the celebrated crux, " the morrow of the Sabbath" (Lev. xxiii, 11, 15). What day is meant by this?

The answer to this question has always been of great importance, because the determination of the proper date for the observance of the Feast of Weeks (Pentecost) depends upon it. The Feast of Weeks is fixed as the fiftieth day from the day when "ye brought the sheaf of the wave offering" (Lev. xxiii, 15). The custom of bringing the wave-sheaf ('omer) to the Temple necessarily ceased with the destruction of the Temple, but the rite of the Counting of the Omer is still practised. The counting begins on " the morrow of the Sabbath ", which, according to orthodox Jewish tradition, is the second night of the Passover. The ceremony shows the very great importance which was attached, from early times, to the exact and proper counting from the correct date. In the *Jewish Encyclopædia*, vol. ix, pp. 398 f., there are photographic reproductions of elaborate Omer Tables, one of them now in the library of the Jewish Theological Seminary of America, New York, and the other in the United National Museum, Washington, D.C. These are indicative, with their elaborate arrangement, of the great importance of a correct count. The minute instructions given in the Mishnah *Men.* vi, 1-10, and the details of the Talmud *b. Men.* 65b-68b are relics of a long and bitter controversy.

Some have held the view that " the morrow of the Sabbath " is the morrow of the seventh day of Maççoth (Unleavened Bread, frequently, though loosely, called Passover). The

THE EXILE AND THE CHANGE OF CALENDAR 125

ground of this contention is, presumably, that the word Sabbath meant the seventh day. Thus "the morrow of the Sabbath" is, on this interpretation, Nisan 22. This is the interpretation adopted by the Falashas of Abyssinia. They make the Feast of Weeks to fall on Sivan 12, their months being of twenty-nine and thirty days alternately. According to Charles,[69] both the Syriac of Lev. xxiii, 11, 15, and also the Book of Jubilees xv, 1, regard "the morrow of the Sabbath" as being Nisan 22. The Syriac reads *bathar yawma' charna'*, which must mean either 'after the latter day' (in which case it means the latter of the two special days, the first and the seventh, and so the seventh day), or 'after the last day' (in which case it means the seventh day). On the basis of the first translation here offered, the word *yawma'* means 'a festival day', and this is easily the more likely meaning; in the second case, it means any day of the feast, and so the last of the seven-days. Charles, therefore, is right in his interpretation of the Syriac. We believe that he is right in his interpretation of Jubilees xv, 1. It is difficult to see how the Feast of Pentecost could be held on Sivan 15, unless the counting is from Nisan 22. The celebration of the Feast of Pentecost on Sivan 15 is also inferred in Jubilees xliv, 1-5. Here Israel is said to have left Harran (but it should be Hebron) on Sivan 1, offered a sacrifice at Beer-sheba on Sivan 7, waited there seven days, then celebrated the Feast of Pentecost ('the harvest festival of the first-fruits'), and on Sivan 16 he saw visions of God.

Another interpretation was that the phrase means the morrow of the Sabbath which fell during the Feast of Passover. This was the interpretation of the Sadducees, the Samaritans, and later of the Karaites. This latter sect, during the time of their initial founder Anan (*c.* 840 A.D.), produced what they called 'lion' reasons for their interpretation. Anan, indeed, is said to have lost his life in riots which arose because of his insistence upon this particular point. It is said that this identification was the basis of the fixing of Whitsuntide by the Council of Nicæa in 325 A.D. This is the council whose decisions fix the incidence of Easter, so that we have the curious state of affairs that the General Council which is

[69] *Apocrypha and Pseudepigrapha*, vol. ii, pp. 34 f.

responsible for our variable Easter was governed by wholly heretical Jewish opinions when it adopted the rule whereby Pentecost always falls upon a Sunday in the Christian Ecclesiastical Calendar. It is the fiftieth day from the Sabbath which falls during Passover. Ibn Ezra argued strongly against Pentecost always being on a Sunday, on the ground that all other holy days were fixed by the month, and that it was not proper that Pentecost alone should be fixed by a day of the week. Here again, incidentally, we find an indication that the seven-day week is not a primary factor in the determination of the ecclesiastical calendar.

The traditional Jewish interpretation is that " the morrow of the Sabbath " means the day after the opening of Passover, i.e. the second day of Passover. The Counting of the Omer is from the second night of Passover, as soon as it grows dark, until the 5th of Sivan, the eve of Pentecost, so that Pentecost is always on the 6th of Sivan. Jewish tradition is strong and steady for this interpretation. Septuagint is clear with its " on the morrow of the first day ". The Mishnah and the Talmud make the matter quite plain, as we would expect since they embody the orthodox Pharisaic arguments against both Samaritans and Sadducees. Both Philo (*de septen.* ii, 20) and Josephus (*Ant. Iud.* iii, 10, 5) support the traditional interpretation.[70]

The orthodox position depends upon making the word *shabbath* in Lev. xxiii, 11, refer to the first day of the Feast of Maççoth. The phrase 'seven sabbaths' of Lev. xxiii, 15, has then to mean seven periods of seven days, and the phrase 'the morrow of the seventh sabbath' in verse 16 means the day after seven completed weeks. The Samaritan and Sadducee case thus rests upon the inference that throughout verses 15 and 16 the word *shabbath* has the same meaning, i.e. 'seven'. Thus 'the morrow of the sabbath' means the morrow of the seventh day. Orthodox Jewry, on the contrary, said that it meant the first day. This is such an extraordinary statement that it must be the right one. No one in the ordinary pos-

---

[70] For further details, see *Jewish Encyclopædia*, vol. ix, articles " Pentecost " and " Omer ". Also G. B. Gray, *Sacrifice in the Old Testament*, pp. 323-36, where he argues that the fixing of particular dates is a later development from an original custom which was much less ordered.

THE EXILE AND THE CHANGE OF CALENDAR 127

session of his senses would ever dream of inventing such an explanation, so apparently contradictory to everything that he would know about the Sabbath. The interpretations of the Samaritans and the Sadducees on the one hand, and of the Falashas on the other, are both understandable on the supposition that they all found the word *shabbath* in the text, and, being verbal inspirationists, all three groups proceeded to interpret the Word of Scripture according to their knowledge of the word *shabbath*. The traditional interpretation can be explained only on the supposition that the Pharisees, ever the faithful custodians of popular custom, knew that the first day was the right day whatever the verse in Leviticus happened to say about it.

The first day of Passover is the 15th[71] day of Nisan. This at first looks like the Mesopotamian *shabattu*, but we do not find the explanation here. Rather we find it in Exod. xii, 16 (P), with its parallels in Num. xxviii, 18, 25. The first and the seventh days of the Feast of Unleavened Bread were rest-days. This is why they were Sabbaths. They were not days of *shabbathon* because such days mark the end of a period of time. Neither the first nor the seventh days of Unleavened Bread are that, but they are Sabbaths in the sense that they are rest-days, days wherein " No manner of work shall be done in them, save that which every man must eat, that only may be done of you " (Exod. xii, 16). We hold this to be the explanation because it provides an explanation of the origin of the Falasha 'heresy', which is supported by the Syriac of Lev. xxiii, 11, 15, and also by the Book of Jubilees. The Syriac, for instance, reads 'after the latter day', i.e. after the latter of two particular days, which we take to be the first day and the seventh day of Exod. xii, 16. The Syriac is thus making clear what the Targum of Onqelos has left indefinite with its " from after the holy day " (*yoma' ṭaba'*), defining ' the holy day ' as the second of the two rest-days of Exod. xii, 16. Thus all the interpretations can be accounted for. The Samaritans take the word *shabbath* to mean the Sabbath, the seventh day

[71] Lev. xxiii, 5, mentions the 14th day, but it is " the fourteenth day between the two evenings ". Without entering into a discussion of the noted crux " between the two evenings ", it can be said that the Passover lamb was slain in the evening following the 14th day, i.e., at the very beginning of the 15th day.

of the week; the other two interpretations both accept the Targum of Onqelos with its reference to 'the holy day', thus realizing that *shabbath* in Lev. xxiii, 11, means a rest-day, but not necessarily the Jewish Sabbath, the seventh day of the week. The Falashas, the Syriac, and the Book of Jubilees take it to be the second of the two days, strengthened perhaps by the fact that it is the seventh day of the Feast, but the orthodox tradition takes it to be the first day, thus ignoring the Sabbath both as the only rest-day and as the seventh day of the week. We hold that they could never have done that except on the knowledge that the word *shabbath* could refer to a rest-day independently of any other considerations.

But the special celebrations of the new-moon days did not pass away without any attempt at survival. The connexion between the Sabbath and the new-month day is preserved in Ezek. xlvi, 1-7. On the two special days, the Sabbath and 'the day of the *chodesh*', "the gate of the inner court that looketh toward the east" is to be kept open. The two days are days of worship, equally and to the same extent so far as the general ritual is concerned. The sole difference lies in the burnt-offering. In this respect the importance of 'the day of the *chodesh*' is greater than that of the Sabbath, for there is an additional offering of a young bullock without blemish with its own proper cereal-offering. We are at a stage where the new-month days and the weekly Sabbaths are both days of penitence and restrictions. But what does *chodesh* mean in this chapter? Does it mean new-month day and full-moon day, or does it mean new-month day and new-moon day? And what are the Sabbaths here? Are they weekly Sabbaths or monthly Sabbaths?

Our belief here is that greater issues are involved than we can deal with in this present study. The offerings of the Sabbaths and the new-month days of Ezek. xlvi, 1-7, are apparently quite distinct from the sin-offerings of the first day of the first month and the first day of the seventh month, as described in Ezek. xlv, 18-20.[72] The equality of the first days of the first and the seventh months reflect the first attempts to deal with the change of the new year from the autumn to the

---

[72] The correct text of verse 20 is preserved in Septuagint and thence in the R.V. margin.

spring.⁷³ This attempt has nothing to do with the provision for all the new-month days and the Sabbaths of Ezek. xlvi, 1-7. Our view of the independence of these two arrangements is confirmed by the double description of the ideal city in Ezek. xlv, 1-8, and in Ezek. xlviii. It is not easy to fit these two descriptions together, and some sort of assimilation seems to be necessary in order to make them agree. Turning back to the double arrangements in respect of the offerings, that in Ezek. xlvi, 1-7, with its emphasis on new-month days and Sabbaths and extra emphasis on the new-month days, fits in generally with the old Assyrian ideas before the reforms of Asshur-bani-pal, the times before the special new-moon days of restrictions were abolished. The other arrangement with its first days of the first and the seventh month, but dealing with no other first days, fits in with a time when the new-moon days have been abolished, and when attempts were being made to adapt the old Hebrew calendar with its full-moon new-month days and its autumn new year to the requirements of the dominating Babylonian calendar with its new-moon new-month days and its spring new year. Whether this means that parts at least of the Book of the Prophet Ezekiel are pre-Deuteronomic or anti-Deuteronomic, and belong to Northern Israel as against the South, as J. Smith[74] and Cameron Mackay[75] suggest, each in his own way, is part of another, and a larger, subject, into which we cannot enter here.

The Spelling of 'Shabbath'

There remains yet the actual spelling of the word *shabbath*.[76] First of all, there is the matter of the final letter *tau*. If there is any connexion with the Babylonian *shabattu*, then

[73] See pp. 141 f. below.
[74] *The Book of the Prophet Ezekiel* (London, 1931), p. 66 f.
[75] *Princeton Theological Review*, vol. xx, pp. 399-417; vol. xxi, pp. 372-88; vol. xxii, pp. 27-45. Also *Expository Times*, vol. xxxiv, 5 (Feb. 1923), pp. 198-201 (criticism by W. F. Lofthouse of the previously mentioned articles); vol. xxxiv, 10 (July, 1923), pp. 475 ff. (Cameron Mackay's reply).
[76] The *sh* of the Hebrew, as against our English *s*, is due to the fact that the Old Testament came to us first through the Greek and the Latin, neither of which could deal with the sound *sh*. 'Sabbath' therefore became established as the English pronunciation before the Hebrew spelling could have its effect.

the final letter *tau* of the Hebrew *shabbath* ought to be doubled. The answer is that it is doubled, and that the doubling shows itself when the suffixes are added. The examples are *shabbatto* (his sabbath) (Num. xxviii, 10; Isa. lxvi, 23); *shabbattekem* (your sabbath) (Lev. xxiii, 32); and *shabbattah* (her sabbath) (Hos. ii, 13; Hebrew, 11). The doubled *tau* is found also in the form *mishbatteha* (Lam. i, 7). This form may be an error in the Masoretic Text, as the Septuagint suggests, but the Masoretes certainly held to the doubled *tau*.

There remains the doubled *beth*. It may be due to the desire to emphasize the idea of rest, in which case the form may be regarded as a piel (intensive) formation. On the other hand, the doubled *beth* may be due to the Babylonian *shabattu* with its first short 'a'. If Hebrew desired to keep this letter firmly and unchangeably short, then, according to Masoretic theories of punctuation, they had no alternative but to double the *beth*. The alternative would be to lengthen the 'a'. Compare what has happened in *shabbathon*, where the second 'a' has become long because the *tau* has not been doubled.

4

THE EXILE AND THE CHANGE OF CALENDAR

B.—New Year's Day

Tishri 10 as New Year's Day

THE changing of the calendar from the old Palestinian system to the Mesopotamian system, so that the new year fell in the spring and not in the autumn, has had a curious effect in Ezek. xl, 1, where Tishri 10 is called Rosh hashShanah. This phrase is the Hebrew equivalent of the Assyrian *resh shatti*, and is the technical name for New Year's Day, not only in the Mishnah and the Talmud, but also in subsequent times.

It is necessary first to defend the Masoretic Text, since some doubt its accuracy, and prefer the rendering of the Septuagint, which has *en to proto meni* (in the first month). This stands elsewhere (Ezek xxix, 17; xxx, 20) for the Hebrew *bari'shon*. Toy[1] and G. B. Gray suppose *bari'shon* to be the original text, with rosh hashShanah as due to a late scribe with whom the phrase was familiar. The scribe could not have been very late, since both the Targum and Syriac support the Masoretic Text. It seems to be more likely that the translator, thinking the Hebrew Text strange, 'corrected' it. Toy and Gray apparently assume that the same Greek rendering presupposes the same Hebrew Text in all three cases. There might be some justification for this if the same translator had been at work, but this is not the case. The translator of Ezek. xxviii-xxxix is not[2] the translator of Ezek. i-xxvii and xl-xlviii. Further, the phrase Rosh hashShanah for the 10th of Tishri was not so familiar to any scribe who would be likely to change the text before the time of the Targums and the Syriac as to induce him to alter an easy text to a difficult one. In any case we see no necessity to assume that *rosh* cannot mean 'the first

[1] *The Book of Ezekiel* (Polychrome Bible, 1899), p. 177.
[2] St. John Thackeray, *The Septuagint and Jewish Worship* (Schweich Lectures, 1920), pp. 37-9, 118-29. The fifteen verses in Ezek. xxxvi, 24-38, are by yet another translator.

day of the year', since it is used of 'the first day of the month', thrice in the Priestly Code, once in the singular (Exod. xii, 2) and twice in the plural (Num. x, 10; xxviii, 11). These three examples also, in our view, dispose of Gray's suggestion that the phrase in Ezek. xl, 1, means "a period of about ten days long" at the beginning of the year. Rosh hashShanah is the technical term for New Year's Day in later times, and we see no reason why it should not mean New Year's Day here, even if it had not come by this time to be a technical term. There is sufficient warrant for this in Mesopotamian usage and sources.

How, then, should the 10th day of a month, and especially the 10th day of the 7th month, ever be called New Year's Day? Tishri 10 is not a full-moon day, nor is it a new-moon day, and it does not correspond with any particular phase of the moon. Further, even if we take into consideration the Greek system of dividing the month into three parts, each of ten days, we would still be a day out, for the day, as the beginning of any period, would have to be the 11th. In any case, the Greek division into three ten-day periods could not possibly have had any influence on sixth-century B.C. Israel in Babylon. Yet again, Tishri 10 bears no relation to any seven system, a number which we have seen to be of peculiar importance in all calendar arrangements which depend upon Babylonian influence.

There must be some proper explanation for Tishri 10 as New Year's Day. It is such an extraordinary day to be thus named. No one would ever have thought of making Tishri 10 into New Year's Day unless there was some adequate reason for it. Indeed, even the removal of the phrase from Ezek. xl, 1, does not solve the problem, for Tishri 10 is actually New Year's Day for the Year of Jubilee, and trumpets were blown to mark the fact of it being the new year, even though it was not New Year's Day according to any known calendar. Wellhausen sees an interpolation in the verse which ordains the blowing of trumpets on this day (Lev. xxv, 9). He says that this very verse acknowledges how strange it is that shofars, the curved trumpets of ram's horn, should be blown on this day.[3] The correct day for the blowing of these particular trumpets,

[3] *Jahrbuch f. d. Theol.* XII, S. 437.

THE EXILE AND THE CHANGE OF CALENDAR

as against ordinary straight trumpets, is Tishri 1. Another peculiarity is that the Year of Jubilee does not appear to be known at all to the writer (compiler?) of Ezek. xl-xlviii. It is therefore of post-exilic growth.[4] This makes it all the more curious that Tishri 10 should be found in Ezek. xl, 1, as *Rosh hashShanah*. The one clear case where orthodox Jewry recognized Tishri 10 as New Year's Day is the one which most obviously is missing in pre-exilic and even in exilic times, except only for this one suggestion of Ezek. xl, 1.

Our explanation is as follows. Tishri 10 is the day on which New Year's Day falls when a solar year is imposed upon a twelve-month lunar year of 354-355 days, counting from Tishri 1 of the preceding year. That ten days, and not eleven days, is reckoned as the period of variance between the solar year and the lunar 'year' so far as the Jews are concerned is confirmed by the tirade in the Book of Jubilees vi, 36: "For there will be those who will assuredly make observations of the moon—how it disturbs the seasons and comes in from year to year ten days too soon". Verse 37 tells how they will confound all the days, the clean with the unclean, "for they will go wrong as to the months and sabbaths and feasts and jubilees", and all because (verse 38) "they will not make the year three hundred and sixty-four days only". This period of ten days crops up again in connexion with the stated duration of Noah's flood. According to the Babylonian sources, the length of the flood was one year, and this is stated to have been the length of it also in the Book of Jubilees (v, 23-32) and in the Septuagint. These latter make the Flood begin on the 27th of the 2nd month of the 600th year, and finish on the 27th of the 2nd month of the 601st year. The Masoretic Text, on the other hand, makes it begin on the 17th day of the 2nd month of the 600th year, and finish on the 27th day of the 2nd month of the next year. Thus the whole duration according to the Masoretic Text is one year and ten days.[5] As we have indicated, the correct difference between the solar year and the lunar year of twelve 'moons' is more accurately eleven

---

[4] Here again we find an indication that the association of 'Sabbath' and 'seven' is a post-exilic development, i.e. the idea here that seven-times-seven should be seven-sabbaths.

[5] See the commentaries, e.g. Skinner, *Genesis* (ICC), pp. 167 f.

days. The Babylonians knew that this was the difference in the seventh century, though probably not earlier. The evidence for this is given in the transcription by Virolleaud[6] of the tablets concerned. In this tablet the list of the twelve months is given and then the *zagmuku*,[7] or new year period, is added " to the end ". That is, we understand the *zagmuku* period to be that period of eleven days, the semi-intercalary period, which completes the period betweeen the twelve lunar months, Nisan, Ayar, and so on to Adar, and the end of the solar year. The reason why we suggest that this period of eleven days was not known by the Assyrians until the seventh century is that previously to the reforms of the seventh century in the time of Asshur-bani-pal the New Year Festival in Assyria lasted for nine days, seven of them for fasting, and the other two for feasting. It is true that later, in Rabbinic times, the Jews recognized that the period of variance between the two years was eleven days, but we are not dealing here with Rabbinic times. We are dealing with a time when, as the Book of Jubilees shows,[8] it was thought that the solar year consisted of 364 days, so that the difference was ten and not eleven, as it would be if the solar year were 365 days.

This curious New Year's Day, Tishri 10, is comparable to April 5th as the Old Lady Day. This Old Lady Day is the day on which the nation's accounts are still opened. We have to make our Income Tax returns up to April 4th. Old Lady Day is the day on which Lady Day would fall in the first year in which the new calendar was adopted, supposing that the same period elapsed between the two Lady Days. When the Act of Parliament to correct the calendar was passed in 1751, and our system was at last brought into line with the rest of Europe, it was ordained that September 2nd, 1752, should be called September 14th, 1752. This would make the old March 25th into the new April 5th.[9] The same curious survival of the

[6] *Babylonica* IV, 112. 57-82. See also Langdon, *ibid.*, pp. 107-9.
[7] *zagmuku* is the Akkadian rendering of the Sumerian ZAG. MU, which means 'the head-of-the year'. The Semitic equivalent is *resh shatti*. See Svend Aage Pallis, *The Babylonian 'akitu' Festival* (Kobenhavn, 1926), p. 12.
[8] See also Enoch lxxiv, 10; lxxv, 2; 2 Enoch (according to Charles's nomenclature) xlviii, 1 (twice one hundred and eighty-two).
[9] For March 25th as new year day, see A. F. Pollard in *English Fortnightly Review* (April, 1940) LV, p. 178.

change in this country in 1752 from the old Julian calendar to the new Gregorian calendar which had been adopted on the Continent in March, 1582, appears also in the way in which the fixing of the dates of village fairs in England is still often governed by the 'Old Style' (Julian) Calendar and not by the 'New Style' (Gregorian) Calendar.

The ten days beginning with Tishri 1 and ending with Tishri 10 are the days which make up the difference between the old lunar and the new solar year. They are not, however, exactly days 'out of the calendar', for they are counted as the first days of the next year. This is exactly what happened in the Babylonian calendar. The eleven days of the *zagmuk* period are the first eleven days of the month Nisan of the next year. Possibly there was a time when this period was an intercalary period 'out of the calendar', but such a state of affairs, if it ever existed,[10] was apparently found too inconvenient, and the system of an intercalary month 'inside the calendar' was adopted.

It is probable that there is a connexion between the ten-day period of the Jews and the eleven-day period of the Mesopotamians. We doubt, however, whether the connexion is direct. Both are probably separate attempts to fill in the difference between the two years. There was never any eleven among the Jews, nor any ten among the Mesopotamians. In the tenth century there was a nine-day period in Assyria. The length of the new-year period was sixteen days in Babylonia before Nebuchadrezzar shortened it to eleven days. Thus in Mesopotamia we have an eleven, a nine, and a sixteen, but never a ten.

These ten days were, as we shall see, days of penitence among the Jews. The reason is probably that they were regarded as being in some sense outside the calendar, just as the *zagmuk* period was in some sense outside the calendar. Something of this feeling that the days were outside the calendar is shown in the statement attributed to R. Ishmael ben Jochana ben Beroka[11] that the slaves who were freed in the year of release feasted from the 1st of Tishri to the 10th of Tishri, and

---

[10] This does actually seem to be the plain meaning of the tablet which Virolleaud transcribed: "and the *zagmuk* to the end".

[11] Tanna of the second century A.D., contemporary of R. Simon ben Gamaliel II. The reference is *b. Baba Qama*, 114 b.

then returned to their old homes of pre-slavery days. These days were thus 'outside' the calendar. The slaves were no longer slaves, but at the same time they were not wholly free.

There are similar ideas in connexion with the development of the Christmas Pantomime. Whilst in some respects its origin is to be found in the old *Pantomimus* of the Roman Empire of the first century A.D., yet the Christmas Pantomime is a peculiarly English development, and it properly belongs to the period between the new Christmas Day and the old Christmas Day. It is said that the reason why the Principal Boy is always a female part[12] is because the days are outside the calendar, and are therefore topsy-turvy days. Parallel to this idea of topsy-turvydom, we have the ancient Twelfth Night custom of the Bean King. A cake containing one bean was cut on the evening of Twelfth Night, and he in whose slice the bean was found was the King of the Bean, and master of the festivities for the rest of the night. There may well be here, as Frazer suggested,[13] an association with the holiday king of the Roman Saturnalia, but there are considerable differences between the two customs,[14] and they are probably quite independent. The mediæval customs of the Bishop of Fools, the Abbot of Unreason, and the Lord of Misrule are just as likely to have sprung from an 'outside the calendar' idea as from the ancient pagan Saturnalia. In this latter feast of the Saturnalia the central idea was the revival of the good old days, but in such a custom as that of the King of the Bean there is no such suggestion.

The season between Christmas Day and Twelfth Night is reckoned as a mystic season in many places. They are days when evil forces have greater freedom than usual, or they are days which are regarded as being in some sort preliminary to the coming year. There is, for instance, a taboo on the word 'wolf' during this period in Thuringen and in Mecklenburg. In the village of Quatzow in Mecklenburg there are yet other

[12] So contrary to English drama generally, where the female parts were taken by men.

[13] *The Golden Bough* (abridged edition, 1923), p. 586.

[14] Frazer tends generally to concentrate on similarities, and to neglect differences. See *The Distinctive Ideas of the Old Testament* (1944), pp. 18 f.

animals which must not be called by their true names during this period. A fox is called 'long-tail' and a mouse 'leg-runner'. Frazer tells[15] of a farmer who had a bailiff named Wolf. During this period the farmer always referred to the bailiff as Herr Undeert (Mr. Monster). All such customs as these arise from a belief that during this 'between' period the wolves, or it may be other animals also, have special freedom and powers.

The connexion between these twelve days and the New Year is established by the popular belief that the weather for the following year is determined by the weather of this period.[16] This is a notion parallel to that which we have already noticed,[17] namely that what is done on New Year's Day will be done all through the year. During this period farm servants in Gloucestershire used to assemble in a cornfield, kindle twelve fires in a row, and round the largest of them to drink to the health of their master and to a good harvest in the following year.

Frazer also gives[18] instances of the hunting of the wren at this period of the year. The reason for the hunting is given in an old song which is said still to be sung in parts of Leinster and Connaught on Christmas Day or on the following day. It runs:

"The wren, the wren, the king of all birds,
St. Stephen's Day was caught in the furze;
Although he is little, his family's great,
I pray you, good landlady, give us a treat".

A similar custom, accompanied by almost identical verses, used to be observed in the County of Essex. These customs of St. Stephen's Day belong properly to the whole period between Christmas Day and Twelfth Day, i.e. from St. Stephen's Day to Twelfth Night. There used to be a Twelfth Day custom observed in Pembrokeshire. Men and boys carried about from house to house a wren in a little box with glass windows surmounted by a wheel. From this wheel were hung various coloured ribbons. Amongst the songs which men and

---

[15] *The Golden Bough* (second ed. in three volumes, 1900), vol. i, p. 454.
[16] Frazer, *ibid.*, vol. iii, p. 143 note.
[17] See p. 62 above.   [18] *Ibid.*, vol. ii, pp. 444 ff.

boys sang was one in which they wished " joy, health, love, and peace " to the people who lived in each house. Here we have an ancient fertility rite. The reason given for the inclusion of the wren in the customs is that the wren above all birds is the bird which has the large family. The songs are songs of good health and prosperity. These are New Year customs, though they are proper to these days between the old and the new Christmas Days. Such customs are found with varying details in the South of France, so that it is evident that they belong to Western Europe generally, and were at one time much more widespread than in the British Isles only. Indeed, there must have been a very wide distribution of the customs connected with the fertility of the wren, if they are to be found as survivals in such unconnected areas as the West of Ireland, South West Wales, Essex, and the South of France. These are not areas which are usually associated in any matter of common custom or interest.

Another instance of a New Year custom connected with fertility rites and belonging to this 'between' period, actually to the eve of Twelfth Day, is quoted by Frazer[19] from books on old customs in Normandy. The men, women and children are said to run wildly through the fields and orchards with lighted torches in their hands. They wave them about the branches and dash them against the tree-trunks. Thus they burn away the moss and drive away the vermin. The object is really a double one. Not only is it to drive away the vermin lest they should multiply beyond measure, but also it is to give fruitfulness to trees, fields, and even cattle. They believe that the longer the ceremony lasts, the greater will be the crop of fruit in the autumn. In Bohemia they wave the torches high, and they say that the corn will grow as high as the torches. On every hand, therefore, in Western Europe, we find that New Year rites are attached to this particular period of the year. It is a 'between' period, depending upon the half-survival of old calendar observances. Popular superstition tends to insist that these things must be done at the time sanctioned by ancient custom whatever the present calendar may have to say. The old time, so to speak, is " God's time ".

An example of the stubborn survival of an old New Year's

[19] Frazer, *ibid.*, vol. ii, pp. 313 ff.

THE EXILE AND THE CHANGE OF CALENDAR 139

Day was to be found, until recent times at any rate, in the Isle of Man. There, according to Frazer,[20] the mummers used to go round on Hallowe'en, and their song was a sort of Hogmanay song, beginning with " To-night is New Year's night, *Hogunaa* ". Here we have a survival of the old Celtic New Year, which has survived in a less disturbed form because of the comparative isolation of the Isle of Man. In Scotland and in the English borderland the Hogmanay rites have largely become detached from Hallowe'en, and have been attracted to the new New Year's Eve.[21]

There was, among the Karaites, a serious attempt to keep Tishri 10 as Rosh hashShanah (New Year's Day). This attempt was on the part of Daniel ben Moses al-Kumasi about 900 A.D. This man was originally an Ananite, and though he revolted from that sect, yet he continued to agree with them in that there ought to be no calculation for the determination of the calendar. He further insisted that *Rosh hashShanah* should be Tishri 10 and not Tishri 1. There is something to be said for his position. It may be that his immediate reason for his insistence on Tishri 10 as New Year's Day is the actual Hebrew Text of Ezek. xl, 1. The Karaites, like their ' parents ' the Ananites, were reformers who were in favour of ancient custom as against modern inventions. They were particularly against such developments as are enshrined in the Talmud, but which have no specific Scriptural warrant. Thus it comes about that when the Scripture under consideration was in the Law, they were in agreement usually with the Sadducees and/or with the Samaritans against the Pharisees. We have seen an instance of this agreement in the interpretation of " the morrow of the Sabbath ".[22] And yet, in this case, there

[20] *The Golden Bough* (abridged ed.), pp. 633 f.
[21] The connexion between the Highlands of Scotland, old Ireland, and the Isle of Man, in the matter of the survival of the ancient Celtic dress is discussed by N. F. McClintock, *Old Irish and Highland Dress* (Dunalgan Press, 1944). It is to be seen in the kilts and plaids of the pipers of the Irish Guards, the cloaks of the Irish, as well as in the kilts and plaids of the Highlanders, and in the old-fashioned Manx dress. He is of the opinion that this is the origin of the shawl as worn by countrywomen in England. It is still worn by older women in such a district as Holbeck in the city of Leeds. The survival of the Celtic New Year in the Isle of Man is not therefore an isolated phenomenon.
[22] See pp. 124 f. above.

seems to have been more in this matter than a stubborn adherence to the actual words of Scripture. In Jerusalem in Mishnaic times the Rabbis apparently discussed the rival claims of Tishri 1 and Tishri 10 as Rosh hashShanah. The evidence is in the Mishnah *Rosh hashShanah* iii, 4, where it is stated that Jubilee (i.e. Tishri 10 in the year of Jubilee) is equal to Rosh hashShanah (Tishri 1) for trumpet blasts and for the recital of Benedictions.[23] Rabbi Judah insisted that there should be a distinction (paragraph 5b), and that on Tishri 10 the trumpets should be straight as against the curved trumpets on Tishri 1. It will appear, therefore, from the Mishnah discussion that Daniel the Karaite was reverting, in part at least, to ancient ideas. This Daniel was indeed a great advocate of ancient custom as against 'modern' Babylonian tendencies. He believed, as we have said, that the calendar ought to be fixed by actual observation of the new moon. This method of observing the crescent of the new moon was that which was established in Palestine (Mishnah *Rosh hashShanah* ii, 5-7). The astronomical element in their decisions was limited to enquiring whether the witnesses saw the crescent of the moon as a C or a D. They knew that if it was a D, then it was the new moon which had been seen, but that if it was a C, then it was the crescent of the old moon. They even went so far as to have diagrams to which they could direct the attention of the witnesses. As late as 853 A.D. the Babylonian Amoraim still deferred to the Palestinians in this custom of determining the beginning of the month, and therefore of the calendar and the feasts, by such primitive methods of observation. It is recorded that in that year an intercalary month was decreed by the patriarch in Palestine in order to keep the sowing season right. Later, however, the Babylonian schools grew stronger and became independent. This independence in the matter of determining the calendar was due partly to their growing ascendancy, and partly also to the obvious efficiency and superiority of their more exact and scientific methods. The climax came in 921 A.D., when there was a definite quarrel between Rabbi Aaron ben Meir on the Palestinian side and Rabbi Sa'adiyah on the Babylonian side, with the result that a rectified Babylonian calendar was

[23] For the New Year Benedictions, see pp. 177-194.

THE EXILE AND THE CHANGE OF CALENDAR 141

instituted.[21] Rabbi Sa'adiyah was a valiant warrior on behalf of the Babylonian schools, against both the heretic Karaites and the orthodox Palestinians.

We see thus that Tishri 10 as New Year's Day is a relic of the change-over of the calendar from a twelve-lunar-month year with occasional intercalary months to some sort of attempt to keep a true solar year. The stage was transitional except in so far as the New Year's Day for the Year of Jubilee is concerned. A further traditional stage in this change-over is to be seen in the equality which was once observed between Nisan 1 and Tishri 1.

Equality of Tishri 1 and Nisan 1

The equality between Tishri 1 and Nisan 1 is to be found in Ezek. xlv, 18-20. They are days of atonement and expiation. This equation, so far as the Jews were concerned, was a transitional arrangement, if indeed it ever did exist in Judah. It belongs to the period when it was uncertain how much, if any at all, of the autumnal old year and new year ceremonies and ideas should be transferred to the spring in company with the civil calendar. In the end none of the old ceremonies gravitated to Nisan 1. So far as traditional Jewry is concerned, Tishri 1 survived as a special day, and, so far as the Temple and synagogue rituals are concerned, Nisan 1 is no different from any other new-month day.

Another scheme in the last chapters of the Book of the Prophet Ezekiel is that of making every new-month day equally a day of atonement and propitiation (Ezek. xlvi, 6). On these days an extra bullock, and that without blemish, was to be offered in addition to the offerings proper to every Sabbath. The final arrangement of the Priestly Code involved an approximation to a compromise between this scheme and that outlined in Ezek. xlv, 18-20. There is the special burnt offering at the beginning of every month throughout all the months of the year: "And one he-goat for a sin offering unto the Lord; it shall be offered beside the continual burnt offering and the drink offering thereof" (Num. xxviii, 11-15). In addition to this there is an additional burnt offering and one he-goat for a sin offering on Tishri 1, the first day of the

[24] Margolis and Merx, *History of the Jewish People*, pp. 261, 213.

seventh month (Num. xxix, 1-6). We thus see that, although the new-month day still retains the connexion with atonement and propitiation proper to the moonless nights of the new moon, yet in Judaism proper the equality of Nisan 1 and Tishri 1 did not exist so far as the offerings in the Temple were concerned.

But there was an equality between Nisan 1 and Tishri 1 for the purposes of fixing the calendar accurately. According to *Rosh hashShanah* I, 4a, particular care was taken to fix the calendar exactly on both Nisan 1 and Tishri 1. The passage reads: " Upon two new-month days they may profane the Sabbath, in Nisan and in Tishri: for in them the messengers set out according to Palestinian custom, and in them the feast times are fixed ". The reference is to the custom whereby the first day of the month was fixed consequent upon the evidence of the two reliable and independent witnesses who made the journey to Jerusalem to testify that they had seen the sickle of the new moon in the sky. It was permissible for this purpose to exceed the prescribed length of the Sabbath day's journey. But there was discussion and doubt concerning this concession, for the next paragraph says: " As long as the Temple was standing, they might profane the Sabbath in addition upon every new-month day, because of the proper arrangement of the new-month offerings ". Here we have a reflexion of the double strand in Ezek. xlv, 18-20, and Ezek. xlvi, 6. The Talmud discusses the double tradition, and comes to the conclusion that originally they were permitted to profane the Sabbath on every new-month day alike, but that since the Temple was destroyed and the new-month offerings had therefore ceased, it was not permissible to profane the Sabbath for the purpose of fixing the beginning of the month with careful exactitude, except in Nisan and in Tishri.

It is probable that the Talmud is wrong in saying that the special importance of Nisan and Tishri above the other new-month days is later, for this double custom of fixing the calendar is found among the Samaritans. To them Nisan 1 is of no importance as being in itself a festival, but they deem it advisable to be sure of accuracy in the month Nisan. The reason is the same as that given in the Mishnah, namely the accurate observance of the Passover, the proper counting of the Omer,

THE EXILE AND THE CHANGE OF CALENDAR 143

and the consequent fixing of Pentecost, all of which are dependent upon the proper and correct fixing of Nisan 1. Both the Jews and the Samaritans would take particular care in this matter, since it was a source of great antagonism between them. There are accounts both in Rabbinic and in Samaritan traditions of bitter fights and bloodshed in connexion with these matters. "The Samaritans endeavoured to mislead the Jews in the Diaspora, and lighted beacons on the hill-tops on wrong days to indicate the new moon as calculated in Jerusalem, for this was the sign agreed upon by the Jews",[25] in order to make sure that they themselves were accurate in fixing their dates according to their own traditions. The Samaritans adopted exactly similar ceremonies in each case, both for Nisan and for Tishri.

This fixing of the calendar twice a year by the Samaritans still persists, as is stated in a letter written by Salamah son of Tabiah to Silvestre Sacy, in 1920, and quoted[26] by Dr. E. Robertson. "We preserve the manuscript of this book (by Phineas son of Eleazar), and every six months we deduce from it the rules which determine the new moons and the festivals, and we send them through Israel". Dr. Robertson has elucidated the astronomical tables of the Samaritans, and it is evident that they are based on the tables of the ninth-century Muslim astronomers Al-battani and Al-khwarizmi. The ceremonies and the double fixing of the new-month days in Nisan and in Tishri are therefore evidently a survival from pre-Muslim days, from before the time when these tables were in the constant use to which evidently they have been subjected.

The most obvious remark to make concerning this double fixing of the calendar is that it was due to the necessity of being accurate in the fixing of these two new-month days, Nisan and Tishri, because these are the two months in which the two great feasts fall, and the other feast, Pentecost, is definitely dependent upon the Passover of the month Nisan. The fact

[25] M. Gaster, *The Samaritans* (Schweich Lectures, 1923; London, 1925), pp. 36 f.
[26] *Notes and Extracts from the Semitic Manuscripts in the John Rylands Library*, VI. *The Astronomical Tables and Calendar of the Samaritans*. Reprinted from *The Bulletin of the John Rylands Library*, vol. 23, No. 2, Oct. 1939, pp. 8 f.

that there were such controversies between the Jews and the Samaritans would appear to confirm this view. On the other hand, we have an equality between the two in Ezek. xlv, 18-20, and this equality is still the subject of discussion in the Mishnah. It is probable, therefore, that the equality of Nisan 1 and Tishri 1 goes back in its origins to the days of the Exile, especially since there is evidence that something of the same kind existed in Mesopotamia. Indeed, the regulations of Ezek. xlv, 18-20, are almost certainly due to the influence of contemporary Babylonian menologies.

The equality of Nisan and Tishri is found through Mesopotamian menologies generally, and also in Sumerian and Babylonian calendars. It is not simply the case that the new Babylonian calendar could not entirely suppress the old Hebrew calendar with its autumnal New Year, with the result that for a little while the Hebrews, even ecclesiastically, paid respect equally to both. Actually the Mesopotamians themselves never managed entirely to suppress an autumnal New Year of their own.

In the old Sumerian times each city seems to have had its own calendar, but during the following millennium (the second) the system of Nippur prevailed. This city, Nippur, was the seat of the greatest of the Mesopotamian cults, since there En-lil was worshipped. It was the centre of learning and culture after the decline of Uruk (Erech). The liturgical books of the priests and schoolmen of Nippur became ultimately the liturgical books of Assyrian and Babylonian Temples generally. It is true that Asshur-bani-pal had many books from Uruk transcribed and placed in his library at Nineveh, but his interest seems to have been mainly antiquarian, though there were certainly wide-sweeping reforms in his time. But about 2300 B.C. the second (Semitic) invasion overran Sumer and Akkad. The invaders adopted the native religion and largely the native civilization also, as their predecessors had done before them. It is not often that invaders ever conquer 'the manner of the land'. Amongst other things, these new invaders adopted the Nippurian system of months and festivals, though they themselves translated the original Nippurian names for the months. These translations are the names for the months which ultimately survived in

THE EXILE AND THE CHANGE OF CALENDAR

common use, and in course of time they found their way into Jewish literature. They are the names of the Jewish months to this day. They are Nisan, Ayar, Sivan, Tammuz, Ab, Elul for the first half of the year; Tishri, Arachsamna (Marchesvan), Kislev, Tebeth, Shebat, and Adar for the second half of the year.

But the complications of the old Sumerian times are not confined to the varying customs of the different cities. The whole question of dating is difficult also. Just as in the Old Testament the pre-exilic months are referred to by post-exilic numeration,[27] so also the names of Sumerian months were sometimes borrowed from the later Nippurian list. An example of this is the Umma list cited by Thureau-Dangin, where three of the month names, the first, the second, and the sixth, are from the Nippur list, whilst the twelfth month is called *Dumu-zi*, which is *shu-KUL-na*, mentioned as the sixth month at Ur, and the fourth at Nippur.[28]

The remarkable thing about the Nippur official list is that although Nisan was undoubtedly the first month of the year in neo-Babylonian times, yet the name of the seventh month, Tishrit, means 'opening, beginning', from the root *seru* (begin). It is clear that Tishritu (opening) and Shibitu (seventh) both refer to the autumn month in the Hammurabi period, and equally clear that in his time Shibitu refers to the month Nisan.[29] The explanation is that in Hammurabi's time the beginning of the civil year was transferred from Tishrit to Nisan. The old Nippurian year had its new year in the autumn, and this was the custom under Sargon of Agade, and under Gudea. There is a later Uruk tablet which speaks of an ancient new year festival there in Tishrit, and another from the time of Hammurabi which tells of its celebration in Nisan. At Ur in Sumerian times the festival was held in *shu-KUL-na* (Du'uzu, the sixth month),[30] but sometimes in *she-KIN-KUD* (at the close of Adar, i.e. the beginning of

---

[27] "The month Ziv, which is the second month" (1 Kings vi, 1); but it was the eighth, whereas Bul was not the eighth (1 Kings xii, 33), but the second.

[28] S. A. Pallis, *The Babylonian 'akitu' Festival*, pp. 29 note, 17.

[29] There are indications that the third month also was sometimes called Shibitu, but some of the early variations are strange.

[30] This obtained at one period also at Adab.

Nisan), and sometimes in Tishrit. But the Nippurian calendar gained the supremacy with its new year festival in Tishrit, until Hammurabi changed this to Nisan. This was the date which finally prevailed throughout Mesopotamia. In the main the ecclesiastical calendar followed the civil calendar.

We thus see that the double new year appears in Babylonia also,[31] and it is probably this age-old variation which is the reason for the equation of Nisan 1 and Tishri 1 in Ezek. xlv, 18-20, though this double emphasis gained new meaning when the times of controversy arose in connexion with the proper observance of the feasts.

The whole position seems to be a compromise between an old Calendar, which celebrated the new year in the autumn, and the Hammurabi innovation, which insisted on the celebration in the spring. Though Hammurabi had his way throughout Mesopotamia, and even in the West because of the Babylonian conquests of the sixth century, yet the local customs tended to survive, especially in Palestine, where the autumn new year maintained its supremacy in the ecclesiastical new year of post-exilic Jewry. They made a temporary compromise with respect to the fixing of the calendar in Nisan, though only because this suited a wider purpose. Their compromise in respect of atonement offerings on Nisan 1 and Tishri 1 soon fell into disuse, if indeed it ever came into use at all. Tishri 1, as we shall see, came into a new prominence. The old Palestinian new year with its autumnal associations persists until this day, though the Babylonian names are supreme. It appears also in the Aramaic-Syrian lists of Christian writers of the first century, where both the civil and the ecclesiastical years are reckoned from Teshrit. The same situation is found in the Greek version of these names found at Baalbek, though there the first month is called *Ag* (for the Hebrew *chag*: it is the pilgrimage month) instead of the Former Teshrit, as in the Aramaic lists, and the second month is called Tishirin instead of the Latter Teshrit.[32]

The attempt to preserve a balance between Nisan and

---

[31] A calendar from Umma calls Tishrit 'the second festival'.

[32] Langdon, *op. cit.*, pp. 65 f. For details as to the Mesopotamian new year celebrations, see Langdon, *op. cit.*, pp. 98. 126, 157; and S. A. Pallis, *op. cit.*, pp. 14-31, especially pp. 30 f.

THE EXILE AND THE CHANGE OF CALENDAR 147

Tishri probably accounts also for the later custom (Exod. xii, 3 f.: P) of choosing the Passover Lamb on Nisan 10, so that Nisan 10 now becomes a special day, just as Tishri 10 is a special day. The Sabbath before the 14th of Nisan is called 'The Great Sabbath' by the modern Jew. This is because the day on which the Passover Lamb was first chosen was a day on which the 10th of Nisan was also a Sabbath. Here we have another indication of the desire to maintain some sort of equality between the two halves of the year, a tendency which we have seen to be marked from Ezekiel onwards. Similarly, after the Exile an eighth day was added to the Feast of Sukkoth (Lev. xxiii, 36); and to correspond with this we have the later institution of an eighth day for the Feast of Passover also.[33]

The double new year with its tendency to equate Nisan and Tishri can also be seen in the variations of the place in the calendar for the insertion of the intercalary month. We have said that the Hebrew year before the Exile was a rough-and-ready lunar year of twelve moons with an intercalary month inserted, almost unwittingly, in case of need. The custom of deliberately inserting an extra month was followed in Mesopotamia in Sumerian times, but the method there, as later in Palestine, was far from being systematized. Towards the end of the year the Sumerians examined the corn-fields, and if it seemed to them that the twelfth month Adar was going to fall too early, then they inserted before it 'a former Adar' in order to keep the months right with the seasons. Islam has never done this, with the result that the Pilgrimage moves round the whole year, being sometimes in the height of summer and sometimes in the depth of winter. Whilst the Sumerian custom was to insert the intercalary month before the twelfth month, the later Mesopotamian custom was to insert it after the twelfth month. As Langdon points out,[34] they had forgotten by this time the actual meaning of the name Adar, which is 'threshing-floor'. This is an example of the effect of the urbanization of these later times, a development upon which S. A. Pallis lays great stress in his study of the Babylonian New Year Festival.

[33] Schultz, *Old Testament Theology* (Eng. tr. by J. A. Paterson, Edinburgh, 1892), vol. i, p. 364.
[34] *Op. cit.*, p. 142.

There are also indications of an intercalation after the first month instead of before it. These all depend upon a calendar with its new year in the spring. There is also a half-yearly parallel, which depends upon a new year in the autumn. This is an intercalation after Elul, the sixth month, the month in which the new year festival was sometimes held at Ur and Adab in early times. However, the intercalation after the twelfth month finally prevailed, and it was this custom which was adopted by the Jews of post-exilic times, especially after the time when the Babylonian schools became supreme in 921 A.D.

The final development in respect of the months Nisan and Tishri, so far as the Old Testament is concerned, is that of the Priestly Code. Nisan 1 has become, from the ecclesiastical point of view, no different from any other new-month day. Tishri 1 has become unique. "In the seventh month, in the first day of the month, shall be a solemn rest (*shabbathon*) to you, a memorial of trumpet-blowing (*zikeron teru'ah*), a holy convocation (*miqra' qodesh*)" (Lev. xxiii, 24). Tishri 10 is the Day of Atonement (*yom hakKippurim*), "an holy convocation, and ye shall afflict your souls" (Lev. xxiii, 27). Tishri 15 is the first day of the Feast of Sukkoth (Tabernacles, Booths) for seven days, with an additional eighth day, which, like the feast, is "an holy convocation" (Lev. xxiii, 34-6). The original Feast of Asiph (Ingathering), with its rejoicing and its penitence, has thus become three festivals, one great Feast and two observances. Instead of one New Year period, we have three New Year Days. First there is that New Year's Day which kept close to the moon and was ultimately called Tishri 15. Next there is the curious New Year's Day, Tishri 10, surviving in its association with the Year of Jubilee, the "Old New Year's Day". Lastly, so far as the ecclesiastical calendar is concerned, there is the true ecclesiastical New Year's Day, Tishri 1, later known as Rosh hashShanah. Apart from this there is the civil New Year's Day, Nisan 1, and various other New Year's Days, which actually are the proper fixed days for certain annual tithing purposes, and so forth.

New Year's Days for Tithes

These other New Year's Days are mentioned in the Mishna, *Rosh hashShanah* I, 1, a-d. The passage runs as follows: "There are four New Years. On the first of Nisan is the New Year for kings and feasts; on the first of Elul is the New Year for the cattle tithe; Rabbi 'Ele'azar and Rabbi Shim'on say 'on the first of Tishri'; on the first of Tishri is the New Year for years, and for years of release and for jubilees, for plants and for herbs; on the first of Shebat is the New Year for trees, according to the House of Shammai: the House of Hillel says 'on the fifteenth of it'."

It is very strange, as Büchler has pointed out,[35] that these dates correspond to the days on which the Books of the Pentateuch were begun according to the Palestinian three-year lectionary. The first Book of the Pentateuch was begun on the first of Nisan, the fifth Book on the first of Elul, the third book on the first of Tishri, and the second and fourth Books on the fifteenth of Shebat. These correspondences form a series of remarkable coincidences, so remarkable that they can scarcely be accidental. This means that they have apparently nothing to do with New Year's Day in the proper calendar sense, and so they are outside our present scope. Why these dates should be the times for the particular purposes which are mentioned is an unsolved puzzle. It is possible, however, that the reason for the fixing of the fifteenth of Shebat as the proper day for the tithing of trees is to be found in one of the Haftaroth for the day. (The Haftarah is the Reading from the Prophets which 'closed' the Reading from the Law.) The passage begins with Isa. xxvii, 6: 'In days to come shall Jacob take root; Israel shall blossom and bud: and they shall fill the face of the world with fruit'.

[35] *J.Q.R.*, vol. v, p. 443.

5
TISHRI 1: THE DAY OF MEMORIAL

THE earliest reference to Tishri 1 is to be found in Ezek. xlv, 18-20, where both Tishri 1 and Nisan 1 are equally days of atonement and expiation. In the Priestly Code, Tishri 1 has gained the pre-eminence among new-month days, and Nisan 1 is in no way different from any other new-month day. Tishri 1 has become "a solemn rest, a memorial of trumpet-blowing, a holy assembly" (Lev. xxiii, 24). For the Hebrew "a memorial of trumpet blowing" (*zikaron teru'ah*) the Septuagint has *mnemosunon salpiggon*. Not only does this confirm the pointing of the Masoretic Text, but it also confirms that at the time when the Hebrew Text of the Law was translated into Greek in the third century B.C., the trumpets of Tishri 1 were interpreted as a memorial, just as was the case at the time when the Hebrew Text was first written.

But whilst Tishri 1 is the only day which is described in the Priestly Code as a Day of Memorial, yet every festival and every new-month day is a day of memorial in respect of trumpet-blowing. "Ye shall blow with the trumpets in respect of your burnt-offerings and over the sacrifices of your peace-offerings; they shall be to you for a memorial before your God" (Num. x, 10). Here the reason for the blowing of trumpets is clearly stated to be that the people may be remembered before God. This is the case also when the trumpets are blown in battle. It is in order that, because of God's remembrance, the people may be saved from their enemies (Num. x, 9). Trumpet-blowing, in the Priestly Code generally, is for a memorial before God. Inasmuch, therefore, as Tishri 1 is a "day of trumpet-blowing" (Num. xxix, 1), it is a day of special remembrance before God. If it should be argued that the trumpets of Tishri 1 were different from other trumpets blown on other occasions, in that they were curved trumpets of ram's horn, then the reply is that there is no mention in Num. xxix, 1, of ram's-horn trumpets (the shofar) for Tishri 1, and that this is a later development.[1]

---
[1] See p. 169 below.

Meanwhile Tishri 10 has become the Day of Atonement, when men must "afflict their souls" (Lev. xxiii, 27; Num. xxix, 7). Tishri 1 ceases to be mentioned as a day of sadness and remorse. The association of Tishri 1 with sorrow and remorse appears, however, in Neh. viii, 12, when, at the reading of the Law, Ezra and the Levites "said to the people, This day is holy unto the Lord your God; mourn not, nor weep. For all the people wept when they heard the words of the Lord (viii, 9) . . . neither be ye grieved; for the joy of the Lord is your strength" (viii, 10). And so the people "went their way to eat, and to drink, and to send portions, and to make great mirth, because they understood the words that were declared unto them" (viii, 12). All this took place on the first day of the seventh month (viii, 2), that is, on Tishri 1. It is clear that the day of joy was an innovation. Was their original sorrow only because of the particular occasion? And was their new-found joy because they understood, thanks to those who took pains to expound, the words which were read to them? It is difficult to be certain in this matter, but the explanations given seem scarcely to be adequate, and we are disposed to assume that the sorrow on this particular Tishri 1 was the survival of a former and ancient custom. Further, in spite of the efforts of Ezra and his Levites, there is no trace of the secure establishment of Tishri 1 as a pre-eminent day of joy such as Neh. viii would suggest. This is probably because the Giving of the Law became associated with the Feast of Weeks (Pentecost) rather than with Tishri 1. The rejoicing which the leaders sought to establish was connected with the understanding of the words of the Law, which for the first time had been read and explained to the people. The modern parallel is *Simchath Torah* (the Rejoicing of the Law), which belongs to Tishri 23 in the modern synagogue. This is the day when the last Seder of the Law is read (Deut. xxxiii-xxxiv), and immediately the first verses of Genesis (i, 1-ii, 3) are read, lest it should ever be said that Israel has finished the Reading of the Law.[2]

[2] The fixing of the Pentateuchal lessons so that they should be completed immediately after the Feast of Sukkoth is an indication not only of the solidarity of the three holy celebrations of Tishri, but also of that aspect of the celebrations which marks the end of the year.

Tishri 1 Among the Samaritans

That penitence rather than joy is the original significance of Tishri 1 is confirmed by the ideas of the Samaritans who separated from the orthodox Jews of Jerusalem sufficiently early for them to have avoided any possible innovations from the time of Ezra onwards. They had, indeed, little reason to regard with anything other than the gravest suspicion whatever the " cursed Ezra " and his companions introduced. This suspicion applies to everything which the Aaronic priesthood of Jerusalem supported during the troubled period of rivalry and bitterness which assumed increased importance from the time of the unconciliatory attitude of Jeshua and Zerubbabel (Ezra iv, 1-6).[3]

Among the Samaritans the Feast of Trumpets of Tishri 1 is not regarded as being in itself a New Year Festival, but rather as being the beginning of the great penitential period of the year.[4] The Samaritan Liturgy, as shown in A. E. Cowley's edition,[5] supports this statement. The prayers for Tishri 1 are followed by the special prayers for the Day of Penitence (Selian), pp. 462-82. The ideas associated with the whole period from Tishri 1 to Tishri 10 are sorrow, penitence, remembrance, and as a background to it all there is the idea of judgement in connection with the turn of the year. For them Tishri 10 has become the Day of Judgement[6] (*Yom alDin*).

Another indication of the significance of Tishri 1 among the Samaritans is to be gleaned from the *qaṭef* for the day. On special occasions the Samaritans have made additions to their liturgies, and these additions are called *Musaph*, just as the Jewish additional services for special days are described. Among these additions are certain songs and prayers, but more particularly a string of verses from the Pentateuch, this being, of course, the only Scripture which the Samaritans ever recognized as such. This string, or more properly ' chain ', of verses

---

[3] For the part which the Zadokite-Aaronite priesthood played in the ejection of the Samaritans from Jerusalem, see *Studies in the Psalter* (London, 1934), pp. 12-6.

[4] Montgomery, *The Samaritans* (1907), pp. 40 f.

[5] *The Samaritan Liturgy* (1909) in 2 vols.; see particularly vol. i, pp. 443-67.

[6] M. Gaster, *Samaritan Oral Law and Ancient Traditions*, vol. i, *Eschatology* (1932), pp. 109, etc.

TISHRI 1: THE DAY OF MEMORIAL

is called the *qaṭef*, and the verses correspond to the character of the day for which they are chosen. It is difficult to identify these verses,[7] but the actual reference itself is probably enough for our purpose. A comparison of the various *qaṭefs* for certain special days, festivals and so forth, will show what is characteristic of Tishri 1. The reference given is, in each case, to the edition of *The Samaritan Liturgy* by A. E. Cowley in two volumes.

For the Eve of the First Day of the Year: *shemesh, ri'shon, mophetin* (vol. i, p. 114).
For the Morning of the First Day of the Year: *berith, zikaron, shemesh, yoṣiph, ri'shon, mophetim* (vol. i, p. 125).
For the Morning of the First Day of Passover: *berith, zikaron, ri'shon, mophetim, maççoth, shabbath, qorban* (vol. 1, p. 161).
For the Feast of Maççoth: *berith, zikaron, terumah, yoṣiph, mophetim, ri'shon, miçraim, ço'n, boqer, shabbath, sammeach, qorban* (vol. i, p. 224).
For the First Sabbath of Pentecost: as usual plus *shabbath, qaçir, hayyam, shebu'oth* (vol. i, p. 284).
For Tabernacles: *shabbath, shebi'i, berith, zikaron, terumah, yoṣiph, sukkoth* (vol. ii, p. 725).
For the eighth day of Tabernacles: *shabbath, shebi'i, shemini* (vol. ii, p. 779).
For the seventh month: *berith, zikaron, terumah, paqad, yoṣiph, shabbath* (vol. ii, p. 428).
For the Eve of the Feast of the seventh month: *shemesh, shebi'i, shabbath* (vol. ii, p. 443).
For the Morning of the Feast of the seventh month: *shabbath, shebi'i, berith, zikaron, terumah, yoṣiph, kipper* (vol. ii, pp. 455 f.).

A comparison of these lists shows that the one distinctive element in the *qaṭef* for the first of Tishri, the seventh month, is *kipper* (atonement). The first of Tishri shares the idea of remembrance with the other festivals. Every other verse connected with Tishri 1 is found also in connexion with at least one other festival. In the remainder of the Tishri 1 liturgy the references are to trumpet-blowing (*teru'ah*) as in Lev. xxiii, 24, to memorial, to *shabbathon*, and to penitence, mercy, and

---
[7] I have tried in every possible way to seek details of these verses, their identity and their extent, but have been unsuccessful.

the forgiveness of sins. These elements are those which are clearly stated in the long declaration as to the significance of the day which is to be found on pp. 453 f. of vol. ii of *The Samaritan Liturgy*. In the list of verses which form the *qaṭef* for the seventh month the word *paqad* is to be noted. This is important in view of the relation between the Hebrew root *p-q-d* (visitation) and the root *z-k-r* (remembrance), which is discussed in the Tosefta *Rosh hashShanah*.[8]

The Bene Israel

We search for other groups of Jews who broke away, for one reason or another, from the main development of Jewish tradition at an early date. One such group is to be found in the Bene Israel.[9] These are a body of Jews in number about ten thousand who inhabit a district in the Bombay Presidency. The date of their immigration into India is certainly not later than the second century A.D., though K. S. Kehimkar believed that they left their mother country before the time of Antiochus Epiphanes, 175 B.C.[10] This date is probably too early. The fact that they did not know of the Feast of Dedication is in itself no evidence that they left Palestine before 165 B.C., when that Feast was instituted, because they did not keep the Feast of Pentecost either. They, however, knew nothing of the doubling of the first and last days of festivals, a custom which seems to have sprung up in Mishnaic times. Generally speaking, they seem to have observed the customs of their ancestors in Palestine of pre-Mishnaic times, but they seem to have been cut off from them completely before 100 A.D. This impression is confirmed by a reference made in conversation by the late Mr. H. Loewe of the Queens' College, Cambridge, that in their ritual of drinking wine they preserved[11] Roman customs of the time of Nero. This date at the end of the first

---

[8] See p. 179 below.

[9] Their history and customs are discussed by J. H. Lord in ERE, ii, pp. 470 ff., and also in a monograph entitled *The Jews in India and the Far East* (Kolhapur, 1907). Both of these studies are founded on studies by K. S. Kehimkar, whose notes were posthumously published under the title *The History of the bene-Israel of India* (Tel-aviv, 1937).

[10] *Ibid.*, p. 12.

[11] These verbs are all in the past tense, because we are dealing with the period before they were 'reformed'.

TISHRI 1: THE DAY OF MEMORIAL 155

century A.D. is important, because the second century A.D. was the time of very great revisions in Jewish prayers. Indeed, the Jewish prayers have not changed materially since that date, the period when the Rabbis set to work to make such alterations in the synagogue prayers as would more effectively compensate for the loss of the Temple and its sacrificial and other ritual.

With respect to the omission of the observance of Pentecost by these Jews of the Bombay Presidency, there may well be a reason for its deliberate omission. In his Schweich Lectures for 1920,[12] St. John Thackeray thought that it was significant that the last chapters of the Book of the Prophet Ezekiel omit all reference to Pentecost. It is certainly a strange omission, since the Feast of Pentecost was undoubtedly observed by the Jews both before and after the Exile, and by the Samaritans also, though by them always on a Sunday. His suggestion was that the omission was deliberate because of recent tendencies to sun worship (Ezek. viii, 14 f.). This may well be a sound suggestion, for it is most likely that of all the festivals of Canaan this one was most closely connected with the sun. The readings from the Prophets proper to the Feast, and the Psalms also which belong to it, all speak of the great chariot-drive through the heavens, and St. John Thackeray is not alone in thinking that here we have an association with the great journey of the midsummer sun from one end of the heaven to the other, and the violent thunderstorms which are characteristic of that period of the year.[13] It may be that there is a similar explanation of the fact that the Bene Israel had no Feast of Pentecost. Was it because of the presence of the Parsees in the Bombay Presidency? The Bene Israel have assimilated many Indian customs during their long sojourn in that country, but the fear of idolatry may have prevented them in this one particular from adopting the customs of the heathen with whom they were surrounded. The history of the Dispersion throughout the centuries has always shown this double characteristic. The Jew may have adopted, and often has adopted, the customs of the country of his sojourning, but he has always stopped short of anything which infringed the

[12] *The Septuagint and Jewish Worship* (London, 1921), p. 43.
[13] *Ibid.*, p. 47.

Unity of God, or of anything which even remotely approached idolatry. Many Jews have lapsed from the strict observances of their religion because of their Gentile environment, but the horror of idolatry or of anything which is contrary to monotheism of the strictest type has been a barrier which can very rarely indeed be overstepped. Whether this explanation of the absence of the Feast of Pentecost from the rites of the Bene Israel is acceptable or not, we are quite content to have it established with a considerable measure of certainty that they were separated from the main body of Jewry before the great revisions of the synagogue prayers at the beginning of the second century A.D.

The Bene Israel have a tradition that some nine hundred years ago a certain David Rahabi came to them and effected a considerable religious revival among them. He may have come from Cochin, where the name still exists as a family name among the Jews there. It is agreed, both by K. S. Kehimkar and by J. H. Lord, that the celebrations, both feasts and fasts, which David Rahabi introduced are distinguishable by the fact that they have Hindustani names, whereas the earlier celebrations have Marathi names. This is the ordinary vernacular of the district in which these Jews have lived for two thousand years or so. It is probable that David Rahabi's visit was somewhat later than nine hundred years ago, since Hindustani as a spoken language in India is scarcely earlier than the beginning of the fifteenth century. Our interest in these reforms of mediæval times is limited to the additional emphasis which they lay upon the differences between the customs of the Bene Israel and the orthodox Jewish traditions. Where there is a difference we may be all the more sure that it goes back to very ancient times.

These Jews speak the ordinary Marathi vernacular, and they adopted Marathi names for their more ancient festivals, revising some of the customs in order to adapt them to their very different environment. They used to observe the Feast of Tabernacles a fortnight out of time. They called it *Khiricha San*, i.e. the Feast of *Khir*, "a confection made of grains of new rice compounded with sugar, scraped cocoanut, and spices".[14] The fact that they kept it a fortnight out

---

[14] J. H. Lord, *ibid.*, p. 34.

of time is most curious. It has been suggested that the difference was due to their not being able to build the booths in a strange and sometimes hostile environment. Against this it can be said that they never had any difficulty about dates, since the local month coincided so satisfactorily with the Jewish new month. Our suggestion is that the variation may have something to do with the change-over in the new-month day which we hold to have taken place during the time of the Babylonian domination, whereby the new-month day was changed by exactly this period, from the full moon to the new moon. This suggestion is supported by the fact that they did not observe the fasts of the fourth, fifth, seventh, and tenth months, which were abolished in the early post-exilic days (Zech. vii, 5; viii, 19). They seem therefore to have left Palestine before these fasts were re-established, and may also therefore have retained some remembrances of the old new-month day.

They observed the Festival of Purim (*Holicha San*), Passover (*Dakhacha San*), and the Fast of Ab (*Budyacha San*). They kept the Day of Atonement (*Dargal-nicha San*, i.e. the day of door closing), and the ten days prior to this were observed as days of penitence. There is evidence that at one time this period was called Ramzam, apparently because of Islamic influence, though later this name was transferred to the whole of the previous month, Elul. On these ten days they recited special prayers. They kept the New Year Festival (*Navyacha San*), and this was followed by the Fast of the New Year (*Navyacha Roja*). This latter fast is important. The word *roja* is Hindustani and not Marathi, and it shows that the fast is not primary among the Bene Israel. It belongs to the time of the revival of David Rahabi. It was held on Tishri 3, which is the date of the Fast of Gedaliah, the fast of the seventh month abolished in Zech. viii, 19. But the Fast is called the Fast of the New Year. K. S. Kehimkar says[15] that it was given this name in order to remind them when it should be held. Our suggestion is that whilst the observance on Tishri 3 is mediæval, yet the fast itself is much older and is a relic of the penitential character of New Year's Day as the first of the ten-day period of penitence (cf. among the Samaritans). The word *roja* is Hindustani, but the word *navyacha* is Marathi.

[15] J. H. Lord, *ibid.*, p. 17.

The fast in that case would originally have nothing to do with the Fast of Gedaliah, but would be a relic of the Tishri 1 of Neh. viii, 9, when Ezra attempted to change the day from mourning to joy. It is significant that the Bene Israel managed in every case to keep the day of the festival or fast exactly, except for the Feast of Tabernacles, a fortnight out of time, and the Fast of the New Year two or three days after the new year.

The Jews of Cochin

Another group of Jews who have been separated from the main body of Jews for centuries is the Black and White Jews of Cochin. It seems to be impossible to discover anything of their liturgies (if any) which belong to the time before they were 'reformed' and their customs brought into line with orthodox Jewry. If they had any liturgical manuscripts extant before this date, either they have not come to light or they have been destroyed.[16]

The Jews of Kai-fung-fu

Yet another colony of long-lost Jews are those (perhaps now entirely disappeared, since they were almost extinct before the present troubles in China) who lived at Kai-fung-fu in the Province of Honan. There is an actual manuscript of the New Year liturgy on its strange Chinese paper in the John Rylands Library, originally delivered to the Reverend Solomon Carpenter at Shanghai in 185(2?), and deposited by him among the Hebrew MSS. at the Mill Yard, London, on March 15th, 1859. Whilst the actual MS. shows that their knowledge of Hebrew pronunciation was traditional rather than intelligent, the liturgy itself is not substantially different from the modern Jewish liturgy for the Additional Service (*Muṣaf*) for the New Year. The most noteworthy feature is that there is one additional sentence among the Zikronoth (passages which contain the word 'remember').[17] There is no agree-

---

[16] I have been in communication with Mr. A. B. Salem, of Cochin Town, who has studied the customs of his own people, and has written a monograph on the subject, but he has no information on these matters.

[17] See further p. 180 below.

ment concerning the settlement of these Jews in China, but it seems to have taken place not earlier than the fourth century A.D., and probably much later. We see, therefore, that so far as it is possible to judge in cases where there has been an early separation of Jews from the main stream of Jewish development in liturgies, the Festival of the New Year is one of penitence and sorrow.

Josephus and Tishri 1

The testimony of Josephus to the significance of the Festival of Tishri 1 is disappointing. He seems to recognize no difference between this day and the first day of any other month, except only for the additional sacrifice. The passage is *Ant. Iud.* III, x, 2, where he is dependent on Num. xxix. However, he expressly mentions trumpet-blowing, following Lev. xxiii, 24. He apparently knew of some tradition, unless he surmised it himself from the Sacred Text, that Tishri 1 has at one time been the beginning of the year (*Ant. Iud.* I, iii, 3). According to him, Ezra read the Law at the Feast of Tabernacles, and not on Tishri 1 (*Ant. Iud.* XI, v, 5). If Tishri 1 was by any means an important festival in his time, it is strange that he should neglect it to the extent to which he has done. On the other hand, if Tishri 1 was the Feast of the Kingdom of God, we would not expect him to say very much about its significance as such, since he wrote in troublous times, and for Roman eyes to see. But even here there does not seem to be any objection to his emphasizing that God is King, since this would deprecate any idea of a Jewish Messiah as a rival to Cæsar. There are, then, two possible explanations for his silence. One is that he did not want to say anything about it. The other is that he had nothing to say. Which is the correct explanation must depend on what others have to say.

Philo and Tishri 1

Philo[18] calls Tishri 1 "the festival of the sacred moon". He gives two reasons for the trumpet-blowing on this day, "one peculiar to the nation (i.e. to the Jews), and the other common to all mankind". The first reason is that it is a commemora-

[18] *De spec. leg.* II, 188.

tion of the Giving of the Law, and the second is that the trumpet is the instrument of war, and "on this account the Law has given the festival the name of a warlike instrument, in order to show the proper gratitude to God as the giver of peace". It is evident that Philo has difficulties over this matter of the trumpets. He stands by himself as an exegete. Neglecting his own explanations, which, so far as the second is concerned, are largely products of his own ingenuity, it is clear that he knew three things about Tishri 1. First, it was a commemoration, a remembrance day; second, it was a day for trumpet-blowing; third, it was the anniversary of the giving of the Law. In this last case he is following Neh. viii, and disagreeing with Josephus. Ultimately the Giving of the Law was connected with the Sabbath and with Pentecost.[19] The Samaritans combine the New Year and the Pentecost traditions, and they recite the Decalogue at both festivals.

The Talmud and the Trumpet-blowing

In the Talmud two explanations of the trumpet-blowing are offered. According to *b. RH* 16b, they were blown "to confuse Satan when he is accusing Israel before the Divine Judge". According to *b. Shabb.* 131b, they were blown "to bring the remembrance of Israel to their Father in Heaven".

Sa'adiyah and the Trumpet-blowing

Rabbi Sa'adiyah (tenth century A.D.) gave ten reasons why God had commanded the Shofar to be sounded on Rosh hashShanah.[20]

They are as follows:

1. Because this day is the beginning of creation, on which God created the world, and began to reign over it. And just as is the custom of kings, in that they sound the cornets and horns to make known and to cause to be heard in every place the commencement of their reign, so also we proclaim the

---

[19] "All agree that the Law was given to Israel on the Sabbath" (*b. Sabb.* 86b. Cf. p. 126); the Samaritans celebrate Pentecost on the Sabbath.

[20] See *Festival Prayers according to the German and Polish Rites*, New Year Service, trans. by David Levi, pp. 84 ff. The translation here given keeps closer to the Hebrew text than does that of David Levi.

TISHRI 1: THE DAY OF MEMORIAL

Creator King over us this day. And thus saith David in Psalm xcviii, 6: "With cornets and the sound of a Shofar shout ye before the King Jehovah".

2. As the day of Rosh hashShanah is the first of the ten days of penitence, so we sound on it the Shofar to proclaim to us as one who admonishes and says, Every one who is willing to return (and repent) let him return, and if he does not, he cannot say that he was not called, for he was fully informed. For so do kings publish their decrees at the beginning of their reigns, so that every passer-by may be informed, and none may plead that they did not hear.

3. To remind us of the standing on Mount Sinai, as it is said in Ex. xix, 16: "And the sound of the Shofar exceeding loud". And that we ought to bind ourselves as our fathers did, when they said, "We will do and hearken".

4. To remind us of the words of the prophets who are likened unto (watchmen) blowing on the Shofar, as it is said (Ezek. xxxiii, 4): "Whoso heareth the sound of the Shofar and taketh not warning, and the sword cometh and taketh him away, his blood be upon his own head; but he that taketh warning shall save his life".

5. To remind us of the destruction of the Temple, and the sound of the enemies' battle-cry, as it is said in Jer. iv, 19: "Because thou hast heard, O my soul, the sound of the Shofar and the alarm of war". Wherefore we, hearing the sound of the Shofar, ought to beseech the Almighty to rebuild the Temple.

6. To remind us of the binding of Isaac, who submitted himself to the will of Heaven. So ought we to submit ourselves for the Sanctification of His Name, and offer our memorial before Him for good.

7. So that when we hear the sound of the Shofar we should fear, and be terrified, and humble ourselves before the Creator, for it is the nature of the Shofar to spread dread and terror, as it is said in Amos iii, 6: "Shall the Shofar be blown in the city, and the people not be afraid?"

8. To remind us of the great and awful day of judgement, as it is said in Zeph. i, 16: "The great day of the Lord is near and hasteneth, a day of shofar and alarm".

9. To remind us of the gathering of the outcasts of Israel, and to pray for it, as it is said in Isa. xxvii, 13: "And it shall come to pass on that day, that the great shofar shall be sounded, and those that were perishing in the land of Assyria . . ."

10. To remind us of the Resurrection of the Dead, and to believe firmly in it, as it is said in Isa. xviii, 3: "All ye that inhabit the earth, and ye dwellers on the earth, when the standard is lifted on the mountains, ye shall behold, and when the shofar is blown, ye shall hear".

An examination of the reasons which Rabbi Sa'adiyah has given shows that they are built up almost entirely on the synagogue prayers for New Year's Day. In no case can we say that they are themselves evidence of the original reasons for the sounding of the shofar. It is noticeable, however, that in seven cases (*i.e.*, except the first, the second, and the seventh) the blowing of the shofar is for remembrance, though with Rabbi Sa'adiyah it is man rather than God who is to be brought to remembrance.

The first reason is because of the creation of the world on Tishri 1. The connexion is through the fifth Shofaroth,[21] which is Ps. xcviii, 6. This psalm is the Mishnah psalm[22] for the sixth day of the week. According to the Talmud (*b. RH* 31a) this choice is "because then He had finished His works, and began to reign over them". All this is the substance of that part of the synagogue prayers which immediately precede the Malkiyyoth, and the same ideas are expressed in the prayers immediately following them. Jehovah is Creator, and therefore He is King. This corresponds to the reasons given in the Tosefta *RH* I, 12, in the name of Rabbi Aqiba (early second century A.D.). The whole passage reads: "Say ye before Him the Malkiyyoth that ye may proclaim Him King over all His works, the Zikronoth that your memorial may rise before Him for good, the Shofaroth that your prayer may ascend before Him with a trumpet-blast (*teru'ah*)". He is mentioned as King, on Tishri 1, therefore, because that day is the Day of Creation. Tradition has not always been unanimous that Tishri 1 was the Day of Creation, since some Rabbis held that it was Nisan 1, but the matter had been settled long before the time of Rabbi Sa'adiyah (tenth century).[23]

---

[21] For the special verses of Scripture recited on Rosh hashShanah, namely the Malkiyyoth, the Shofaroth and the Zikronoth, see pp. 177 f. below.

[22] *Tamid* vii, 4; *b. RH* 30b, 31a; *Sopherim* xviii, 1.

[23] See p. 192 below.

The second reason advanced by Rabbi Saʿadiyah is that Tishri 1 is the first of the ten days of penitence. This is important because we have seen that this is the characteristic feature of the day among the Samaritans, who have in many ways preserved the pre-Ezra traditions, as, indeed, it is also among the Bene-Israel of the Bombay Presidency. Here, therefore, we have a very early tradition, and there is other evidence of this survival in the conception of this day as the Day of Judgement amongst the Jews.[24] Rabbi Saʿadiyah goes on to illustrate from the accession of kings, when they ascend the throne, that they blow a shofar to declare the laws. Even here, however, the point is not so much that Jehovah has become king, as that the blowing of the shofars is a warning to the people to repent and obey His laws. The reference to the king, therefore, does but emphasize the fact that Tishri 1 is the first of the days of penitence.

The third reason is because of the Giving of the Law. The passage which is quoted is the first of the Shofaroth (Ex. xix, 16), and all the three Shofaroth which are taken from the Law are concerned with this event. Further, it is the subject of the prayer which introduces the Shofaroth in the synagogue liturgy.

The fourth, seventh, and eighth reasons are connected directly with Rosh hashShanah as the Day of Judgement. This association is made very clear in the introductory prayers to the Zikronoth. The fifth and the ninth deal with the hope of the restoration and of the return of the scattered exiles. This is the burden of the prayer which follows the Shofaroth, though the restoration of the Temple is not specifically mentioned there. It is, nevertheless, a repeated theme in the synagogue prayers generally. The sixth reason is the binding of Isaac. This is mentioned in the prayers which immediately follow the Zikronoth, though the emphasis has changed. Originally the significance was to remind Jehovah of the "covenant and the loving-kindness and the oath which thou swarest unto our father Abraham on Mount Moriah". The next stage, as also in the prayers, was that just as Abraham overbore his compassion to perform God's will with a perfect heart, so may God's compassion overbear His anger. The next

---

[24] See p. 166 below.

stage in the development of the explanation is that given by Rabbi Sa'adiyah, that just as Isaac submitted himself to the Divine Will, so also may Israel on the Day of Rosh hashShanah. Something of this idea is to be found in the Talmud (*b. RH* 16a): "Rabbi Abbahu said, Why do we blow a shofar (ram's horn)? The Holy One, Blessed be He, said: Sound before Me a ram's horn, so that I may remember on your behalf the binding of Isaac son of Abraham, and account it to you as if you had bound yourselves before Me."

The last reason which Rabbi Sa'adiyah gives is in connexion with the Resurrection of the Dead. Here it is clear that he has been working on the basis of the synagogue prayers, since he quotes the eighth of the Shofaroth, which is connected with the hope of the return, an idea with which all the three prophetic Shofaroth are connected. He does not quote any passage which might reasonably be associated with the theme of the resurrection of the body.

Maimonides and the Trumpet-blowing

The reasons given by Maimonides[25] (Rambam, 1135-1204) for the blowing of the shofars are Repentance and the need for awakening men from sleep. "So the beginning of the year is celebrated for one day because it is the day of retrospect, or of returning and awakening men from their sleep, which is the reason why the shofar is blown on that day, as we have stated in the Mishnah. It is also the preparation for the Day of Fasting (that is, the Day of Atonement), as is shown by those ten days, whereon they intercede between the Beginning of the year and the Day of Atonement." This explanation is in line with the customs and ideas of the Samaritans, and also, as we see immediately below, with the statements of the Mishnah.

According to the Mishnah (RH I, 2c), on which Maimonides has clearly based his explanation, as indeed he said himself that he did, "On Rosh hashShanah, all who come into the world pass before Him like lambs, as it is said, He that fashioneth the hearts of them all, that considereth their ways." This means that Rosh hashShanah is conceived of as a Day of Judgement. A variant expression of these ideas is to be found

[25] *Moreh Nev.* iii, 43.

TISHRI 1: THE DAY OF MEMORIAL

in *Eccles. Rabba* on ix, 7: "On the eve of the New Year the pure ones of a given generation fast, and God remits to them a third of their sins; from New Year to the Day of Atonement individuals fast, and God remits to them a third of their sins; and on the Day of Atonement all fast, and God says, What is done is done; from this time a new reckoning begins." A parallel development is found in the Talmud, in the Gemara on the above-mentioned passage in the Mishnah (*b. RH* 16b, 17a): Rabbi Kruspedai said in the name of Rabbi Jochanan: "Three books are opened on New Year's Day, one for the wholly wicked, one for the wholly righteous, and one for the intermediate ones. The wholly righteous are inscribed and forthwith sealed for life; the wholly wicked ones are inscribed and forthwith sealed for death; the intermediate ones are suspended, and stand over from Rosh hashShanah until the Day of Atonement. If they are then pure, they are inscribed for life, and if they are not pure, they are inscribed for death." Rabbi Jochanan belonged to the second generation of Palestinian Amoraim, who flourished c. 280-320 A.D.

Tishri 1 is a Day of Penitence

We see, then, that in all these cases Rosh hashShanah is associated primarily with the ten days of penitence, and in this respect the Samaritan custom is confirmed as being sound. G. B. Gray pointed out that there is confirmation of Rosh hashShanah as a Day of Destiny in the Book of Jubilees, where Abraham "sat up through the night of the new moon of the seventh month to observe the stars from the evening to the morning in order to see what would be the character of the New Year with regard to rains (xii, 16)". Here, incidentally, is a clear case of the survival of pre-exilic ideas which we found in connexion with the Feast of Asiph (Ingathering), namely, the necessity of praying for the rains which were due almost immediately after the conclusion of the Feast. A still further development is to be found in the Tosefta *Sanhedrin* 13, where the passage is associated with Dan. xii, 3; Zech. xiii, 9; 1 Sam. ii, 6, and through them with the resurrection of the dead.

The significance of New Year's Day as the first of the ten days of penitence, and itself the great Day of Judgement and Awfulness, is clear again and again in the synagogue prayers.

"The fearful day of judgement is come; all creatures are dismayed with fearful expectation. . . ."[26] Particularly see *Unethanneh toqef*, the meditation which is ascribed by tradition to Rabbi Amnon of Mainz c. 1000 A.D. in the day of his martyr's death.[27] "We will celebrate the mighty holiness of this day, for it is one of awe and terror. In it is Thy kingdom exalted, and Thy throne is established in steadfast-mercy (*cheṣed*), and Thou sittest thereon in truth. Verily it is Thou Thyself who art judge and arbiter, who knowest and art witness, who writest down and dost fix the seal, who recordest and dost tell. Thou rememberest all forgotten things, and Thou dost open the book of remembrances, and from itself it is read aloud (i.e. the deeds recorded in it proclaim themselves), for the seal of every man's hand is set thereto. The great trumpet is sounded; the still small voice is heard; the angels are dismayed; fear and terror seize hold of them, and they proclaim: 'Behold the Day of Judgement, when the host of heaven are to visited in judgement'. For they are not pure in Thine eyes, and all who enter the world Thou dost cause to pass before Thee like a flock of sheep. As a shepherd seeketh out his flock, and causeth them to pass under his crook, so dost Thou cause to pass and number and count and visit every living soul. Thou dost fix the measure of every creature's life, and dost decree their destiny."

It is customary to think of the Day of Atonement (Yom Kippur) as the Day of Judgement, and as such to be distinct from New Year's Day. There is no such distinction. The emphasis is certainly stronger in the prayers for the Day of Atonement, but New Year's Day is nevertheless quite clearly a Day of Judgement and the first of the ten penitential days. For instance, in the Liturgy for the Day of Atonement, according to the Machzor of Aragon, there is to be found an admonitory poem by the famous Solomon ibn Gabriol. It is an acrostic on the name Solomon, and like many of the *Penitentialia* is a *shelishiayyah*, i.e. in stanza of three lines, each line rhyming. It opens:

---

[26] The prayer *'ath chil*: see the New Year Machzor, e.g. The Festival Prayers (German and Polish), D. Levi's translation, vol. i, Cologne 1898 edition, p. 55.
[27] Ibid. for the tradition p. 109a, and for D. Levi's translation, p. 110.

TISHRI 1: THE DAY OF MEMORIAL

"I was desolated by the multitude of pains;
In the day when my pride was visited upon me
What shall I say to my Lord?"

But although in the Aragon Machzor this admonition is found in the Day of Atonement liturgy, yet in the Ashkenazi rite it belongs to the Eve of the New Year.[28]

Tishri 1 and the Readings from the Law

Further evidence of the ideas connected with Rosh hash-Shanah can be found in the Readings from the Law and the Prophets appointed for that day. This is evidence which in part dates from a time prior to the Mishnah. With respect to the Mishnah, it is doubtless true that it contains traditions from a date much earlier than the earliest date which can be given for the compilation of the Mishnah itself, but we can never be wholly sure of the date unless the name of the teacher himself is given. But however early the earliest of these traditions may be, it is certain that the first choice of special Readings from the Law for special days is earlier. It is probable that, as early as 300 B.C.,[29] readings from the Law were introduced at certain festivals. At first the relevant passages from Lev. xxiii were read. In time these readings were extended from the festivals to the four special Sabbaths of Adar, and finally to all Sabbaths. Ultimately, in Palestine, the whole of the Law was arranged so that it was read consecutively Sabbath by Sabbath over a period of three years. The modern system is annual, and not triennial, since the Babylonian annual lectionary was finally adopted. In the course of time a 'concluding' passage was read from the Prophets, and this was therefore called the Haftarah. Ultimately there was a reading from the Prophets to correspond to every reading from the Law.[30] There may also have been a system whereby the Psalter was recited over a three-year period, and it is probable that the actual order of the psalms was to some extent fixed with this in view.[31] We are concerned here, however, only

---

[28] Zunz, *Die Ritus des synagogalen Gottesdienstes*, S. 109.

[29] Büchler, *Jewish Quarterly Review* (old series), vol. v (1893), suggests c. 200 B.C., but see St. John Thackeray, *Journal of Theological Studies*, vol. xii, p. 212.

[30] Büchler, *J.Q.R.*, vol. vi (1894), pp. 1 ff.   [31] Cf. p. 26 (note).

with Rosh hashShanah, and the evidence is good for the period 300 B.C. onwards.

The earliest *Seder* (Reading from the Law) for Rosh hashShanah was from Lev. xxiii, 24 f. (*Meg.* iii, 5). This reading, together with the readings from the same chapter for other special days, presently fell into disuse, and others were substituted. *Sopherim* xvii, 6, gives Num. xxix, 1-6, as a Reading for Rosh hashShanah. The Tosefta *Meg.* iii, 6, gives Gen. xxi as the New Year Seder, and adds that "some say" Lev. xxiii, 24. These two readings are given also in *b. Meg.* 31a and *j. Meg.* iii, 7, and in both *Pesiktas*, though they all insist that Gen. xxi is first. An earlier Seder, however, than Gen. xxi was Gen. xxx, 22, where Rachel, and not Sarah, is 'remembered'. Further, according to *b. RH* 10b, the *Midrash Tadse*, and the Book of Jubilees xxviii, 24, Rachel was 'remembered' on Tishri 1. The question arises, Which came first? Did the tradition that Rachel was remembered on Tishri 1 arise from the Seder, or the Seder from the tradition? Büchler maintained that the reading came first, and there can be little doubt of the correctness of his statement. He took the 155 Sedarim and allocated them to the Sabbaths and Feasts in succession throughout the three-year cycle, beginning with Nisan. He found that the traditional dates of various events which are recorded in the Pentateuch according to *Seder Olam* fit in with the readings of this triennial cycle. On this arrangement, Gen. xxx, 22, is the Seder for Rosh hashShanah, Tishri 1. Büchler therefore held, and rightly, that the order of development was, first the reading, then the remembering of Rachel, and finally the remembering of Sarah. This does not mean that there was no idea of remembrance associated with Tishri 1 until the second stage of the development of its Sedarim. On the contrary, a certain amount of choice would naturally be exercised in the divisions of the Sedarim, and, as St. John Thackeray said,[32] "the remembrance of Rachel here recorded, linked on to, and gave a new connotation to the already existing conception of New Year's Day as a Day of Memorial". We have seen that one of the reasons for blowing shofars on Rosh hashShanah was, according to Rabbi Saʻadiyah, because of the binding of Isaac.[33] We see

[32] *J.T.S.*, xvi, 1.   [33] See p. 161 above.

TISHRI 1: THE DAY OF MEMORIAL

now that this was not primarily a New Year idea, but that it arose, and is embedded in the New Year Prayers, because of the choice of Gen. xxi as the Seder for the New Year. After Gen. xxi had supplanted Gen. xxx, 22, as the New Year Seder in the first year of the cycle, Gen. xxii came to be read on Tishri 2, the second of the two New Year Days, and a link was found with Rosh hashShanah as the Feast of Trumpets in Gen. xxii, 13, "a ram caught in the thicket by his horns", since the trumpets in use were the curved trumpets made of ram's horn and named shofar. The portion was not chosen because of this verse. As Büchler pointed out,[34] the chapter Gen. xxii came to be read first by the Babylonian Jews because the sages did not permit the rolling of the scroll to another portion. It has to be read through portion after portion, 'so that Israel should read through the Torah in continuous fashion'. This stage of development for the readings for Rosh hashShanah is given in *b. Meg.* 31a: "On Rosh hashShanah (the Seder is) Lev. xxiii, 24, and the Haftarah is Jer. xxxi, 19; but some say Gen. xxi and the Haftarah is Hannah (i.e. some portion from 1 Sam. i, ii). And now when there are two days we read on the first day 'as some say' (i.e. Gen. xxi and Hannah), and on the morrow Gen. xxii and Jer. xxxi, 19."

The various prayer books give different readings for New Year's Day. The Machzor *Vitry* (p. 384) gives Gen. xxi and Num. xxix with the Haftarah 1 Sam. i, 1, for the first day, and Gen. xxii with the Haftarah Jer. xxxi, 2-30, for the second day. According to Seligmann, *Gebetbuch* II, pp. 43 f., the readings are Gen. xxii and 1 Sam. i, 1, for the first day and Deut. xxx, 11-20, with Jer. xxxi, 2-30, for the second day. The reading from Deut. xxx, 11-20, is a development from the idea of Rosh hashShanah as the Day of Destiny as given in *b. RH* 16b, 17a.[35]

It seems probable that the use of ram's horns as against straight trumpets on New Year's Day is really due to the adoption of Gen. xxii as a reading for New Year's Day. Here there is the reference to the ram caught in the thicket. Shofars are not mentioned either in Lev. xxiii, 24, or in Num. xxix, 1. In

---

[34] *J.Q.R.*, v, p. 445. See also St. John Thackeray, *J.T.S.*, xvi, p. 181; and *H.D.B.*, iv, p. 815b.

[35] Cf. pp. 165 f. above.

each case the word used is *teru'ah*, a word which can mean any kind of loud noise, with or without any sort of trumpet. The word *shofar* occurs first in connexion with New Year's Day in the Mishnah *RH* III, 5b, where it is stated that Rabbi Judah (i.e. R. Judah ben Ilai) established it firmly that curved trumpets of ram's horns were to be used for Rosh hashShanah. The passage reads: " Rabbi Judah said: At New Year one blows with curved trumpets (*zekarim*), and at Jubilee (i.e. Tishri 10 in the Jubilee year) with straight trumpets (*ye'alim*)". This statement is followed immediately by the statement that New Year's Day and Jubilee are alike for trumpet-blasts and benedictions. At first sight this seems to contradict the former statement, but the reference to trumpet-blasts refers to the kind of noises made, whether long or short and so forth, and not to the kind of horn with which they were made. The comment of the Gemara (*b. RH* 26b) is that the shofars of New Year's Day were of antelope's horn and were straight, and thus it was also for Jubilee and for rains,[36] but that Rabbi Judah said it should be ram's horns for New Year and antelope's horn for Jubilee. This opinion of Rabbi Judah's is given also in the Tosefta *RH* III, 3b, but with such other statements as suggest even more clearly that the custom of using ram's horns was an innovation due to Rabbi Judah. " With what do they blow? With trumpets (*haççoçeroth*, not *shofaroth*) as Moses did. Rabbi Judah says, In New Year they blow with rams' horns (*zekarim*) and at Jubilee with antelopes' (*ye'alim*). The wise gave what was most handy to the one who was most handy ('*eth-hammaçuy lammaçuy*) and what was not most handy to the one who was not most handy ".

There is evidence also from Josephus,[37] who says that the same silver trumpets (the word is *haççoçeroth*) made by Moses for the assembling and the marching of the tribes (Num. x, 3-10), were used in their sacred ministrations when they were bringing their sacrifices to the altar, as well on the Sabbaths as on the rest of the festival days. This actually is what is stated in Num. x, 3-10, and the word *haççoçeroth* is used regularly by the Chronicler, twice only paralleled with *shofar*, in his descriptions of Temple ceremonies. Apparently Josephus

---

[36] For the meaning of this reference to the rains, see p. 174 below.
[37] *Ant. Iud.* III, xii, 6.

knew of no difference between the trumpets used on Rosh hashShanah and those used at any other time.

Three conclusions may be drawn from the evidence. There seems to have been no fixed ruling on the matter during the time when the Temple was standing. If the trumpets used had always been shofars (i.e. made of rams' horns), there would never have been any discussion at all. If the change had not been recent, the discussion in the Talmud (Gemara) and the Tosefta would not have been such as it was. On the supposition that change came subsequently to the adoption of Gen. xxii as the New Year Reading (Seder), the whole discussion is readily intelligible. In the end, even in the Talmud b. RH 16a, the binding of Isaac comes to be given as the definite reason for the use of the ram's horn shofar. "Rabbi Abbahu said: Why do we blow on a ram's horn? The Holy One (blessed be He) said, Sound before me on a ram's horn, so that I may remember on your behalf the binding of Isaac son of Abraham, and account it to you as if you had bound yourselves before Me".

The complete list of Sedarim and Haftaroth for Rosh hash-Shanah came ultimately to be as follows:[38] Gen. xxi with its Haftarah 1 Sam. ii, 21-28, for the first year of the cycle; Lev. i with Jer. xxxi, 19, for the second year; Deut. v with Joel ii, 1, for the third year. In respect of the first of these Haftaroth there is a certain amount of confusion, since 1 Sam. i, 11-22, is also mentioned. According, however, to an Oxford MS. mentioned by Büchler,[39] this latter Haftarah was associated with Gen. xxx, 22, one of the supplanted Sedarim, and the connexion is "And God *remembered* Rachel" and "If thou wilt indeed look upon the affliction of thine handmaid and *remember*". This connexion of remembrance provides also, as Rashi pointed out, the reason for the choice of Jer. xxxi, 19.

The importance of these 'connexions' for the understanding of the significance of the festival is worthy of emphasis. It gives an indication of the chief motif of the festival in these formative days. The use of catchwords is much more common

[38] This is in Palestine under the triennial system. The passages mentioned in the Prayer-books belong to later times after the triennial system had been superseded by the annual lectionaries.
[39] *Jewish Quarterly Review* vi (1893), p. 22.

in Hebrew literature and ritual than was formerly supposed. It is being realized more and more that the four books of the Later Prophets, Isaiah, Jeremiah, Ezekiel and the Twelve, are not long continuous books, neither does the continuity often extend even to one chapter. On the contrary they are composed, for the most part, of quite short sections or oracles, pieced together by an editor (the prophet himself or another), and arranged in their present order by catchwords or linkwords. For instance, the reference to Sodom and Gomorrah provides the link between two very different paragraphs in the first chapter of the Book of the Prophet Isaiah, namely the section composed of verses 4-9 and the section composed of verses 10-17.[40] The whole theory has been worked out in detail for Second-Isaiah by Mowinckel.[41] The sections are sometimes very short, as for instance in the Books of Amos, Hosea and Micah.[42] There is evidently a very great deal indeed to be said for this thesis, and no one can study the choice of the various Haftaroth for very long without realizing that they also were chosen because of certain words common to the Haftarah and the Seder. In particular the Sedarim and the Haftaroth chosen for special occasions are chosen because of the occurrence in them of certain words. This means that beyond any shadow of doubt the leading motif in the choice of the readings for Rosh hashShanah during the two centuries or so before Christ was Remembrance. This is confirmed by the Talmud (*b. RH* 11a): "'On New Year Sarah, Rachel and Hannah were visited'. How do we know this? Rabbi Eliezer said, We learn it from the two occurrences of the word 'visiting', and the two occurrences of the word 'remembering'. It is written concerning Rachel, 'and God remembered Rachel', and it is written concerning Hannah, 'and the Lord remembered Hannah', and there is an analogous mentioning of 'remembering' in connexion with Rosh hashShanah, as it is

---

[40] This example is given by T. H. Robinson: 'After fifty years: higher criticism and the Prophetic Literature', *Exp. Times* (Feb.), 1939), pp. 198-202.
[41] 'Die Komposition des deuterojesajanischen Buches' in *ZAW* (1931), SS. 87-112. Also W. Caspari, *Lieder und Gottessprüche der Rückwanderer* (Jes. 40-55), 1934.
[42] E. Balla, *Die Droh- und Scheltwörte des Amos*, 1926; A. Weiser, *Die Profetie des Amos*, 1929; T. H. Robinson, *Hosea bis Micha* (Tübingen, 1936).

written, 'a solemn rest, a remembering of the blast of the trumpet'". The passage then goes on to connect Sarah and Hannah in a similar way by the word 'visiting'. This word 'visiting' (*paqad*) is one of the references in the Samaritan *qaṭef* for the seventh month,[43] Tishri. The connexion between 'visiting' and 'remembering' is shown also by the discussion in the Tosefta *RH* IV, 7a: " Piqdonoth (i.e. verses mentioning 'visiting') are the same as Zikronoth (i.e. verses mentioning 'remembering'), and so it is said, 'And the Lord visited Sarah' (Gen. xxi, 1), and 'I have surely visited you and that which is done to you in Egypt' (Ex. iii, 16). Rabbi Jose says, They say them with Zikronoth. Rabbi Judah says, One does not say them with them."

Lev. i and Deut. v, however, have no such connexions with Rosh hashShanah. These readings chanced to fall on that day, and the Rabbis were severely restricted hereabouts in their choice by the contents of the Torah. Deut. v, with its Deuteronomic version of the Ten Commandments, may owe its precise allocation for the day to the tradition which at one time connected this day with the Giving of the Law. Possibly, however, the Seder came first and the tradition arose afterwards, as is the case with the dates assigned in *Seder Olam* to the various incidents related in the Pentateuch. In this case Philo may well have been doing more than depend simply on Neh. viii.[44] In any case the Giving of the Law on Sinai provides the link with the Haftarah Joel ii, 1, since both the Haftarah and Ex. xix, 16 ff., speak of shofar-blasts, thick clouds, and a fire upon a mountain.

The Proper Psalms for Tishri 1

The allocation of psalms to this festival of the New Year also provides evidence of the early associations of this day. One of the New Year Psalms is Ps. lxxxi, chosen because of verse 4 (EVV 3) with its reference to the blowing of the shofar on the New Moon. St. John Thackeray has shown[45] how to some extent the text of this psalm has been influenced by the Sedarim and the Haftaroth for Rosh hashShanah. That the selection of this psalm was in fact due to the mention of the

---

[43] See p. 154 above. [44] See p. 151 above.
[45] *Journal of Theological Studies*, xvi, pp. 177 ff.

shofar is confirmed by the Talmud *b. RH* 16a: "Rabbi Isaac said: Why do we sound the horn on Rosh hashShanah? You ask why do we sound. The All-merciful told us to sound", and the reference given is Ps. lxxxi, 4. The other New Year Psalm is Ps. xlvii. This psalm has reference to the Kingship of Jehovah, but its associations with Rosh hashShanah are in connexion with shofar-blowing, because Ps. xlvii, 5, is one of the Shofaroth. In addition Ps. xxix, 8 (xxix is a general festival psalm), is mentioned in *b. RH* 30b.

There is, then, abundant evidence that Rosh hashShanah is essentially a day of repentance and sorrow. We agree entirely with Eerdmann when he argues[46] that the idea of New Year's Day as a day of destiny was current in pre-exilic times, though this does not by any means involve our acceptance of his theory of the Day of Atonement as a pre-exilic observance.[47] We find a continuous stream of development in Israelitish thought along these lines from the very earliest times. We find, on the other hand, no evidence that this day was a day of destiny after the pattern of, or due to the influence of the Babylonian ritual whereby Marduk in the council chamber determines the fate of the ensuing year. More probably the blowing of the trumpets on Rosh hashShanah goes back to an early belief in the presence of numerous demons on that day, but as G. B. Gray pointed out,[48] there is no evidence of this in Hebrew tradition, and there is indeed just as little evidence of the other.

Trumpet-Blowing and the Delayed Rains

On the contrary, a definite relationship can be established between the Feast of Asiph and its need for offering prayers for rain, thereby ensuring a good fate for the following year, and post-exilic times and the performance of those rites which may be expected to bring rain, including, above all things, the recital of the Zikronoth and the Shofaroth. According to the Mishnah *Ta'anith* I, 1-III, 8, part of the ceremonies to ensure the falling of the delayed monsoon rains was the recital of the Zikronoth and the Shofaroth. If Marcheshvan 17[49] had

[46] *Altt. Stud., Leviticus*, iv, p. 79. [47] *Op. cit.*, pp. 73 ff.
[48] *Sacrifice in the Old Testament*, p. 304.
[49] Marcheshvan 17 in the year 5708 is October 31, 1947.

come and the rains had not fallen, single persons began to observe a three-day fast. If still no rain had fallen in Kislev 1,[50] then a public three-day fast was instituted. After three days, another three-day fast was called, and if still there was no rain a seven-day fast. After suitable acts of penitence and the recital of such words as " And God saw their works that they turned from their evil ways ", they " stood up in prayer and sent down before the Ark (i.e. the Ark which had been taken out of the Synagogue, in which also the scrolls of the Law were preserved) an old man. . . . He recited before them twenty-four Benedictions, namely the eighteen of daily use, adding to them yet six more ".[51] These six were the Zikronoth and the Shofaroth and four other passages, Pss. cxx, cxxi, cxxx, and cii. According to Rabbi Judah, he need not recite the Zikronoth and the Shofaroth, but in their stead 1 Kgs. viii, 37 ff., and Jer. xiv, 1 ff., two passages which speak explicitly of drought. " And he seals each with its proper ending (II, 3) ". The meaning of this last sentence is made clear in the next paragraph, II, 4. The six extra Benedictions are inserted into the Eighteen Benedictions after the seventh.[52] After this seventh, and after each of the extra six Benedictions, a sentence, different in each case, was inserted as the seal. Each sentence called upon God to hear and answer prayer just as He had answered " Abraham our father on Mount Moriah ", " our fathers at the Red Sea ", " Joshua in Gilgal ", " Samuel at Mizpah ", " Jonah in the belly of the fish ", and " David and his son Solomon in Jerusalem ". There is nothing of moment for our present purposes in these seven references. They are the seven outstanding examples in Hebrew history of answer to prayer. The variations in custom are mentioned in connexion with the days of Rabbi Halafta and Rabbi Hananiah ben Teradion. This latter belonged to the third generation of Rabbinic teachers, c. 120-140 A.D. We see, therefore, that the use of the Zikronoth and the Shofaroth on days other than Rosh hashShanah was still under discussion in the first part of the second century A.D., and that this use was associated with the twin ideas of penitence and prayers for rain. These

[50] Kislev 1, 5708, is November 14, 1947.
[51] Mishnah, *Taanith* II, 2 ff. See Danby, *The Mishnah*, pp. 195 f.
[52] Danby, *The Mishnah*, p. 196, note 9.

apparently are the primary reasons why these sentences were recited on Rosh hashShanah, i.e. the need of the change of fortune and of a good fate for the ensuing year, dependent upon penitence and followed by such good rains as would ensure good harvests. The presumption is that these are also the primary associations of the day.

It has been suggested, in an effort to connect the post-exilic Feast of Sukkoth (Tabernacles) with a supposed Feast of Jehovah the King on Rosh hashShanah, that Zech. xiv, 16, 17, brings the idea of Jehovah the King and prayers for rain into close association.[53] If there is anything in this argument, one would have thought that, whatever else was excluded, the Malkiyyoth would certainly have been included together with these other two Rosh hashShanah groups of verses, the Zikronoth and the Shofaroth, in these prayers for rain. Nothing could, on Mowinckel's theory, have been more suitable, or indeed more essential for the support of it. The fact of the matter is that they are not mentioned. In pre-Mishnaic times there is no connexion between Jehovah the King and Rosh hashShanah.

[53] S. Mowinckel, *Psalmenstudien*, II, p. 43.

6
THE BENEDICTIONS FOR NEW YEAR'S DAY

APART from the blowing of shofars, perhaps the most significant feature of the synagogue ritual for Rosh hashShanah is the recital of certain passages of Scripture, to which we have already referred. The passages are in three groups: first, the Malkiyyoth, passages in which there is a reference to the Kingship of Jehovah; secondly, the Zikronoth, passages in which there is a reference to Jehovah remembering Israel; thirdly, the Shofaroth, passages in which the blowing of the shofar is mentioned. All these verses of Scripture are recited during the Musaph, or Additional Service, for Rosh hashShanah.

The Malkiyyoth

There are ten Malkiyyoth, and they are in three groups of three, with a concluding verse from the Law. The first three are from the Law, the second three from the Psalms, and the last three from the Prophets, with the opening sentence of the Shema as the conclusion. The order Psalms before the Prophets is in accordance with the rule in *Sopherim* xviii, 3, though in the Tosefta *RH* IV, 6, the reference is to the Prophets first and then to the Psalms. In P. Fiebig's edition of the Mishnaic tract *Rosh hashShanah*,[1] the number of the Malkiyyoth is given as nine, and so also for the Shofaroth. This is definitely wrong, and is contrary to the Tosefta *RH* IV, 6, where the number ten is quite definitely and clearly given in respect of each of the three sets of sentences. Fiebig actually has omitted the first of the Malkiyyoth, and he has taken the closing verse of the Shofaroth (i.e. the additional and closing verse from the Law, ' the seal ') to be in the concluding prayer.

The ten Malkiyyoth are: —

1. Jehovah shall reign for ever and ever (Ex. xv, 18).[2]
2. He hath not beheld iniquity in Jacob, neither hath he

[1] Beer and Holtzmann's edition, *Die Mischna* IIb (Giessen, 1914), pp. 51 f. and 56.
[2] This verse ensures that the Exodus Song of Moses is the seed-bed for all ideas of Jehovah as King, just as 2 Sam. vii is the seed-bed for all ideas of the Messianic King.

seen perverseness in Israel; Jehovah his God is with him, and the trumpet-blast of a King is among them (Num. xxiii, 21).

3. And he became King in Jeshurun, when the heads of the people were gathered, the tribes of Israel together (Deut. xxxiii, 5).

4. For the Kingdom is Jehovah's, and he is ruler over all the nations (Ps. xxii, 29).

5. Jehovah reigneth: he hath robed himself in majesty: Jehovah hath robed him, yea, he hath girded himself with strength: the world also is set firm that it cannot be moved (Ps. xciii, 1).

6. Lift up your heads, O ye gates, and be ye lift up, ye everlasting doors, that the King of glory may come in. Who then is the King of glory? Jehovah strong and mighty, Jehovah, mighty in battle. Lift up your heads, O ye gates; yea, lift them up, ye everlasting doors, that the King of glory may come in. Who then is the King of glory? Jehovah of Hosts, he is the King of glory. Selah (Ps. xxiv, 7-10).

7. Thus saith Jehovah, the King of Israel, and his Redeemer, Jehovah of Hosts; I am the first and the last, and beside me there is no God (Isa. xliv, 6).

8. And strangers shall come up on Mount Zion to judge the mount of Esau, and the Kingdom shall be Jehovah's (Obad. 21).

9. And Jehovah shall be King over all the earth; in that day shall Jehovah be one, and his name one (Zech. xiv, 9).

10. Hear, O Israel, Jehovah our God, Jehovah is One (Deut. vi, 5) (this being the first sentence of the Shema and the Declaration of the Unity of God).

There has evidently been some confusion at one time as to the exact constitution of the ten Malkiyyoth. In a liturgical MS. of the Honan Jews of Kai-fung-fu, now in the John Rylands Library, another verse is inserted between the fifth and the sixth of the Malkiyyoth, namely Ps. cxlvi, 10: 'Jehovah shall reign for ever; Thy God, O Zion, unto all generations. Praise ye Jehovah'. This verse is found in the Benediction *Qedushath hashShem*.[3] It brings the number up to ten without the concluding Shema. The inclusion of the Shema belongs to the second century, when the recitation of the Shema came to be regarded as the equivalent of the accept-

---

[3] *The Authorised Daily Prayer Book* (with commentary), ed. Chief Rabbi J. H. Hertz (London, 1942), vol. i, p. 137.

THE BENEDICTIONS FOR NEW YEAR'S DAY 179

ance of the Kingdom of God. This idea was established before 120 A.D., and was observed by Rabbi Gamaliel II and his fellows. The Tosefta *RH* IV, 6, makes it clear that the Shema is to be included in the Malkiyyoth, for it says, " Begin with the Law and end with the Law, and say what is from the Prophets and what is from the Hagiographa in the middle ". At the same time there is on record (*ibid.* IV, 7e) a discussion between Rabbi Judah ben Ilai and Rabbi Jose ben Chalapta (130-160 A.D.) as to whether the Shema should be said with the Malkiyyoth. The discussion actually is in connexion with the phrase ' Jehovah He is God '. Rabbi Jose advocated the inclusion, but Rabbi Judah (i.e. Rabbi Judah ben Ilai) was against it. Both passages, the first verse of the Shema and the phrase ' Jehovah He is God ' had similar significance with respect to the Kingdom of God, though the Shema had first place.[4] We are therefore driven to the conclusion that the inclusion of the Shema in the number of the Malkiyyoth does not belong to the first stage of their development. Rabbi Judah ben Ilai, for instance, was against the inclusion of it. His attitude generally was to resist innovations, and to see to it generally that the proper and exact tradition was followed. He resisted the use of Piqdonoth (verses which contained the root *paqad* ' visit ') as equivalents of Zikronoth.[5] He held to the proper use of curved trumpets (shofars) on New Year's Day, for his opinion is given in the Mishnah *Rosh hashShanah* III, 5b, and variations for this are not found until later, in the Talmud *b. RH* 26b and in the Tosefta *RH* III, 3b.[6] He objected to verses which contain double (or treble) references being counted more than once. His objections referred to Lev. xxvi, 42, the third of the Zikronoth, and he held that Ps. xxiv, 7, 8, 9, should count as one of the Malkiyyoth and not as three.

The Zikronoth

The Zikronoth are also ten in number, and also, like the Malkiyyoth, begin with the Law and end with the Law, having

[4] *Mishnah Berakoth* I, 3, and numerous other passages. See A. Büchler, *Studies in Sin and Atonement in the Rabbinic Literature of the First Century*, Jews' College Publications No. 11 (1928), p. 86, note 2.
[5] See p. 173 above.   [6] See pp. 170 f. above.

first three verses from the Law, then three from the Psalms, three from the Prophets, and concluding with one verse from the Law. This division into three sections is doubtless the reason why the Zikronoth and the Shofaroth alone may be referred to as the 'six Benedictions' in the ritual for the sending of the delayed rains in the month Kislev.[7]

The ten Zikronoth are: —

1. And God remembered Noah and every living thing and all the cattle that were with him in the ark: and God made a wind to pass over the earth, and the waters subsided (Gen. viii, 1).
2. And God heard their groaning, and God remembered his covenant with Abraham, with Isaac, and with Jacob (Ex. ii, 24).
3. Then will I remember my covenant with Jacob; and also my covenant with Isaac, and also my covenant with Abraham will I remember; and I will remember the land (Lev. xxvi, 42).
4. He hath made a memorial for his wondrous works: Jehovah is gracious and full of compassion (Ps. cxi, 4).
5. He hath given food to them that fear him: he will ever remember his covenant (Ps. cxi, 5).
6. And he remembered his covenant, and repented according to the multitude of his loving-kindnesses (Ps. cvi, 45).
7. Go and cry in the ears of Jerusalem, saying, Thus saith Jehovah, I remember thee for the kindness of thy youth, the love of thy bridal state; how thou wentest after me in the wilderness, in a land that was not sown (Jer. ii, 2).
8. Nevertheless, I will remember my covenant with thee in the days of thy youth, and I will establish unto thee an everlasting covenant (Ezek. xvi, 60).
9. Is Ephraim a precious son to me? Is he a caressed child? As often as I spoke against him, I earnestly remembered him; therefore my heart yearneth for him; I will surely have mercy upon him, saith Jehovah (Jer. xxxi, 19).
10. But I will for their sakes remember the covenant of their ancestors, whom I brought forth out of the land of Egypt in the sight of the nations, that I might be their God: I am Jehovah (Lev. xxvi, 45).

Once again, in the liturgical MS. of the Honan Jews there is another Zikronah, inserted as before between the fifth and

---

[7] See above, p. 174.

the sixth, once more from the Psalms, and once more making ten without the last verse from the Law which is embedded in the concluding prayer. It is "He hath remembered his covenant for ever, the word which he commanded to a thousand generations (Ps. cv, 8)".

The Shofaroth

The Shofaroth are ten in number, but arranged differently. There are four in the middle group which, as usual, is from the Psalms, instead of three as in the case of the orthodox tradition of the Malkiyyoth and the Zikronoth. It may be that this is the explanation of the vagaries of the Honan liturgy, it being an attempt to bring all three exactly into line, so as to build up the number ten in exactly the same way for each group.

The ten Shofaroth are: —

1. And it came to pass on the third day, when it was morning, that there were thunders and lightnings, and a thick cloud upon the mount, and the sound of the shofar exceeding loud, and all the people trembled (Ex. xix, 16).
2. And the sound of the shofar waxed louder and louder: Moses spake, and God answered him with a voice (Ex. xix, 19).
3. And all the people perceived the thunderings and lightnings, and the sound of the shofar, and the mountain smoking; and when the people saw it, they were moved and stood afar off (Ex. xx, 18).
4. God is gone up with a shout, Jehovah with the sound of a shofar (Ps. xlvii, 5-6).
5. With trumpets and with the sound of a shofar, shout joyously before the King Jehovah (Ps. xcviii, 6).
6. Blow the shofar on the new moon, at the beginning of the month, for our day of festival, for it is a statute for Israel, a decree of the God of Jacob (Ps. lxxxi, 3-4).
7. Psalm cl.
8. All ye inhabitants of the world, and ye dwellers on the earth, when an ensign is lifted up on the mountains, see ye, when the shofar is blown, hear ye (Isa. xviii, 3).
9. And it shall come to pass on that day, that a great shofar shall be blown; and they shall come who were outcasts in the land of Egypt; and they shall worship Jehovah in the holy mountain in Jerusalem (Isa. xxvii, 13).

10. And Jehovah shall be seen over them, and his arrow shall go forth as lightning; and the Lord Jehovah shall blow the shofar, and shall go with the whirlwinds of the south. Jehovah of Hosts shall be a shield unto them (Zech. ix, 14).

Earliest References to the Recitation of the Benedictions

The earliest reference to the recitation of these three Benedictions, the Malkiyyoth, the Zikronoth, and the Shofaroth, is found in the Mishnah *Rosh hashShanah* IV, 5, in the order of Benedictions for New Year's Day. The passage reads: —

The order of the Benedictions. They say, Aboth, Geburah, and Qedushath hashShem, and associate the Malkiyyoth with them, but no shofar-blast. Then Qedushath hayYom and a shofar-blast, the Zikronoth and a shofar-blast, the Shofaroth and a shofar-blast. Then Abodah, Hodaah and Birkath Kohanim. These are the words of Johanan ben Nuri. Rabbi Aqiba said to him, If there is no shofar-blast to the Malkiyyoth, how shall a man ensure remembrance? Rather it is this wise, They say, Aboth, Geburah, and Qedushath hashShem, and connect the Malkiyyoth and the Qedushath hayYom and a shofar-blast. Then the Zikronoth and a shofar-blast, the Shofaroth and a shofar-blast, and then they say Abodah, Hodaah and Birkath Kohanim.

This passage refers to the first three and the last three of the Eighteen Benedictions, or *Shemone Esreh*, or *Tefillah*, or *Amidah*, as these prayers, which are the foundation of the Synagogue service, are variously called. According to the Mishnah *Berakoth* IV, 1, *Shemone Esreh* (the Amidah) consists of three groups of prayers or benedictions, the first three, Aboth, Geburah, and Qedushath hashShem, the last three, Abodah, Hodaah, and Birkath Cohanim, and the middle ones. The first three and the last three are recited every day, whatever the day (Mishnah, *Ta'anith* II, 2), but on Sabbaths, Festivals, and on Yom Kippur, the middle ones are replaced by prayers special to the day. For New Year's Day (Rosh hashShanah) the order of the insertion is the Festival prayer, preceded by the Malkiyyoth and succeeded by the Zikronoth and the Shofaroth. The Mishnah passage giving the order of the benedictions for New Year's Day dates from the beginning of

The Insertion of the Malkiyyoth

the second century, since both the Rabbis mentioned flourished about that time.

It has been suggested by L. Ginsberg, and, following him, by Finkelstein,[8] that the Malkiyyoth were probably inserted in the prayers for Rosh hashShanah in the time of Rabbi Aqiba. Certainly Rabbi Aqiba is said to have established the prayer *Abinu Malkenu*, wherein the Kingdom of God receives the same emphasis as the Divine Fatherhood. Finkelstein points out that in the Mishnah[9] quoted at length above (*Rosh hashShanah* IV, 5) the statements of Rabbis Johanan ben Nuri and Aqiba differ only in respect of the Malkiyyoth. His presumption is that they both had an old Mishnah which contained no reference at all to the Malkiyyoth. This may seem to be an unwarranted assumption, but there is a certain amount of evidence, in addition to that which Finkelstein gives, in favour of the position that the Malkiyyoth are indeed a later insertion. Firstly, the assumption that there was an older Mishnah which did not refer to the Malkiyyoth is supported by the Tosefta *RH* IV, 4: "Rabbi Judah says Rabbi El'azar says, *Shabbathon*, that is *Qedushath hayYom*; *zikaron*, that is the Zikronoth; *teru'ah*, that is the Shofaroth; *miqre-qodesh*, sanctify it". Rabbi Aqiba differed from Rabbi Judah in respect of the first and last items, holding that the first referred to cessation from ordinary labour since He of old rested in the Beginning, and that the last referred to *Qedushath hayYom*. The Rabbis are both of them working on the basis of Lev. xxiii, 24, and it is a reasonable deduction that they are seeking to deduce from that verse the order of the special prayers which were inserted into the Amidah for New Year's Day. It will be seen[10] that if we omit from the Mishnah *Rosh hashShanah* IV, 5, the words "and associate the Malkiyyoth with them, but no shofar-blast", then we get exactly the conclusion at which Rabbi El'azar arrived in his exegesis of Lev. xxiii, 24. His equation of *shabbathon*

---

[8] *Jewish Quarterly Review* (new series), vol. 16 (1925-6), pp. 17 f.
[9] *b. Taanith* 25b. K. Kohler (*Jewish Encyclopædia*, i, p. 65) denies this, says that the prayer is earlier, and tends to date the beginning of the growing emphasis on the Kingdom of God from the previous century, from (say) the time of Caligula.
[10] See p. 182 above ('The earliest reference . . .').

with *Qedushath hayYom* is quite arbitrary, and has no apparent justification except as a means of establishing a predetermined state of affairs.

Secondly, in the Talmud *b. RH* 32a, reasons are given for the recital of the Malkiyyoth. It is difficult to see how the discussion could have taken place in the particular form in which it is given, unless the Malkiyyoth are an addition to prayers already established. It will be seen that the passage is actually a development from the Tosefta *RH* IV, 4, which we have discussed in the previous paragraph. The passage from the Talmud confirms the suspicion shown in the previous paragraph that the introduction of the Malkiyyoth was not earlier than the time of Rabbi El'azar (c. 130 A.D.). The passage reads: "When do we learn that we are to say the Malkiyyoth, the Zikronoth and the Shofaroth? Rabbi El'azar says, Because it is written, A solemn rest, a memorial proclaimed with blast of trumpets, a holy convocation. 'A solemn rest' (*shabbathon*) means Qedushath hayYom, 'a memorial' (*zikaron*) means the Shofaroth, 'a holy convocation' (*miqre qodesh*) means 'sanctify it by not doing any work'. Whence do we learn that we say the Malkiyyoth? It has been taught, Rabbi says 'I am the Lord your God ... in the seventh month'. This means the Malkiyyoth (i.e. the fact that the two phrases occur so closely together means that the seventh month is intimately connected with that for which the Divine declaration stands, namely the Kingdom of Heaven). Rabbi Jose ben Judah said, There is no need for such an exegesis, for it is written, 'And they (the trumpets) shall be to you for a sign before your God'. This makes 'I am the Lord your God' superfluous."

For the elucidation of this passage, two statements are necessary. One is that the declaration 'I am the Lord your God' was taken to be a declaration of God's Kingship.[11] The other is that it was one of the canons of Rabbinic exegesis that if any phrase could be deemed superfluous, then there was a special reason for its presence.

As we have indicated, the first part of the Gemara is similar to the passage in the Tosefta *RH* IV, 4. Büchler holds[12] that

---

[11] Büchler, *Studies in Sin and Atonement*, etc., pp. 39 ff.
[12] *Op. cit.*, p. 42.

Rabbi El'azar is trying to find Biblical support for the three additional paragraphs, the Malkiyyoth, the Zikronoth, and the Shofaroth, and so would argue that the Malkiyyoth were added before his time, i.e. before the year 70 A.D. This contention is parallel with that which would place the beginning of the growing emphasis on the Divine Kingdom in Caligula's time. But all this is exactly what Rabbi El'azar did not do, as we have indicated in our discussion of the passage from the Tosefta. On the contrary, he does not appear to know that they existed, and so rests satisfied that he has proved from Scripture all that was required of him, that is, he has justified the *Qedushath hayYom*, the Zikronoth and the Shofaroth. It might be argued that he intended the Malkiyyoth to be included in *Qedushath hayYom*, but the Talmud evidently did not think so, for it goes on to say, 'Yes, but what of the Malkiyyoth?', saying, so to speak, 'Yes, that accounts for the Zikronoth and the Shofaroth, but it does not account for the Malkiyyoth'. The further discussion is between Rabbi and Rabbi Jose ben Judah, and is of later date than the time of Rabbi El'azar. It provides evidence that the insertion of the Malkiyyoth into the New Year prayers was later than the insertion of the Zikronoth and the Shofaroth, and further it shows that the justification for the insertion of the Malkiyyoth is not an immediate inference from Scripture, but that it depends upon one or other of two developed canons of Rabbinic exegesis. This latter fact makes it all the more likely that the Malkiyyoth are a later insertion.

Thirdly, it is more strange that the Malkiyyoth are separated from the other two groups of verses, the Zikronoth and the Shofaroth, both in the list in the Mishnah *Rosh hash-Shanah* IV, 5, and in the synagogue prayers. One would have thought that if the three groups of verses, the Malkiyyoth, the Zikronoth, and the Shofaroth, were all equally and similarly collections of verses from Scripture, then they would all three have come together, and all three would have followed the *Qedushath hayYom*. But the Malkiyyoth stand out from this. The only likely explanation of the curious position of the Malkiyyoth is that they were placed in their extraordinary position at a time when it was desired to place more than ordinary emphasis upon them, and upon New Year's Day in connexion with them. If the development of New Year's Day as the Festival of Jehovah the King had grown up in the ordinary natural course of development, we would naturally expect the Malkiyyoth to take first place among the three collections of verses, but after the *Qedushath hayYom*, the Benediction which 'sanctified' the day. The position before the *Qedushath hayYom* is so anomalous that it must have been established because of a new and significant emphasis on the day. The strange position of the Malkiyyoth as separate from the other selections of verses is commented on, though not explained, in *Sifre* 77, 19b (on Num. x, 10), in a discussion on 'I am the Lord your God' as a declaration of the Divine Kingdom over Israel. "Rabbi Nathan says 'I am the Lord your God' (Num. x, 10) prescribes the Malkiyyoth. If so (considering that the words are the last in the verse), why did the scholars place the Malkiyyoth first, and the Zikronoth and Shofaroth later?" So ends the discussion from the *Sifre*, and it is clear that the anomalous position of the Malkiyyoth has been a source of comment from an early date.

Fourthly, whilst *Qedushath hayYom* has a shofar-blast, and also the Zikronoth a shofar-blast, and also the Shofaroth a shofar-blast, yet it is explicitly stated that the Malkiyyoth have no shofar-blast of their own.[13] This is most amazing, if indeed the Malkiyyoth were introduced because Rosh hashShanah was primarily, essentially, and from time immemorial, the Festival of Jehovah the King. Even more amazing is it if all that Mowinckel and his successors have said concerning the Königsjubel is right. They connect the shofar-blast with the Coronation of the King, and refer to the acclamations and the flourish of trumpets with which the kings of Israel and Judah were greeted on their accession. They make a very great deal of all these shouts and trumpet-blasts in order to emphasize the existence of this Coronation Feast (Thronbesteigungsfest) of Jehovah from early pre-exilic times down to this present era. And yet there is no shofar-blast for the Malkiyyoth in the New Year Service. Whatever had no shofar-blast, it certainly ought not to have been the Malkiyyoth. But the Malkiyyoth are the only ones of the special 'benedictions' which have no shofar-blast. The only way in which Rabbi Aqiba, whose

[13] Mishnah *RH* iv, 5. See p. 183 above.

THE BENEDICTIONS FOR NEW YEAR'S DAY 187

devotion to the Kingdom of God led him to take part in the Bar-kokba revolt, and of whom there are numerous stories concerning his persistence in repeating the Shema as the acknowledgement of the Kingdom of God, could secure a shofar-blast for the Malkiyyoth was by combining them with the *Qedushath hayYom*, and by reckoning the shofar-blast of that Benediction to belong to the Malkiyyoth. Even then the order of Rabbi Aqiba was followed only in Judæa, whilst that of Rabbi Johanan ben Nuri, who denied that the Malkiyyoth had a shofar-blast, was followed in Galilee.[14] Still further, even Rabbi Aqiba said that the shofar-blast is for remembrance. It is very difficult to make all this agree with the theory that the blowing of the shofar on New Year's Day was the Königsjubel.

Fifthly, there was a dispute between the schools of Hillel and Shammai as to the order of Benedictions for Rosh hashShanah. This took place about the beginning of the second century, and it provides another indication that the Malkiyyoth were introduced during the second century A.D. The account of the dispute is preserved in the Tosefta *Rosh hashShanah* IV, 11, and in the Tosefta *Berakoth* 13 : — " When a feast-day of Rosh hashShanah falls on the Sabbath, the House of Shammai says, Ten prayers are used, but the House of Hillel says, Nine. When a feast day (i.e. any feast day other than the two feast days of Rosh hashShanah) falls on the Sabbath, the House of Shammai says, Eight prayers are used, Sabbath prayers for the Sabbath, feast prayers for the feast day, and begins with the Sabbath. But the House of Hillel says, Seven prayers are used, beginning with the Sabbath, and ending with the Sabbath, with Qedushath hayYom in the middle."

All this means that both schools were agreed that whenever any feast day falls on the Sabbath the first three and the last three of the Benedictions of the Amidah were to be recited. These are the original six quoted from the Mishnah *RH* IV, 5.[15] The difference of opinion between the two schools was in respect of the intermediary Benedictions. The

[14] *Jer. RH* iv, 7.
[15] See p. 182 above. For the use of shortened forms of the Amidah, in which the original six were recited at length, but the remainder summarized, see Chief Rabbi J. H. Hertz, *The Authorised Daily Prayerbook*, vol. i, pp. 159 f.

House of Shammai maintained that on any feast day that fell on a Sabbath, both the Sabbath Benediction and the Festival Benediction were to be recited, but the House of Hillel held that only the latter was necessary. When, however, the festival happened to be on one of the two New Year's Days, then two were added by each school, making ten instead of eight for the House of Shammai, and nine instead of seven for the House of Hillel. But it ought to have been eleven and ten respectively, if the Malkiyyoth, the Zikronoth and the Shofaroth were all extant at the time. Lest this should seem to be a prejudiced inference on our part from the Tosefta, it is to be pointed out that the very same question was raised later, and is to be found in the Talmud *b. Erub.* 40a (end), where the problem is again discussed: —"If Rosh hashShanah fell on a Sabbath, the House of Shammai ruled, One shall recite ten Benedictions, and the House of Hillel ruled, One recites only nine. Now, if that were so, should it not be necessary according to the House of Shammai to order eleven?" Clearly in the time to which the Tosefta refers, i.e. in the first century A.D., one of the three special New Year Benedictions was missing. Equally clearly by the time to which the Talmud refers it was not missing. The missing one must be the Malkiyyoth.

Sixthly, we have seen that the Zikronoth and the Shofaroth could be used apart from the Malkiyyoth, namely in the ceremonies of the delayed rains, Mishnah *Ta'anith* I, 2-4.[16] This custom must have been in existence, as we have seen, before the time of Rabbi Hanania ben Teradion (c. 120-140 A.D.), since already there were variations. We assume, therefore, that they were so used before the Malkiyyoth were added to them for the Rosh hashShanah prayers. If the rain prayers were associated with prayers to Jehovah as King, as Mowinckel alleges partly on the basis of Zech. xiv, 16 f.,[17] then it is as certain as anything can be that the Jews would never have used both the Zikronoth and the Shofaroth, and left out the Malkiyyoth, provided that the last were in existence.

Seventhly, it is stated that Rosh hashShanah and the Day of Atonement are equal for blasts and blessings. So says the Mishnah *RH* III, 5a, but this is denied by Rabbi Judah in the next paragraph so far as the kind of trumpets used is con-

[16] See p. 174 above.   [17] *Psalmenstudien* II, p. 43.

cerned. This statement of the Mishnah is part of a general tendency to equate the two days, New Year's Day and the Day of Atonement. For instance in Babylonia the prayers for the coming of the Kingdom of God were recited on New Year's Day and on the day of Atonement, and on no other days, whereas in Palestine they were recited at all festivals.[18] The same attitude is found in respect of the prayer *Abinu Malkenu*, the prayer which is said to have been instituted by Rabbi Aqiba.[19] According to Amram Gaon this prayer was regarded as an ancient institution and was recited on the Ten Penitential Days, and it became a German custom to recite Amram Gaon's version of the prayer with its twenty-two verses after the Amidah morning and evening during the Ten Penitential days. The number of verses varies in the different liturgies, twenty-five, twenty-nine, thirty-eight, forty-four, and fifty-three, but, apart from the rigidly pious who repeated it every day (except, of course, Sabbaths and holy days), custom restricted it either to the Ten Penitential Days, or, as in the Reform Ritual following a custom at one time observed by the Sephardis, to New Year's Day and to the Day of Atonement.[20] Our conclusion is that the prayer *Abinu Malkenu*, which perhaps more than any prayer is concerned with Jehovah as King, is not at all restricted to New Year's Day, but belongs properly to the first ten days of penitence.

Eighthly, in the Book of Jubilees (2nd cent. B.C.) there is a curious extension of the special new-month days. At most, as we have seen,[21] these special days should be Nisan 1 and Tishri 1, but the Book of Jubilees makes them the new moon of the first, fourth, seventh and tenth months. The fact that the Book of Jubilees thus divides the year up into four equal divisions of thirteen weeks is of no particular account, for this book has many strange and unique suggestions about the calendar. The important thing from our present point of view is that it calls all these special new-month days "days of remembrance, and the days of the seasons, the four divisions of the year" (vi, 23, 25). Evidently, these first days of the month meant remembrance so far as the author was concerned. The details which are to be remembered are worthy

[18] Elbogen, *Monatsschrift*, 55, 437.
[19] See p. 183 above.
[20] *Jewish Encyclopædia*, vol. i (1901), p. 65.
[21] See p. 141 above.

of notice. The first month is to be remembered because Noah made an ark, and also because the earth became dry. The fourth is because the mouths of the depths of the abyss were closed. The seventh is because all the mouths of the abyss of the earth were opened, and the waters began to descend into them. The tenth is because the tops of the mountains were seen. The curious thing is that the reason for the first month corresponds exactly to the first of the Zikronoth, and further the whole setting of the Zikronoth in the New Year prayers is Noah's flood. Apparently the first of the first month meant remembrance exactly as the first of the Zikronoth, and it is difficult to resist the conclusion that in the second century B.C., New Year's Day meant Remembrance. Further, it seems as though the author of the Book of Jubilees knew the Zikronoth, and regarded them as being essentially the centre and core of the New Year liturgy.

Lastly, there are many indications that the closing years of the first century A.D. and the first years of the second century were marked by a great activity in the redaction of the synagogue prayers. This indeed is only to be expected in view of the destruction of the Temple in 70 A.D. Henceforth the synagogue alone must serve until in the Providence of God the Temple is rebuilt. According to *Sifre* (Deut. 343), 'the first wise men' were responsible for the Amidah (Eighteen Benedictions, *Shemone Esreh*), or, according to the Talmud *b. Meg.* 17b, 'one hundred and twenty elders and among these a number of prophets'. The general Talmudic tradition refers the Prayer Service to the Men of the Great Synagogue (*b. Ber.* 33a). All these are the usual statements which are commonly made concerning matters of ancient tradition. Parallel with all these, are the traditions associated with the name of Simeon hapPaqoli, who was commissioned to act as editor by Rabbi Gamaliel II in the academy of Jabneh (*b. Ber.* 28b). The basis of these apparently contradictory traditions is that some of the Benedictions were already extant in the second century B.C., whilst the first three and the last three may be very much earlier than that.[22] The twelfth, *Birkath hamMinim* or *Birkath haçÇaduqim*, was added

[22] See W. O. E. Oesterley, *The Jewish Background of the Christian Liturgy* (1925), pp. 54 ff., and the authorities there quoted.

about 100 A.D. by Gamaliel II, and the fifteenth in the middle of the third century A.D., this latter actually making nineteen, though the original Eighteen still survives in the title of the Benedictions. The fourteenth must at least have been remodelled after the destruction of the Temple, when the whole of the *Shemone Esreh* were redacted—"And build her speedily in our days as an everlasting structure." Elbogen, Zunz and others have shown that the original text of the Eighteen Benedictions was much shorter than at present, and it is reasonable to hold, as Hirsch says,[23] that " the Maccabæan period seems to furnish adequate background for the national petitions (Benedictions X-XIV), though the experience of the Roman War and the subsequent disasters may have heightened the colouring in many details ".

In the recital of the Shema, for instance, in the synagogue prayers, the first sentence is followed by " Blessed be His Name, whose glorious Kingdom is for ever and ever ". According to Friedmann,[24] this insertion was due to the fact that the recitation of the Shema came, in the days of the Roman War, to be regarded as proof of allegiance to the Divine Kingdom. Nor is this the only case in which a reference to the Divine Kingdom seems to be an insertion, during this period, into the synagogue prayers. The *Qedushah*, which follows the third Benediction and is found thrice in the liturgy, consisted in its original form of " And one cried unto another and said, Holy, Holy, Holy is the Lord of Hosts: the whole earth is full of His glory (Isa. vi, 3). Blessed be the glory of the Lord from His Place (Ezek. iii, 12)." The earliest addition was "The Lord shall reign for ever and ever: Thy God, O Zion, unto all generations."[25] That this addition was not made until the first half of the second century A.D. at the earliest is shown by the Tosefta *Ber.* I, 9, which reads " We do not respond with him who pronounced the Benediction ' Holy, holy, etc.' and ' Blessed be the glory of the Lord from His Place.' All the words Rabbi Judah used to say together

[23] *Jewish Encyclopædia*, vol. xi, p. 281a.
[24] Note on Deut. xxxi in his edition of *Sifre*, and quoted in this connexion by Finkelstein, to whom much of the material in this chapter is due.
[25] Oesterley, *ibid.*, pp. 67 f. Curiously this is the extra verse in the Malkiyyoth of the Honan (Kai-fung-fu) Jews, see p. 178 above.

with the Benediction." Dr. Oesterley instances this as evidence that the custom of responses was not as old as Dembitz alleged, since, contrary to what Dembitz said, there is, both here in the Tosefta and also in Sopherim xvii, 12, an echo of the dispute as to the responses. But our present interest in the passage from the Tosefta is that only two out of the three responses are quoted, and the one that is omitted is the one which refers to the Divine Kingdom, "The Lord shall reign for ever and ever...." It is evident, therefore, that the whole of this Benediction, as known in the first years of the second century A.D., did not include the reference to the Divine Kingdom.

We therefore ascribe the passages which refer to the Divine Kingdom to the period of the redaction under the guidance of Gamaliel II in the first half of the second century A.D., the period of the later Roman Wars. This is confirmed by the opinion of Derenbourg, who holds[26] that even the Rosh hashShanah interpolations are later than the controversies with Jewish heretics and Romans, and belong to the time when some answer had to be made to the Messianic claims of Christianity. He even goes so far as to say that whenever the word *melek* (king) is found in the text, it is an interpolation.

It is unlikely, then, to the highest degree that the Malkiyyoth were introduced into the order of the Benedictions for Rosh hashShanah because it had been from time immemorial, or was even in later times, the Festival of the Divine Kingdom. The reason for their introduction, occasioned immediately by the difficulties of the Roman Wars, was rather because Jehovah was Creator and Judge. In the Talmud *b. RH* 10b, 11a, there is the record of a dispute handed down from the closing years of the first century A.D. The controversy was between Rabbi Eleazar ben Hyrcanus and Rabbi Joshua ben Chanaya. The former said that 'In Tishri the world was created,' but the latter held that it was created in Nisan. Here is an echo of the old rivalry between Tishri and Nisan. An insertion of the Malkiyyoth, following the settlement of this controversy in favour of Tishri, would account for the discussion between Rabbis Aqiba and Johanan ben Nuri, in the next

[26] *R.E.J.*, xiv, pp. 26 f.

THE BENEDICTIONS FOR NEW YEAR'S DAY 193

generation, as to the association of the Malkiyyoth with a shofar-blast.[27] Jehovah is King because He is Creator. At the same time we have found that the association of Jehovah and the Kingship is connected with the whole of the Ten Penitential Days, and not with the New Year's Day only. This latter association is with the turn of the year, and with ideas of Judgement associated with that season. These developed during the same general period. Jehovah is Judge because it is the New Year. The order is Judge and King, rather than King and Judge.

The conclusion of the matter is this. Undoubtedly there was, from the first century A.D. onwards, a closer connexion between the Kingdom of God and Rosh hashShanah than between the Divine Kingdom and any other festival, the Sabbath only excepted,[28] though in Palestine it must be remembered that the prayer for the Coming of the Divine Kingdom was used at every festival. The connexion between Rosh hashShanah and the Kingdom of God cannot be used as evidence of any connexion between Rosh hashShanah and any King-festival after the Babylonian pattern, since the association in Palestine is not earlier than the second century A.D. Pre-exilic Israelitish cults may very well have been an off-shoot from some far-off Myth-Ritual-Pattern common to most of the Middle East, but we do not find any association in this particular development of the Jewish New Year Festival. There are very great differences between what we know of the Mesopotamian cults and what we may conjecture concerning the Hebrew New Year cults. The Israelitish cults of pre-exilic days probably followed rather the agricultural pattern of the Ras Shamra texts, and not the highly developed urbanized cults of the cities of Mesopotamia. Or if reference must be made to Mesopotamia, then the association is with the old Tammuz cult, rather than with the Marduk-Tiamat elements or the astrological developments of Mesopotamian cults.[29] At the Exile an almost complete break

[27] See p. 186 above. [28] See p. 203 below.
[29] S. A. Pallis, *The Babylonian Akitu Festival* (Kobenhavn, 1926); S. H. Hooke, *The Origins of Early Semitic Ritual* (Schweich Lectures, 1935). This latter book makes use not only of the carefully documented material in Pallis, but, with the availability of the Ras Shamra

occurred with the cults of former days. Another break, though perhaps not so clean-cut as the former because of the bridge which the synagogue provided, came with the destruction of the Second Temple. This turning-point in Jewish religion led, during the next generation or so, to a considerable revision of the synagogue prayers. It was during this period, with a renewed emphasis on the Divine Kingdom heightened by the distresses of the Roman Wars, that Tishri 1 (Rosh hashShanah), the first day of the Jewish Ecclesiastical Year, became the Festival of Jehovah the King.

---

material, avoids many of the extremes of the earlier *Myth and Ritual* (ed. S. H. Hooke, 1933). Some of the essay-writers in that volume, whilst rightly sure that early Hebrew ritual had much in common with that of near-by cultures, were driven to make what, in our view, seem to be many unjustifiable assumptions with respect to the gaps in our knowledge of the Babylonian rituals. The discovery of the Ras Shamra material has opened up a variant from an old original Tammuz-basis which provides very much closer parallels to the small amount of evidence which reforming prophets and priests have left in the Old Testament.

7

THE CORONATION PSALMS

No Connexion with the New Year Liturgy

SINCE Mowinckel published in 1922 his *Psalmenstudien* II with the sub-title *Das Thronbesteigungsfest Jahwas und der Ursprung der Eschatologie*, following on Volz's *Das Neujahrsfest Jahwes* (1912), it has been accepted, practically without question, that Pss. xciii, xcv-xcix with xlvii formed the central part of the liturgy of a Coronation Feast of Jehovah celebrated at the New Year, and dramatically represented in the ritual after the general pattern of the Babylonian New Year liturgies. It needs to be pointed out that, even if there was such a festival in Old Israel (and this has been surmised rather than proved), there has never been produced, except in one instance with which we shall deal below,[1] one shred of evidence that any of the Psalms, other than xlvii, has ever been associated with Tishri 1 or indeed any of the festivals of Tishri. No theory has ever received such a measure of general approbation with so little critical examination.

Ps. xlvii is one of the New Year psalms. We have seen[2] that it was chosen because of the mention of the shofar, that the blowing of the trumpets was for remembrance and not because of anything to do with the Kingship of Jehovah,[3] and, further, that the introduction of the curved trumpet of ram's horn is comparatively late and it follows the adoption of the last of all the Readings from the Law which came to be associated with the Festival.[4] In any case, trumpets were blown on all sorts of occasions in the ritual,[5] and especially on the Sabbaths. According to the Talmud *b. Shabb.* 35b, six trumpets were blown to introduce the Sabbath. When, therefore, great stress is laid upon the fact of the blowing of trumpets in order to emphasize similarities with Babylonian rites, it must be remembered that most of what can be said, could be said of the Sabbath also.

[1] See p. 196.　　[2] See p. 174 above.　　[3] See p. 150 above.
[4] See p. 169 above.　　　　　　　　　　　　[5] See p. 150 above.

We are left with Pss. xciii, xcv-xcix. The claim in respect of these psalms has been made in the following terms. " Here let it be said, in passing, that in many cases there is direct evidence that the Psalms from which quotations will be made were sung during the festivals: in some cases, where such direct evidence is wanting, there are indications in the Psalm itself that it was sung during a festival."[6] The psalms from which these quotations are made are these same Coronation Psalms, xciii, xcv-xcix. It has to be said that apart from xcvi (for which, see below) there has never been produced any direct evidence whatever which would connect any or all of these psalms with the New Year Festival. The whole of what evidence there is, is of that subjective kind which seeks references to a problematic liturgy which itself is built up almost entirely from non-Palestinian sources. No one who has ever sought to break new ground can fail to realize that such a course is fraught with peril, and without the greatest care serious and false deductions may ensue. Our charge is that the whole of Mowinckel's position in respect of these Coronation Psalms has been built up independently of any definite evidence either from the Old Testament or from Jewish sources generally.

Actually the alleged connexion of these Coronation Psalms with the Harvest-New-Year feast is confined to Ps. xcvi. It comprises the first of the reasons which Mowinckel gives to support his contention of the existence of such an Annual Feast after the Babylonian pattern.[7] He holds that the bringing up of the Ark by Solomon (1 Kgs. viii) at the New Year Feast was a repetition of what David did, and was *probably* (the italics are mine) on the self-same day. Both these ceremonies, Mowinckel claims, were in Chronicles brought into association with our Coronation Psalms. With regard to this claim, we point out in the first instance that the reference is to Chronicles and not to the Books of Samuel and Kings. Also, it has to be said that there is no reference to any psalm in the Chronicler's story of Solomon's installation of the Ark, beyond the statement that He gave thanks unto the Lord " for He is good, for His mercy endureth for ever " (2 Chr. v, 13; vii, 3).

[6] This quotation is from the essay entitled: ' Early Hebrew Festival Rituals ', p. 125 in *Myth and Ritual* (ed. S. H. Hooke, 1933).
[7] *Psalmenstudien* II, S. 42.

It is true that this verse is given also in 1 Chr. xvi, 34, which is in the account of David's removal of the Ark, but this cannot legitimately be adduced as evidence of the use of the Coronation Psalms. This phrase is invariably quoted by the Chronicler whenever his Levites sing, either in the Temple or out of it, and was apparently a ritual call to praise in the Chronicler's time.[8] It was used, for instance, in the second month (Ezra iii, 11), and also in the Wilderness of Tekoa when Jehoshaphat took the Temple choirs with him in order to defeat his enemies (2 Chr. xx, 21). If the use of this phrase is evidence of the use of the Coronation Psalms, then they were always being used, and their use at any New Year Feast signifies nothing at all.

Further, with regard to the alleged connexion between David's removal of the Ark and the Coronation Psalms according to the Chronicler's account, the passage occurs, not so much in the account of the removal of the Ark, as in the account of the inauguration of the Temple choirs. The Chronicler has given a sample of Asaphite psalmody. He has introduced Pss. cxvi, 1-15, and xcvi, 1-15, with the ritual call added, and then, after a rubric, Pss. cvi, 47 and 48, concluding with the Benediction which is found at the end of the First Book of the Psalter, Ps. xli, 13. The use of xcvi, 1-15, is the sole connexion which can be found in 1 Chr. xvi. But is Ps. xcvi, 1-13, used here in its capacity as a Coronation Psalm? And if so, then why does not Mowinckel make any reference to Ps. cvi in his book? Surely if the mention of Ps. xcvi in this chapter is evidence that this was the New Year Feast and that David used this psalm, then the same is true of Ps. cvi.

In *Seder Olam* xiv, there is a very ancient tradition which says that 1 Chr. xvi, 8-36, continued to be sung daily until the erection of the Temple, the first part in the morning and the second part in the evening, immediately after the sacrifices had been offered. In the Sephardi ritual of the present time, the whole passage does actually occur immediately after the description of the sacrifices, though in the modern Ashkenazi ritual its position is a little earlier, namely after the Retsuah has been wound around the middle finger. *Seder Olam* is a

[8] 'The Psalter of the Chronicler', *London Quarterly and Holborn Review* (January, 1934), pp. 39-46.

writing which is generally most reliable concerning the ancient traditions. Büchler used it to great purpose in his study of the ancient Palestinian lectionaries,[9] and there are details preserved in it which can be used concerning the destruction of the Temple.[10] No ancient writing is more reliable concerning the details of half-forgotten days. Whatever the exact meaning of this tradition concerning the singing of 1 Chr. xvi, 8-36, it is reasonably safe, in view of the confirmation in the Sephardi ritual, to assume that it reflects a very early practice. It will therefore be seen that it is most likely that the inclusion of Ps. xcvi, 1-13, in the passage 1 Chr. xvi, 8-36, has nothing at all to do with the fact that it is one of the Coronation Psalms, but that it is due to another and entirely different use. It should be noted, further, that in 1 Chr. xvi the singing of the Levites follows the conclusion of the sacrifices, so that evidently the Chronicler knew exactly what he was doing so far as the two psalms were concerned, just as he knew very well that Ps. cvi, 48 c and d, were both actually rubrics (cf. 1 Chr. xvi, 36, end). The presumption is that here, as often elsewhere, the Chronicler is describing the events of the past in the environment of his own time. What he says about David and the Levitical choirs is evidence not of what happened in David's time, but of what happened in his own.

Further, if these psalms were indeed connected with the New Year Feast in post-exilic times, and if this feast was particularly concerned with the Kingship of Jehovah, then we should surely expect to find that they had an important, if not a pre-eminent place in the liturgy of Rosh hashShanah. This would apply particularly to those verses of Scripture, the recital of which is characteristic of the Festival.

Consider first the Malkiyyoth. There are ten of them altogether, and three of them from the psalms. One of them only is from the Coronation Psalms, namely the fifth, xciii, 1; the other two are xxii, 29, and xxiv, 7-10. Even the extra verse found in the Kai-fung-fu liturgical MS. is not from the Coronation psalms, but is cxlvi, 10. There are five verses which could have been chosen from the Coronation Psalms, namely xcv, 3; xcvi, 10; xcvii, 1; xcviii, 6; xcix, 1. In addi-

---

[9] See p. 168 above.
[10] *Studies in the Psalter* (1934), pp. 79-84.

tion there are three possible verses in Ps. xlvii, namely verses 3, 7, 8. There are twenty-one possibilities altogether from the whole of the Psalter, of which five (or eight) are from Psalms which Mowinckel especially indicated as being psalms connected with this Festival. Of these two were definitely rejected, namely Ps. xlvii, 7, 8. In the Text edited by Paul Fiebig (Bonn, 1914), the Tosefta *Rosh hashShanah* gives no reason, though D. Ugolini gives the reason as being because there was no mention of the shofar also. This is curious, because it was on the ground of the mention of the shofar and the Kingship that Rabbi Jose wanted to include Ps. xcviii, 6, among the Malkiyyoth as well as among the Shofaroth (Tosefta *RH* IV, 7d), which opinion Rabbi Judah resisted, so that the verse is found in the Shofaroth only. It should therefore be omitted from the list of possible Malkiyyoth, making seven possibilities out of twenty. But what is still more curious, if Mowinckel is right in his emphasis on the Kingship of Jehovah in connexion with the New Year, is that the mention of the shofar in Ps. xcviii, 6, should take precedence over the mention of the Kingdom.

Among the Shofaroth, the four psalm verses are Pss. xlvii, 6 (EVV 5), xcviii, 6; lxxxi, 4 (3); and cl. There two are from the Coronation Psalms, and a third, lxxxi, 4, is from the New Year Psalm. This, however, signifies nothing in this particular case, since there are only four possible verses altogether in the Psalter, and all have been included.

Among the Zikronoth, there are three verses from the Psalter, namely Pss. cxi, 4; cxi, 5; cvi, 45. Surely, if there was any sort of connexion between these Coronation Psalms and Rosh hashShanah, then Ps. xcviii, 3, ought to have been included, since no verse could possibly have been more suitable. And yet, even though successive verses have been chosen in Ps. cxi, still Ps. xcviii, 3, was neglected. The additional verse in the Kai-fung-fu liturgy is Ps. cv. 8, once again not from one of the Coronation Psalms.

Yet again, if the Coronation Psalms ever had any association with a Coronation Feast Day of Jehovah, then it is extraordinary that more use is not made of them in the synagogue prayers for the day. The fact of the matter is that the Kingship of Jehovah was not the deciding factor in the choice of the liturgy generally or of the psalms in particular, when the synagogue prayers were in process of development, either prior to the destruction of the Temple by Titus, or subsequent to it. The 'catch-words' for the Festival were *zakar* (remember) and *shofar* (curved trumpet) and not *malak* (be king) at all.

They are Sabbath Psalms

On the contrary, the Coronation Psalms (xciii, xcv-c) are, every one of them, Sabbath Psalms in the Jewish liturgies. We have shown elsewhere[11] that these psalms belong to a group of Sabbath psalms, xc-xcix, with xxix substituted for xciv. We have shown that Pss. xc, xci, xcii, xciv, xcv have close associations with the ancient Sabbath Canticle, Deut. xxxii, 1-43, the Deuteronomic Song of Moses. That is why Ps. xc is entitled 'a prayer of Moses the man of God', and why the following psalms are all 'orphan' psalms, that is, psalms without titles. Further, we have shown that where Pss. xciii, xcvi-xcix are not dependent upon Isa. xl-lv, they are closely connected with the other ancient Sabbath Canticle, Ex. xv, 1-18, the Exodus Song of Moses. Also there are associations between some of these psalms and Rev. xiv in the New Testament, where the setting is the great Heavenly Temple and the service of the great Sabbath at the End of Days. The new Sabbath Song which was sung then is called 'the song of Moses and the Lamb' (Rev. xv, 3), and it was sung on the shores of the glassy sea, just as the great Sabbath Song of deliverance in the Old Testament, Ex. xv, 1-18, was sung on the shores of the Red Sea.

It may perhaps be argued that the Coronation Psalms were used in an original form in the ritual before the Exile. The reply is that the Psalms xciii, xcvi-xcviii are so thoroughly dependent upon Isa. xl-lv that if the Deutero-Isaianic elements are removed the residue is negligible. It is impossible to say anything other than that these psalms are post-exilic, unless the phrases post-exilic and pre-exilic are reduced to meaning nothing at all. The instances of direct depend-

---

[11] *Studies in the Psalter* (1934), pp. 47-87, where there is an attempt to trace the development of the Sabbath liturgy, so far as psalms and canticles are concerned.

ence are too numerous,[12] and it is difficult to see what other conclusion is possible.

In modern times the Ashkenazi Jews recite xcv-xcix, xxix, xcii, and xciii at the Service for the Inauguration of the Sabbath. At the Morning Service of the Sabbath, they omit c, which is sung every weekday, and recite xix, xxxiv, xc, xci, cxxxv, cxxxvi, xxxiii, xcii, xciii, and also, as on weekdays, cxlv-cl. These psalms are also recited at the Morning Service for Festivals, but if a Festival or one of the Intermediate days of a Festival is a Sabbath, then xcv-xcix, xxix and the Bridal Song are omitted from the Inauguration Service.

The Sephardi Jews recite Pss. xxix, xcii, xciii, xxxiii at the Service of the Eve of the Sabbath. At the Morning Service on the Sabbath they recite xxxiii, xxxiv, xc, xci, xcviii, cxxi-cxxxiv, cxxxv, xcii, xciii, cxlv. On the Sabbath which falls during Passover, they recite xciii after the Reading of the Law. When a Festival falls on the Sabbath, they recite xcii, xciii on the Eve of the Festival.

It will be seen, therefore, that to this day, xc and xci, xcii and xciii, xcv-xcix are essentially Sabbath psalms. Indeed, it seems as if there is a tendency to take care that they shall not be regarded in any other light, since xcv-xcix and xxix and the Bridal Song are omitted by the Ashkenazi Jews when the Sabbath is also a Festival, or one of the Intermediate Days. All this is apart from the Mishnah tradition (*Tamid* vii, 4) of the special psalms for the days of the week, which gives Ps. xcii as the Sabbath Psalm. The Mishnah also gives Ps. xciii as the Friday Psalm, but there is also a tradition concerning this psalm preserved in the Arabic Version which gives it the title, " Of David, who spake it for praise on the Sabbath Day when the earth rested ". From many points of view, therefore, we see that the evidence which connects these psalms with the Sabbath is strong, just as that which connects them with New Year's Day is weak.

It is quite clear, as Mowinckel pointed out,[13] that the Coronation Psalms xciii, xcv-xcix deal with the Enthronement of Jehovah, the Judgement which He utters, His fight with the gods of the Under-world. He is both King and Judge because

---
[12] *Studies in the Psalter*, pp. 66-69.
[13] *Ibid.*, SS. 3, 8, 45, 50, etc.

He is Creator. According to Ps. xciii, Jehovah has become king, He has robed Himself in majesty just as the earthly kings put on their royal attire when they take their seat upon their royal thrones, cf. Ahab and Jehoshaphat, 1 Kgs. xxii, 10. He has put on strength as in the ancient time (cf. Isa. li, 9), when He overcame the Monster of the Deep. This feat is connected with His establishing the world so that it cannot be moved. His throne was established from primeval times. The last verses tell how Jehovah was mighty of old, and is still mighty above the waters and the floods. The reference is to the primeval flood of the ancient myth, how Jehovah set a limit to the mighty waters, a limit over which they might not pass. Here also is an example of the tendency to equate the enemies of God and the heathen generally with the waters of the sea.[14] In Ps. xcv the psalmist deals particularly with the deliverance which Jehovah wrought when He rescued His people from Egypt, though here His power is first shown by the fact that He is Creator (verses 3, 5). That is why He is a great God above all gods. Then in the second part of the psalm we get the specific references to the wonders of the Exodus and the journeyings through the desert. Ps. xcvi contrasts the heathen gods, who are things of nought, with Jehovah who made the heavens. Jehovah has become king because He has established the world (verse 10). Because He is Creator and King, therefore He is Judge also. Similar motifs of Kingship, Judge, and Deliverer, are found in Pss. xcvii-xcix.

Mowinckel is certainly on sound ground here, but when he seeks to find the parallel in the Babylonian myth and ritual, he is neglecting a source which is very near to hand. It is true that interwoven with these elements in Ps. xciii, for instance, there are pronounced elements of the ancient Creation-dragon myth. But this is what has happened in Ex. xv, 1-18, where the conclusion is that Jehovah shall reign for ever and ever. This ancient Sabbath Canticle is the *fons et origo* of all the Kingdom of God passages in the Old Testament. Furthermore, in Deutero-Isaiah the association of the Creation-myth, the Kingship of Jehovah, and the Deliverance from Egypt are all three brought into close association with the promised Deliverance from Babylon. There are close

[14] *Studies in the Psalter*, pp. 106 f.

associations between these Coronation Psalms and Deutero-Isaiah.

The Sabbath and the Kingdom of God

We have shown elsewhere that just as Pss. xciii, xcvi-xcix have close associations with the Sabbath Canticle Ex. xv, 1-18,[15] so the other psalms xc-xcii, xciv, and xcv have close association with the other Sabbath Canticle, Deut. xxxii, 1-43. The conclusion to which we are forced is that, whilst undoubtedly there was after the beginning of the second century an ever closer association between Rosh hashShanah and the Kingdom of God, yet before that time, and in the post-exilic period, the association was between the Divine Kingdom and the Sabbath. This would explain, not only the position of Pss. xc-xcix in the Psalter, where they are the first of the liturgical psalms of the Fourth and Fifth Books, and their time-honoured association with Moses,[16] whose two great Songs were Sabbath Canticles from an early date, but also such passages as "They shall delight in thy sovereignty, all those who keep the Sabbath",[17] and the reason given in the Talmud *b. RH* 31a for the choice of Ps. xciii as the Friday Psalm, "He completed His work, and reigned over His Creation."

[15] *Studies in the Psalter*, pp. 62 f.
[16] The first three books of the Psalter are made up from earlier collections, but the last two books are made up, for the most part, of liturgical groups.
[17] *Seder Ram Amram*, i, 29b.

8

NEW YEAR FESTIVALS IN MESOPOTAMIA AND SYRIA

The Three 'Breaks' in Hebrew Religious Development

THE story of the Jewish people has, as we have indicated, three marked points of discontinuity, three occasions on which the development of the people, both religiously and politically, was sharply interrupted, and the whole current of change diverted. The first occasion was the invasion of Canaan, when the nomad Hebrews were introduced to an agricultural civilization dominated by fertility cults. The second occasion was the destruction of Solomon's Temple, when something like a complete break was made with many of the customs and ideas of the past. The third occasion was the destruction of Herod's Temple, when the synagogue alone remained as the centre for Jewry. On each of these occasions we have a change-over into a new environment, followed by conscious and determined efforts to rebuild on a new foundation.

The problem which confronts the student of Hebrew religion is the extent to which in each case the elements of one phase were carried over into the next. These changes are all the more important in relation to the study of ritual, because the ritual necessarily was closely connected with the Temple. Further, the Temple had already become, certainly in theory and probably to a great extent in practice, the one centre for all Hebrew-Jewish rites, and this, before the destruction of Solomon's Temple. Not only so, but we have the problem of the extent of the reforms in the Temple itself of such reforming kings as Hezekiah and Josiah, and, not least important, the evident reversion to more ancient heathen practices during the last days of Solomon's Temple.

To what extent did the fertility rites of Canaan maintain their place at the local shrines, Jerusalem included, when the invading Hebrews began to worship there? To what extent was the pre-exilic cultus of the Jerusalem Temple carried over into the reformed cult of post-exilic days? To what extent did the ideas which were maintained by means of the Temple cultus and traditions find a place in the Temple-less worship of the synagogue in the revision of Jewish prayers of the early second century A.D.?

Our view of the origins of the association of the Kingship of Jehovah and Tishri 1 is that it belongs to the last period, and dates from the troublous times which followed the destruction of the Temple by Titus, that period when loyal Jews prayed ever more insistently for the setting up of the Kingdom of God on earth. We hold that during the third phase, i.e. during the time of the Second (post-exilic) Temple, the prevailing ideas associated with Tishri 1 (Rosh hash-Shanah, as it came to be called) were those of penitence. Whatever the dominant ideas which were carried over into the Tishri feasts from the pre-exilic Feast of Asiph (Ingathering), we hold that the ideas which gravitated to Tishri 1 were those ideas of penitence and reform which are common to all peoples at the turn of the year, summed up in our modern phrases 'turning over a new leaf' and 'making new resolutions'.

Is there anything to be said concerning pre-exilic ideas and rites which belonged to the pre-exilic Old-New Year Feast? Was there any outstanding ritual of pre-exilic days which was abrogated, either in whole or in part, when the great Reformation of post-exilic times took place? We know of most elaborate New Year Festivals in Mesopotamia, extending through the larger part of three millenniums. We have, especially latterly, a considerable amount of detailed information concerning the myths of Syria, made known through the recent (1929) discovery of the Ras Shamra tablets. Did something similar exist in the Israelite cultus of pre-exilic times? And if so, was this carried over, to any marked extent, into the post-exilic cultus?

Mowinckel's Theory of the Coronation Feast of Jehovah

Mowinckel maintained[1] that the origin of the Jewish New Year Festival of Rosh hashShanah was an annual Coronation

[1] *Psalmenstudien* II (Kristiania, 1922).

Feast of Jehovah. Following chiefly in the footsteps of Paul Volz,[2] he maintained that on New Year's Day there was, from a very early date, an annual ceremony in which Jehovah came in procession to His shrine and was enthroned anew. This 'kultisch Thronbesteigungstag Jahwas' was the first day of the pre-exilic Feast of Asiph (Ingathering). In pre-exilic times the Ark, as representing, or actually being in some sense, Jehovah Himself, was carried in procession up to the Temple Mount with great ceremony. There Jehovah was established in His place, and having once again assumed His royal dignity, He proceeded to decide the fate of the coming year. After the Exile, there was an ark-less variant, but in the main the old pre-exilic ideas prevailed. Mowinckel is convinced that there is enough evidence to show that this ceremony was continued in one form or another right down to the last days of the Second Temple. Mowinckel makes no particular use of the synagogue liturgy for Rosh hashShanah, but there are references to this liturgy in Professor S. H. Hooke's Schweich Lectures.[3] Our thesis, which we trust we have demonstrated satisfactorily in previous chapters, is that there is no discernible connexion between the Tishri 1 of pre-Mishnaic times, and the Rosh hashShanah of the days after the Temple had been destroyed. We hold that the association of the Kingdom of God with Rosh hashShanah is a new growth from those days, independent of any early association which there may have been.

Mowinckel actually began his argument with the Coronation Psalms, namely xlvii, xciii, and xcv-c. To these he added a number of other psalms, twenty in number, together with the Exodus Song of Moses (Ex. xv, 1-18), and in a lesser degree, some eighteen others.[4] We have sought to show[5] that it is impossible for Pss. xciii and xcv-xcix to have been used in pre-

---

[2] *Das Neujahrsfest Jahwes* (Tübingen, 1912); for later works see especially Hans Schmidt, *Die Thronfahrt Jahves* (Tübingen, 1927), and, most recently, Ivan Engnell, *Studies in Divine Kingship in the Ancient Near East* (Uppsala, 1943).

[3] *The Origins of Early Semitic Ritual*, pp. 59 f.

[4] The first group are viii, xv, xxiv, xxix, xxxiii, xlvi, xlviii, l, lxvi A, lxxv, lxxvi, lxxxi, lxxxii, lxxxiv, lxxxvii, cxiv, cxviii, cxxxii, cxlix. The second group is lxv, lxvii, lxxxv, cxx-cxxxiv.

[5] See pp. 200 f. above, and *Studies in the Psalter* (1934), pp. 88-109.

exilic times, since they are demonstrably dependent on Deutero-Isaiah. Further there is no particular connexion between these Coronation Psalms and the liturgy of Rosh hash-Shanah.[6] Nevertheless it has been held[7] that, though we have established this particular point, " Mowinckel would still have plenty of evidence for his theory, even if he gave up the Coronation Psalms." The general position is that Mowinckel has not established his case of a yearly accession Feast in Israel.[8] For instance, W. E. Barnes writes[9] that there is no "fact conveyed to us in the Historical Books of the Old Testament" which "will support the hypothesis". But, as Professor S. H. Hooke points out, there is a distinct "cleavage between the early pre-prophetic religion of Israel and the religion which is reflected in the present form of the Pentateuch and in the prophet books".[10] We do not expect to find any definite and specific evidence of what the prophets regarded with abhorrence as a Baal-cult, and must, in the nature of the case, be content with such accidental references as the zeal of the reformers omitted to excise. But whether there is 'plenty of evidence' is another matter. The whole position needs reconsideration in the light of the new material which has become available with the discovery, from 1929 onwards, of the Ras Shamra material. Such reconsideration is the basis of Professor Hooke's Schweich Lectures (*The Origins of Early Semitic Ritual*), and the tendency there to move away from the urban Mesopotamian rites to the agricultural Ras Shamra rites is most marked and, indeed, acceptable. Many scholars who viewed with reserve what seemed to them to be an undue element of 'we may suppose' and 'probably' in the earlier studies, will be much more disposed to view the Myth-Ritual-Pattern theory with sympathy now that it involves comparisons with a similar culture and environment.

[6] See pp. 198 f. above.
[7] Professor N. W. Porteous, *The Kingship of Adonai in Pre-exilic Hebrew Religion*, p. 1. This monograph was originally a paper read before the Society for Old Testament Study in 1938, and was subsequently printed as Lectio No. 3 in a series of such Lectiones by Shapiro, Vallentine and Co.
[8] Cf. Professor S. H. Hooke's reference to the reluctance of Old Testament scholars to accept Mowinckel's theory, *Myth and Ritual*, p. 13.
[9] *The Psalms* (Westminster Commentaries, 1931), vol. i, p. lxxiv.
[10] *The Origins of Early Semitic Ritual*, p. 45.

Babylonian Influence in Palestine

Mowinckel's theory is the outcome of that tendency which has been so marked in recent years to look to Mesopotamia for Hebrew origins, especially in relation to the cultus. This tendency has been most marked in the work of Winckler, Gressmann, and Gunkel. Indeed, there have been occasions, both on the Continent and in this country, when the seal of Babylonian approval has seemed to be necessary in order to secure willing acceptance. Within this acclamation of Babylonian influence our attention has been directed chiefly to the time of Nebuchadrezzar, those last days of Mesopotamian influence and power, and to later times generally, since there has been more material available from these times.

That Palestine is midway between the two ancient centres of civilization of the rivers of Mesopotamia and the river of Egypt must never be forgotten. Still more important is the fact that the highway from one to the other was established long before there was any Persia or Greece or Rome. This highway was through Palestine, or close by its eastern border, so that from time immemorial Palestine was subject to influences from both quarters. We know that there was a time when Egypt exercised some sort of suzerainty over Palestine. This is evident from the story of the campaigns of such warrior Pharaohs as Thothmes III (c. 1501-1447 B.C.), who established Egyptian power in Palestine. There are also the Tell-el-Amarna letters, written from Palestine to Egypt in the time of Amenhotep III c. 1375 B.C., when Egyptian power in Palestine was on the wane. We know also that Egypt was in contact with South-west Asia before 3000 B.C.

On the other hand, the Tell-el-Amarna letters were written in cuneiform, so that this Palestinian-Egyptian correspondence makes it clear that there had been considerable Mesopotamian influence in Palestine long before the fifteenth century B.C. This has been further confirmed by the fact that amongst the languages which have been found at Ras Shamra there are Sumerian and Akkadian, and in addition a North Canaanite language, apparently an ancestor of Phœnician and Hebrew, but written in a hitherto unknown cuneiform script which is alphabetical and not syllabic and ideographic as are

Sumerian and Akkadian. All this evidence of early contact with Mesopotamia is confirmed by the traditions of the Hebrews themselves, which make it clear that the ancestors of the Hebrews came from Mesopotamia, just as it is clear also that Abraham and the other patriarchs had sporadic contacts with Egypt even before the time of the Egyptian bondage. But the contact with Mesopotamia was much more extensive and continued. We know that the Sumerians reached the Mediterranean coast in the time of Lugal-zaqqisi of Erech (c. 2776 B.C.), and that the Semites were there twice during the next hundred years or so, under Sargon in 2750 B.C. and again under Naram-Sin in 2670 B.C., all these dates being some six hundred years or so before the reputed time of Abraham. Further, the evidence of contact with Mesopotamia is shown most clearly in all extant Hebrew, both in the words and in the construction of the language.

The general evidence suggests that the first contacts with Mesopotamia belong to the earlier half of the third millennium, or some earlier period when the idea of cuneiform writing was in a comparatively early stage, sufficiently early for the alphabetical Ras Shamra script to develop independently of the Mesopotamian scripts. It is probable that there was a cessation of Mesopotamian influence for some few hundred years until the migrations from Mesopotamia began c. 2000 B.C., and that apart from nomads who wandered to and fro in the Fertile Crescent, Mesopotamian influence in Palestine (Southern Syria) was limited until the rise of the later Assyrian war-lords. Such influence as there was probably came through Syria, and is shown in those Ras Shamra tablets which are written in Sumerian and Akkadian. Direct Mesopotamian influence on Judah is limited and not earlier than the time of Sennacherib, so far as Assyria is concerned; and not earlier than the time of Nebuchadrezzar so far as Babylon is concerned. Further the Hebrew traditions tell of Abraham's migration as being through Harran, and there is a certain amount of evidence that his sojourn in Harran was prolonged. All this suggests that we must look to North Syria rather than to Mesopotamia for early Mesopotamian influence on Palestinian cults, and directly to Mesopotamia only from the seventh century onwards.

The Myth-Ritual Pattern

In particular, amongst the general Mesopotamian cults, attention has been given to the great New Year Festivals of Mesopotamia, especially of Babylon itself. In this connection considerable prominence has been accorded[11] to the theory of a common Myth-Ritual pattern as underlying all the liturgies and rituals of the Near East, including even those of Egypt. These liturgies and rituals are associated chiefly with the great New Year festivals, and part of the Myth-Ritual-Pattern theory involves the idea that the three feasts of Palestine are remnants of the break-up of an old original New Year Festival, seen at its fulness in the Spring Festival of Babylon.

In our view, much of this work neglects the true canons of criticism. The Graf-Wellhausen theory of the constitution of the Pentateuch has been accepted without question in the realm of Old Testament studies, together with the necessary accompanying theory of development and reformations in the Hebrew-Jewish cultus. It is extraordinary to what an extent the developments and reformations of Mesopotamia have been left out of account. Mowinckel, for instance, makes no attempt to date either his psalms or his Babylonian material, and seems to assume that any evidence from Mesopotamia of whatever date is equally at his disposal for any period of Hebrew history. Indeed, S. A. Pallis complains,[12] and we think with a considerable amount of justification, that the texts published by Zimmern and Thureau-Dangin have not "hitherto been studied with a view to extracting information about the akitu festival", and he adds in a note that "almost all German orientalists who occupy themselves with the Mesopotamian cultures belong to this school", i.e. to the pan-Babylonian school which largely was founded by H. Winckler (1901).

All this is part of the general attitude of modern times which shows itself in the study of the origins of religion. It is to be seen in the assumption of the orthodox Tylor-Frazer school that development of religion can be paralleled all the world over, and that all people have passed through similar stages of development. On this basis they have built up a massive pat-

[11] See p. 193 above.
[12] *The Babylonian Akitu Festival* (Kobenhavn, 1926), p. 9.

tern of world religion, all marshalled into line and all marching in time, adding one element from here and another element from there, largely neglecting the differences in their eagerness to emphasize the similarities. We have given in detail elsewhere[13] one example where Frazer's neglect of the one part of the evidence which showed the essential difference has led him to false conclusions. The instance is his build-up of the theory of the 'divine king', where he argues that even Zeus dies.[14] He neglects the essential fact that this statement is made of Zeus only because he has been equated with the 'low-god' Zan. The whole context is dealing with the Zagrean mysteries of the cult of the Idæan Zeus on Mount Dikte in Crete. This omission is all the more serious because the theory of the 'divine king' plays a large part in the general pattern of primitive religion on which in part the Myth-Ritual-Pattern depends. It is most unfortunate because, from the actual evidence which Frazer produces, the man apparently was killed neither because he was divine, nor because he was a king.[15] Further, the phrase 'divine king' has been used very loosely to cover two quite different and distinct conceptions. It has been used in reference to a set of ideas where the king is supposed to take the place of an actual god in the cult ceremonies. He takes the part of the god in a mimic drama or perhaps in an actual marriage which itself is regarded as having a 'magical' effect on the fertility of the land and nation. It has also been used in reference to another set of ideas, usually more primitive, where the king is not representative of a personal god, so much as the possessor of that supra-human power which belongs to the other world. He has *mana*, and it is because he has this *mana*, showing itself chiefly in his personal fertility, that the nation prospers. Here he is identified not with one personal God, but with general impersonal supernatural power. We hold that the whole attitude which neglects the differences has led scholars into assuming that there is a very great deal more to be said for the Myth-Ritual-Pattern theory than is actually the case.

[13] *The Distinctive Ideas of the Old Testament* (London, 1944), pp. 18 f.
[14] *The Golden Bough* (1900 edition in 3 vols.), vol. i, pp. 1-5.
[15] *Ibid.*, p. 19.

Variations in Mesopotamia

Our knowledge of the New Year celebrations of Mesopotamia is largely confined to "a number of texts all of the late period ".[16] This late period is the time of Nebuchadrezzar, early sixth century B.C., and the days of Babylon's supremacy, when Marduk was the supreme god of the Babylonian pantheon. It is dangerous to assume without careful qualifications that evidence from this period is good for earlier periods elsewhere in Mesopotamia, or even in Babylon itself. We know, for instance, that in the seventh century Asshur-bani-pal abolished the new-month days of Mesopotamia, and it is equally certain that Nebuchadrezzar introduced changes into the ritual. The extent of the seventh-century Assyrian changes can be seen in the variations of the rules for the days of Nisan which Dr. Langdon gives, and also in the rules for the New Year in Teshrit.[17] Not only does he show the differences between the old (tenth-century) Assyrian Calendar and Asshur-bani-pal's Calendar, but he also gives rules which he has culled from other sources, e.g. from Uruk (Erech) and other ancient shrines. These differences are by no means slight. In fact in some cases they are radical. For instance, in the old tenth-century Assyrian Calendar, Nisan 1 was sinister, but in Asshur-bani-pal's calendar it was lucky, whilst in other areas it was 'entirely lucky'. The same is true of Nisan 17 and 21. Many of the days do indeed bear the same character throughout, but often the name of the deity is changed. Either therefore the various deities were worshipped with precisely the same ritual, or the ritual was changed with the name of the god. Indeed, if the day changed from being unlucky to being lucky, the ritual must certainly have been changed, and that radically, since a great deal of Mesopotamian religion was apparently concerned with omens and magical rites, and in these elements the change from unlucky to lucky is fundamental. If these rites had not played a very large part in Mesopotamian ritual, Mowinckel would not have been able to find the evidence which he did find in order to build up his

[16] C. J. Gadd, Essay 'Babylonian Myth and Ritual' in *Myth and Ritual*, p. 47.
[17] *Babylonian Menologies and the Semitic Calendars*, pp. 73-82, 101-104.

theory that the 'workers of iniquity' of the Psalms were actually sorcerers.[18]

Additional evidence of variations are to be seen in connection with the New Year Festivals themselves. What happened at Uruk on the seventh day of Teshrit corresponds to what happened at Babylon on the tenth day of Nisan, and it is evident that the ritual at Uruk was 'of a somewhat different character from that at Babylon'.[19]

The Different Strata of the Babylonian New Year Festival

Most of the great Mesopotamian Creation Epic known as *Enuma elish* has been recovered. This was recited by the high-priest late in the evening of the fourth day of the New Year Festival of Babylon. In the accounts which we have of the festival, there is nothing up to the end of the fifth day 'indicated as happening which could be compared with the story of the Epic. Therefore if the Epic be taken (as it certainly can) for part of the myth connected with the festival, it must refer to happenings which found their place between the sixth and the eleventh (the last) day, for all of which days the ritual is lost'.[20] It is generally supposed, on the basis of a commentary on the rites of the Festival (the text VAT 9555) that there was an acted drama in which Marduk was first slain and then restored to life. This is an incident wholly at variance with the Epic, in which there is not the slightest hint of Marduk's defeat or death. We therefore find the writer having to admit that 'the myth and the ritual do not in this case mutually illustrate each other to the extent we might have expected'.[21] The explanation is to be found in the suggestion that we are dealing with two different strata. In the form in which it is now found, it is no longer a cult text, but is a poetic production detached from the cult, and was recited 'as a powerful magic formula which would exorcize all that is evil'.[22] Further, there are in the poem itself different strata, as illustrated by the two fixings of fate and the varying sense

[18] *Psalmenstudien* I (Kristiania, 1921).
[19] S. A. Pallis, *ibid.*, pp. 127 f.
[20] *Myth and Ritual*, p. 47.   [21] *Ibid.*, p. 47.
[22] S. A. Pallis, *The Babylonian Akitu Festival*, p. 298. See also p. 297.

of the word *shimtu* in the epic.²³ The one 'fixing of the fate' is a purely magical conception by which Kingu, having possession of the tablets of destiny, thereby himself possesses *mana* (i.e. his *shimtu*). The other is the use of the tablets in order to determine the destiny of the following year, so that *shimtu* means the 'destiny' of the coming year. This idea is a later conception, and is far removed from the earlier.

Akitu and the New Year

But the whole Babylonian *akitu* festival itself is a composite festival. It is clear that in sixth-century Babylon the *akitu* festival was the New Year Festival, but was this always the case?

There has been considerable discussion as to the actual meaning of the word *akitu*. The net result of all enquiries is that the attempt to explain the word as a Semitic word must be abandoned. It is probably an old Sumerian word, modified into an Akkadian form. The word is ancient and is found in the third millennium B.C. We know that an *akitu* festival was celebrated at Ga-esh-(ki), at Ur, and probably also at Nippur in the third millennium. The word is found at all periods down to the end of the Mesopotamian civilization.

The chief religious festival of the year was called in Babylon *isinnu zagmuku* or *isinnu akitu*.²⁴ Of these three words, the significance of two of them is clear and certain. The word *isinnu* is good Akkadian for 'periodical festival', and we can safely assume that, perhaps always, but certainly here, it means an annual festival. The word *zagmuku* is the Akkadian form of the old Sumerian ZAG.MU, which means 'head, beginning of year'. The Semitic equivalent is *resh shatti* (in Hebrew *rosh hashShanah*), and, as S. A. Pallis points out, the Semitic translation is often added after the Sumerian loanword. Now it is clear that in the later Babylonian period the word *akitu* is to be interpreted to mean 'new year festival'. This is the case, for instance, in all the Nebuchadrezzar inscriptions, and there is not the slightest doubt that in Nebuchadrezzar's time at Babylon the festival took place in the month Nisan. Thureau-Dangin holds that 'the akitu had not always, so it seems, the character of a new year feast; for it is very probable, as we

²³ S. A. Pallis, *ibid.*, pp. 191-193.   ²⁴ *Ibid.*, p. 11.

shall see [here he refers to p. 111 in his book], that the akitu of Ishtar of Nineveh took place in the month Tebet, and that of Ishtar of Arba-ilu in the month Ab'.[25] We would hold that Thureau-Dangin is right in dating the *akitu* of Ishtar of Arba-ilu in the month Ab, but that the *akitu* of Ishtar of Nineveh was in the month Elul (Ululu). Pallis argues[26] that Thureau-Dangin is not justified in assuming that his references are to *akitu* festivals. Pallis's argument is that when we read of a procession of a deity, it is not essential that it should be an *akitu* procession, since he holds that there were other processions than that of the *akitu*. But the point seems to us to be, not whether there were processions on other occasions, but whether this particular procession, that described in Asshur-bani-pal's Annals (Cyl.B) V, 16 ff., was an *akitu* procession. We hold that this particular festival was actually the *akitu* festival of Ishtar of Arba-ilu. It was *isinnu sharrati*, i.e. 'the yearly festival of the queen of the gods', and it was held in the month of *kakkab qashti*, i.e. the Bow-star. This star is Alpha Canis Major, i.e. Sirius, which in the Assyrian system was the star of Ishtar-Venus. In the time of Asshur-bani-pal it had its helical rising in the month of Ab, and this therefore is the month of the Bow-star. Our argument depends on the following considerations: since we know that each deity was closely associated in the Assyrian astrological-religious system with a heavenly body, the annual high festivals of the deities were necessarily bound up with the movement of the heavenly bodies. For instance, at the Babylonian *akitu* festival in the time of Nebuchadrezzar, towards the end of the fifth day the king and the priest join together in a prayer which opens with the words 'Divine Bull, glorious light which lightens the darkness', this following immediately after their kindling with a torch a bundle of forty reeds.[27] Here we have the festival fixed by the time when the star-equivalent of the deity is at a critical point of the heavens. In this case it is the time when the Sun (Marduk's " star ") crosses the equator on its journey north. This is now known as 'the first point of Aries', but in the far-off days when the prayer was first composed for use at this festival, 'the first point of Aries' was in the next constella-

[25] *Rituels Accadiens* (Paris, 1921), p. 88.   [26] *Op. cit.*, pp. 43-49.
[27] Cf. *Myth and Ritual*, p. 54.

tion, Taurus, the Bull. We thus have the reason for the fixing of the great festival of Marduk in the Spring. This is the *akitu* festival of Marduk the Sun. Similarly we hold that the great annual festival of Ishtar of Arba-ilu was fixed by the time of the helical rising of her star, Sirius, which was in the month of Ab.

The other case which Thureau-Dangin mentioned is the date of the *akitu* festival of Ishtar of Nineveh. The date mentioned in the tablet K 1296[28] is the sixteenth of Tebet. To Pallis, it is 'precisely this exceptional date' which excites his 'just doubts'.[29] We have 'just doubts' also, but on different grounds. Pallis doubts the date as being that of an *akitu* festival because 'otherwise during the Assyro-Babylonian period we always find the *akitu* festival mentioned in connection with Nisan'. Our judgement here is that it is an error to assume that the *akitu* festival necessarily coincided with the New Year festival of the calendar at this comparatively late period, and that is the underlying assumption of Pallis's objection. We doubt the sixteenth of Tebet because there is no astronomical reason for it. The proper date for the *akitu* festival of Ishtar of Nineveh is in the month Ululu (Elul), the sixth month, because this is Ishtar's month,[30] just as Nisan was Marduk's month because the sun was then in Taurus and later in Aries. There is a reference to an Ishtar festival in the Esar-haddon building inscription (K 2711, Rev. 25) in the Kouyunik Collection, and this festival was in the month Ululu. We judge, therefore, that this Ululu festival was the *akitu* festival of Ishtar of Nineveh. We agree with Pallis that there is no reason why the processions, 'the egress of the gods' from their temples, should take place only on the occasion of an *akitu* festival. We imagine that in any temple where there are priests and any organized ritual, there is bound to be plenty of processions, indeed, processions on every possible occasion. Where we part company from him is in his assumption that an undated procession must necessarily be an *akitu* procession in Nisan or not an *akitu* procession at all.

[28] Kouyunik Collection, British Museum.
[29] *Op. cit.*, p. 46.
[30] So the text K 2049, 6. See also Jastrow, *Die Religion Babyloniens und Assyriens*, II, 609; and also the menology in Rawlinson, *Cuneiform Inscriptions of Western Asia* (London, 1861-1884), IV², Pl. 33, 6.

Strack held[31] that *akitu* originally meant 'new-year festival', and that later it came to mean the chief festival of any deity. The evidence, in our view, points exactly the other way. We know that *isinnu* means a regular periodic festival, and we know that *isinnu zagmuku* was the annual new year festival. We know also that *isinnu akitu* means an annual festival of some kind, and that in certain texts these two are equated. There is no evidence at all that *akitu* actually equals *zagmuku*. The two words are not equal either in Sumerian or in Akkadian, i.e. *akitu* cannot be made to equal *zagmuku* etymologically in either language. Our judgement is that originally it meant something else, but came to be equated with *zagmuku* in the development of the cultus. This happened when and where the *akitu* festival coincided with the official new year, i.e. in the last days of Babylon, and earlier also because it was so at Nippur, and it was ultimately the Nippur calendar with its new year in Nisan which triumphed everywhere. We hold therefore that the *akitu* festival was not originally any festival, nor was it necessarily the new year festival. Originally it was the annual high festival of the local deity. In Mesopotamia the date of this high festival was fixed with reference to the heavenly bodies, e.g. the helical rising of the star or some unique position of the sun or the moon. In the case of the sun, the particular and unique position is that which is known as 'the first point of Aries', a time which is most naturally reckoned as the new year in a solar worship environment. It seems to us that, in spite of his claim that the *akitu* festival is the Assyro-Babylonian "New Year's Feast", Pallis is really involved[32] in our position by his note on p. 51, where he says that 'each city god has his *akitu* festival', a comment which he supports with a reference to a text to be found in the Louvre.[33]

The Fixing of the Fate

Arising out of our contention that the *akitu* festival was fixed with reference to the position of the heavenly bodies, and seeing that astrology played a prominent part in Mesopotamian religious cults, it seems to be most probable that the

[31] *Orientalistiche Litteratur-Zeitung* (1905), pp. 375-381.
[32] *Op. cit.*, p. 43.   [33] *Antiquités Orientales* 6463, Obv. 21.

true[34] fixing of the fate for the forthcoming year belongs to the realm of astrology rather than to anything connected with the agricultural year. If this is the case, then the fact that the Hebrews had an idea of a 'change of fortune' at the new year has nothing directly to do with what was done in the Babylonian cultus. Both go back to the same original, but in the Babylonian form we have a new and different association, one which was unknown to the agricultural inhabitants of Palestine, who were not interested in the heavenly bodies.

Astral Mesopotamian Cults

This leads us to what is a fundamental difference between the cults of Mesopotamia and those of Palestine. In the Mesopotamian cults we have a development which is unknown in Palestine, namely the astrological element. In Palestine we have a development from the Tammuz-Adonis fertility cults, these being more suitable to an agricultural environment. There are Tammuz elements in the Mesopotamian cults, and it is in these that the common elements are to be found. But it seems to us to be very much more likely that the Hebrew cult is dependent upon some such cult as we find in the Ras Shamra tablets, and this is the position, for the most part, which is set forth in the later writings of the Myth-Ritual-Pattern School, especially in Professor S. H. Hooke's recent Schweich Lectures on *The Origins of Early Semitic Ritual*.

The King in the Cultus

We should hold it to be very unlikely that the Hebrew-Israelitish kings ever took the part of the god in any ritual ceremony, but that they were regarded as being possessors of *mana* is beyond question. Further it is clear that the well-being of the nation was regarded as being intimately bound up with the well-being of the king. It was a tragedy of the first magnitude that the king should be slain; it meant the quenching of the Light of Israel.[35] We can see also from the

---

[34] I.e. the second reference to the tablets of destiny in the Creation Epic, and the assembly of the gods in the Judgement Hall of Marduk (at Babylon in the sixth century). The first reference belongs to primitive ideas of *mana*, see p. 214 above.

[35] 2 Sam. xxi, 17. Cf. A. R. Johnson, 'The Rôle of the King in the Jerusalem Cultus' in *The Labyrinth* (ed. S. H. Hooke, 1935), p. 73.

story of 1 Kgs. i how important it was for the fertility of the nation that the king should be full of vigour. Whether this particular incident involves us in the idea of a 'sacred marriage' of any particular type, it is not easy to say, since from the story itself the whole incident seems to depend upon the doubt as to the king's sexual vigour. But, if there was some such rite, then it would seem to belong not so much to the type of Mesopotamia where the king definitely represents the god in the sacred marriage, but rather to the type which is portrayed in Naomi Mitchison's *The Corn King and the Spring Queen*, where there is no actual representation of a personal deity. If this is what is meant by the phrase 'divine king', then we have no quarrel with the term when it is used of Israelitish kings. The incident of 1 Kgs. i, however, seems to be much more in line with a custom of our own time, such as is told in H. C. Armstrong's *Lord of Arabia*, where Ibn Saud restored the wavering allegiance of his Arabs by taking a virgin from a neighbouring village, and consummating the marriage there and then, in spite of a deep flesh wound in the thigh. He consummated the marriage in the midst of the camp to show that he was not unmanned, and ordered all the camp to celebrate the occasion.[36]

Parallel Rites

Or again, whilst it is certain that there was actually a ritual combat in the Babylonian ritual, this does not involve a similar rite in Palestine. That the Hebrews knew the ancient Dragon-myth is certain, though the name of the Monster of Chaos is not Tiamat, but Rahab. The fact that the Mesopotamian Tiamat is represented in Hebrew by the depersonalized noun *tehom* (the vasty, primeval deep), shows that the connexion between the two areas is not immediate and direct. On the other hand a connexion between the Tishri festivals and the Mesopotamian rites is to be seen in the foot-race up the altar ramp on the Day of Atonement, a custom which was discontinued because of an accident which once occurred.[37] There was a foot-race in the Babylonian New Year Festival which symbolized the victory of Bel over Zu. But here again

[36] Penguin edition, p. 106.
[37] *Yoma* ii, 1-2, cf. S. H. Hooke, *ibid.*, p. 53.

the differences between the foot-race of Babylon and the scramble of many priests in Jerusalem, and the general intentions of both races, show that there is a marked divergence between the two traditions.

Conclusion

Our conclusion in this matter, therefore, is that the similarities between Mesopotamian ritual and Hebrew rites are not so marked as to involve any direct borrowing during and before the times of the kings. Such association as there is belongs to the distant past, and is confined to fertility rites generally. In Syria we have a development along the lines demanded by a predominantly agricultural community, with Tammuz-Adonis associations prevailing. In Mesopotamia we have an urban development, always inclining away from agricultural habits, with a much more definite pantheon. In Mesopotamia the deities tend to be more separate each from the other. They have their astral associations, and a whole world of astrological lore comes to be introduced. On the other hand in Palestine the tendency is for the ancient *mana* ideas to prevail, and also for fertility cults to prevail, especially the weeping for Tammuz (Ezek. viii, 14), the cult of creeping beasts (verse 10), the worship of the rising sun (verse 16). This latter is the type of cultus which shows most traces in the Old Testament, until the time when the kings who were tributary to Assyria and Babylonia introduced the cults of their overlords, but these new ideas were of comparatively late date, and few of them seem to have survived the exile.

The exile itself led to a new contact with Babylon, and the effect of this is to be seen in the new ideas concerning the Sabbath, in a revival of the ancient Rahab-myth (e.g. Second Isaiah), and in such cult innovations as the introduction of incense. But we find no adoption of Babylonian cult-ceremonies after the pattern which Mowinckel presupposes. The new Israel had a tremendous horror of all such associations, and it is unlikely that any new dramatizations were introduced which in any way allowed the Deity to be represented by mortal man, nor was there any king who could take a rôle anything approaching that which was demanded of the Babylonian kings.

INDEX

(a) OLD TESTAMENT

Genesis.

i, 1-ii, 4a	... ...	119, 151
ii, 2	... ...	123
ii, 4b-iv, 26	... ...	12
ii, 5	... ...	64
iv, 3	... ...	12
iv, 15	... ...	12 n., 115
iv, 23	... ...	115
vii, 2 f. ...	... ...	115
viii, 1 ...	... ...	180
xvii, 12 ...	... ...	117
xix, 23 ...	... ...	60
xxi	... ...	168 f., 171
xxi, 1	... ...	173
xxii	... ...	169, 171
xxii, 13 ...	... ...	169
xxiii, 16 f.	... ...	49 n.
xxvi, 8 ...	... ...	41
xxix, 27	... ...	116
xxx, 22 ...	... ...	168 f.
xxxiii, 3	... ...	115
xxxiii, 19	... ...	49 n.
xxxix, 17	... ...	41
xli	... ...	116
xlv, 6 ...	... ...	85
xlvi, 32-34	... ...	28
xlvii, 3 ...	... ...	28
l, 10	... ...	116, 117

Exodus.

ii, 24	... ...	180
iii, 16 ...	... ...	173
xii, 2	... ...	132
xii, 3 f. ...	... ...	147
xii, 5	... ...	14
xii, 6	... ...	95
xii, 15 ...	... ...	116
xii, 16 ...	... ...	127
xii, 22-27	... ...	14
xii, 27, 29	... ...	15
xii, 40 ...	... ...	95
xiii, 2-16	... ...	15, 24
xiii, 4 ...	... ...	96
xiv, 10-14	... ...	41
xv, 1-18	...	200, 202 f., 206
xv, 18 ...	... ...	177
xvi, 1	... ...	95

xvi, 2 f.	... ...	41
xvi, 23 ...	... ...	122
xvi, 29 ...	... ...	106
xvii, 1-7	... ...	41
xix, 1 ...	... ...	95
xix, 16 ...	... ...	161, 181
xix, 16 ff.	... ...	173
xix, 19 ...	... ...	181
xx, 11 ...	... ...	122
xx, 18 ...	... ...	181
xxii, 29 ...	... ...	14 n., 15 f.
xxiii, 15	... ...	96
xxiii, 16	... ...	56, 58
xxviii, 23 f.	... ...	69
xxxi, 15, 17	... ...	122
xxxii, 1-5	... ...	49
xxxii, 4, 5 f.	... ...	40 f.
xxxii, 20, 27 f.	... ...	41
xxxiv, 18	... ...	96
xxxiv, 22	... ...	53, 56
xxxv, 2 ...	... ...	122
xxxix, 24-26	... ...	69

Leviticus.

i ...	... ...	171, 173
xvi, 31 ...	... ...	121
xix, 23-25	... ...	16
xxii, 27 ...	... ...	14 n.
xxiii, 3 ...	... ...	122
xxiii, 5 ...	... ...	127 n.
xxiii, 11, 15	... ...	124-128
xxiii, 24	...	121, 148, 150, 168 f.
xxiii, 27	... ...	148, 151
xxiii, 32	... ...	121, 130
xxiii, 36	... ...	116, 122
xxiii, 43	... ...	16
xxv, 4 ...	... ...	122
xxv, 9 ...	... ...	132
xxvi, 5 ...	... ...	84
xxvi, 19	... ...	67
xxvi, 42	... ...	179 f.
xxvi, 45	... ...	180

Numbers.

i, 1 ...	... ...	95
iii, 3-10	... ...	170
ix, 1 ...	... ...	95

x, 9	150
x, 10	132, 150, 186
xv, 32-36	106
xxiii, 21	178
xxviii, 10	130
xxviii, 11 f.	41, 132
xxix	159, 169
xxix, 1	150
xxix, 1-6	142, 168
xxix, 7	151
xxix, 35	122
xxxii, 11 f.	41

Deuteronomy.

i, 3	95
v	171, 173
vi, 5	178
xi, 17	64
xvi, 8	122
xvi, 10, 13	116
xvi, 13-15	122
xxvi, 5-11	16
xxviii, 30	71
xxx, 3	75
xxxi, 10	56
xxxii, 1-43	200, 203
xxxiii-xxxiv	151
xxxiii, 5	178

Joshua.

iii, 15	34
iv, 18	34
xxiv, 1	49 n.

Judges.

vi, 4, 11	33
viii, 14	84
viii, 21, 28	97 n.
ix	49 n.
ix, 2, 4	39
ix, 27-29	39, 77
ix, 37-40	34
xi, 40	54
xiv, 12	117
xvi, 7	115
xvi, 17, 19 f.	46, 115
xvi, 22-31	41
xvi, 22	46
xxi, 21	54

1 Samuel.

i, ii	169
i, 3	24, 39
i, 7	40
i, 9-13	39
i, 11-22	171
i, 22-28	56
ii, 6	165
ii, 21-28	171
xii, 17 f.	63
xx, 6	44, 98
xx, 27	96, 98
xx, 34	98, 100
xxiii, 1	33

2 Samuel.

i, 21	64
ii, 14	41
vii	177 n.
xi, 1	32, 59
xiv, 25 f.	45, 77
xiv, 28, 30	76
xv, 2	77 n.
xv, 7	76
xv, 10	77
xv, 12	76
xvi, 21	80
xvii, 19	33
xvii, 20	59
xviii, 9	46
xxiii, 20	52

1 Kings.

i, 1	80, 219
i, 9, 25	79
i, 40, 41	79
ii, 35	48
vi, 1	95
vi, 38	50, 97
vii, 18, 20, 42	69
vii, 21, 22 f.	69
viii	196
viii, 2	25, 37, 46
viii, 37 ff.	175
xi, 28, 29 f.	47
xii, 1, 25	49 n.
xii, 27, 28	49
xii, 28-33	40
xii, 32	25, 47, 100
xiv, 1-18	49
xviii,	66
xviii, 1, 41	67
xviii, 43 f.	115
xx, 22, 26	32
xxii, 10	202

INDEX

2 *Kings.*
iv, 8-37 117
iv, 23 96
iv, 35 115
ix, 1-10 48
x, 19 48
x, 20 122
xi, 4 77
xvi, 9-16 120
xxiii, 8 51
xxiii, 9 48
xxiii, 22 24

Isaiah.
i, 4-9, 10-17 172
i, 12 117
i, 13 122
iii, 18 ... ... 97 n.
vi, 3 191
xii, 3 ... ... 68, 87
xiii, 10 60
xiv, 12 97
xviii, 3 ... ... 162, 181
xxvii, 6 149
xxvii, 13 ... ... 161, 181
xxix, 1 53
xl-lv 36, 200
xl, 2 74
xlii, 13 ... ... 32 n., 59
xliv, 6 178
xliv, 19 82
li, 9 202
lii, 10 36
lxv, 21 f. 71
lxv, 23 130

Jeremiah.
ii, 2 180
iv, 19 161
vii, 11 48
viii, 20 64
xiv, 1 ff. 175
xiv, 2-4 64
xxx, 18 ... ... 75 n.
xxxi, 19 ... 75, 169, 171, 180
xxxiii, 7, 11, 26 ... 75 n.
xli, 1 53
xli, 4 ff. 53
xliv, 15-23 92

Ezekiel.
i-xxvii 131
iii, 12 191

viii, 10 220
viii, 14 ... ... 55, 155, 220
viii, 16 ... ... 91, 220
xvi, 53 ... ... 75, 75 n.
xvi, 60 180
xxiv, 17 131
xxviii-xxxix 131
xxx, 20 131
xxxiii, 4 161
xxxvi, 24-38 ... ... 131 n.
xl-xlviii 131, 133
xl, 1 ... ... 131-3, 139
xlv, 1-8 129
xlv, 18-20 128, 141 f., 144, 146, 150
xlvi, 1-7 ... ... 128 f.
xlvi, 6 ... ... 141 f.
xlviii 129

Hosea.
ii, 11 117
ii, 13 130
ii, 15 72
vii, 5 43
ix, 5 72

Joel.
ii, 1 ... ... 171, 173
iv, 1 75

Amos.
i, 1 95
ii, 8 43
iii, 6 161
iv, 4 51
v, 4 51
v, 21 122
v, 18-20 70
v, 24 82
vii, 1 84
vii, 10-13 50
viii, 5 ... ... 96, 117

Obadiah.
21 178

Micah.
iv, 4 69

Zephaniah.
i, 16 161

INDEX

Zechariah.

vii, 5	157
viii, 19	157
ix, 9	27
ix, 14	182
xiii, 9	165
xiv, 5	95
xiv, 9	178
xiv, 16 f.	63, 176, 188

Malachi.

iii, 1	26

Psalms.

ii	26
ii, 3-5	72
xix	201
xix, 6	59
xxii, 29	178, 198
xxiv, 7-10	178 f., 198
xxix,	200 f.
xxix, 8	174
xxxiii,	201
xxxiv,	201
xli, 13	197
xlvii	36, 174, 195 ff., 199
xlvii, 5	174, 199
xlvii, 5, 6	181
xlvii, 7, 8	199
lxxiv, 15	82
lxxv, 7	59
lxxxi, 3, 4	181, 199
lxxxi, 4	99 ff., 173, 174, 199
xc, xci, xcii	200 f.
xcii	36, 200 f.
xciii, 1	178
xciv	200
xcv-xcix	36, 195 ff., 200 ff.
xcv, 3, 5	198, 202
xcvi, 1-15	151 f., 197 f.
xcvi, 6	63
xcvi, 10	198
xcvii, 1	198
xcviii, 3	36, 199
xcviii, 6	161 f., 181, 198 f.
xcix, 1	198
cii	175
civ, 2	99
civ, 19, 22	59
cv, 8	181, 199
cvi, 1-15	197 f.
cvi, 45	180, 199
cvi, 48	198
cxi, 4, 5	180, 199
cxx-cxxxiv	57, 91, 201
cxx, cxxi, cxxx	175
cxxxv, cxxxvi	201
cxlv	201
cxlvi	201
cxlvi, 10	178, 198
cl	181

Proverbs.

vii, 20	100, 102

Job.

ii, 8	79 n.
viii, 12	83
xlii, 10	74 f.

Canticles.

i-viii	55
vi, 11	83

Ruth.

i, 22; ii, 23	84

Lamentations.

i, 7	130
ii, 14	75

Daniel.

ii, 31	83
xii, 3	165

Ezra.

iii, 11	197
x, 9	63

Nehemiah.

iv, 21	60
viii	151, 173
viii, 18	122

1 Chronicles.

xvi	197 f.
xx, 1	35

2 Chronicles.

v, 13	196
vii, 3	196
vii, 10	100
xx, 21	197
xxi, 2	78 n.
xxiii, 2	78

INDEX

(b) APOCRYPHA AND NEW TESTAMENT

Tobit.
xi, 19 117

Ecclus.
xxxix, 12 113
xliii, 8 97
xlvi, 16 f. 63

Matthew.
xii, 1 106
xxvi, 5 27

Mark.
ii, 43 106
iii, 1-16 106

Luke.
ii, 43 57
vi, 1 106

John.
vii, 2 26

Acts.
xx, 16 27
xxi, 33 27

1 *Cor.*
v, 7 25

Rev.
xv, 3 200

Jubilees.
vi, 23, 25 189
vi, 23-32 133
vi, 36-38 133
xii, 16 165
xv, 1 125
xxviii, 24 168
xlv, 1-5 125
xlix, 1, 16 ... ... 16 n.

(c) JEWISH WRITINGS

MISHNAH

Berakoth.
I, 3 ... ... 179 n.
IV, 1 182

Shebi'ith.
IV, 2 61

Shabbath.
VII, 1 106

Sukkah.
IV, 9 67
V, 1-4 ... ... 41, 86
V, 2, 4 90

Rosh hashShanah.
I, 1a 37
I, 1a-d 149
I, 2c 164
I, 4a 142
II, 5-7 140
III, 4 140
III, 5a 188
III, 5b 140, 170, 179

IV, 5 ... ... 182 f., 187
V, 1-4 86

Ta'anith.
I, 1-III, 8 ... ... 64, 174
I, 2-4 188
II, 2 ff. 175, 182
IV, 8 54

Megillah.
III, 5 168

Menakoth.
VI, 1-10 124

Tamid.
VII, 4 ... ... 162, 201

Middoth.
I, 4 43
II, 3 43

TOSEFTA

Berakoth.
I, 9 191
I, 13 187

INDEX

Shabbath.

| III, 5 | ... | ... | ... | ... 61 |

Sukkah.

| IV, 1 | ... | ... | ... | ... 41 f. |
| V, 2, 4 | ... | ... | ... | ... 90 |

Rosh hashShanah.

I, 12	...	...	...	... 162
III, 3b	...	...	170, 179
IV, 4	...	...	...	... 183
IV, 6	...	...	...	177, 179
IV, 7	...	...	173, 179, 183
IV, 11	...	...	...	... 187

Megillah.

| III, 6 | ... | ... | ... | ... 168 |

Sanhedrin.

| I, 13 | ... | ... | ... | ... 165 |

BABYLONIAN TALMUD

Berakoth.

| 28b | ... | ... | ... | ... 190 |
| 33a | ... | ... | ... | ... 190 |

Shabbat.

35b	...	...	...	... 195
45a	...	...	...	... 61
75a	...	...	...	... 35
86b	...	...	...	160 n.
89a	...	...	...	49 n.
118b	...	...	...	... 61
131b	...	...	...	... 160

Erubin.

| 40a | ... | ... | ... | ... 188 |
| 63a | ... | ... | ... | ... 61 |

Beça.

| 16a | ... | ... | ... | ... 101 |
| 30b | ... | ... | ... | ... 61 |

Mo'ed Qaton.

| 19a | ... | ... | ... | 118 n. |
| 30b | ... | ... | ... | 118 n. |

Rosh hashShanah.

| 4b | ... | ... | ... | 116, 122 |
| 7b, 8a | ... | ... | ... | ... 101 |

10b	...	...	...	... 168
10b, 11a	...	...	...	... 192
11a	...	...	...	... 172
16a	...	17 n., 160, 165, 169
17a	...	...	...	... 169
26b	...	...	...	170, 179
30b	...	...	...	... 174
30b, 31a	...	...	162 n.
31a	...	...	...	162, 203
32a	...	...	...	... 184

Megillah.

| 17b | ... | ... | ... | ... 190 |
| 31a | ... | ... | ... | 168 f. |

Menakoth.

| 65b-68b | ... | ... | ... | ... 124 |

Chullin.

| 15a | ... | ... | ... | ... 61 |

Ta'anith.

| 25b | ... | ... | ... | 183 n. |

JERUSALEM TALMUD

Berakoth.

| I, 2c | ... | ... | ... | ... 60 |
| VIII, 12b | ... | ... | ... | ... 61 |

Sukkah.

| V, 1 | ... | ... | ... | ... 68 |

Rosh hashShanah.

| IV, 7 | ... | ... | ... | ... 187 |

Megillah.

| III, 7 | ... | ... | ... | ... 168 |

Bereshith Rabba.

| ad init. | ... | ... | ... | ... 60 |
| lxx, 8 | ... | ... | ... | ... 68 |

Wayyiqra Rabba.

| p. 29 | ... | ... | ... | ... 101 |

Ruth Rabba.

| iv, 10 | ... | ... | ... | ... 68 |

Ecclesiastes Rabba.

| ix, 7 | ... | ... | ... | ... 165 |

INDEX

Sifre (Num. x, 10).
lxxvii, 19b 186

Sopherim.
xvii, 6 168
xvii, 12 ... ... 187, 192
xviii, 1 ... ... 162 *n.*
xviii, 3 177

Enoch.
lxxv, 2 ... ... 134 *n.*
lxxxiv, 10 ... ... 134 *n.*

2 Enoch.
xlviii, 1 ... ... 134 *n.*

Jubilees.
vi, 23, 25 189
vi, 23-32 133
vi, 36-38 133
xii, 16 165
xv, 1 125
xxviii, 24 168
xlv, 1-5 125
xlix, 1, 16 ... ... 16 *n.*

Seder Olam.
xiv 168

Seder Ram Amram.
l, 296 203

Pirqe de Rabbi Eliezer.
VII 101

Pesiqta Bachodesh.
153a 101

Pesiqta Rabbathi.
39 101

JOSEPHUS

Bel. Iud.
II, xiv, 3 26
III, ix, 5 126
VI, ix, 3 26
VIII, v, 1 28

Ant. Iud.
I, iii, 3 159
III, x, 2 159
III, xii, 6 170
XI, v, 5 159
XVII, ix, 3 27
XX, v, 3 27

(d) PROPER NAMES

Aaron ben Meir 141
Abel und Winckler ... 115
Al-Battani ... ... 81 f., 143
Al-Khwarismi ... 81, 143
Amnon of Mainz 166
Anan the Karaite 125
Armstrong, H. C. 219

Balla, E. 172
Bar Hebræus 100
Barnes, W. E. 207
Browne, G. F. 47
Büchler, A. ... 27 *n.*, 40 *n.*, 149,
167 f., 171, 179, 184, 197
Budge, Sir E. A. Wallis ... 35

Carpenter, S. 158
Caspari, W. 172
Charles, R. H. ... 125, 134

Cook, S. A. 69
Cowley, A. E. ... ... 29, 152 f.

Danby, H. 175
David ben Moses al-Kumasi ... 139
Delitzsch, Fr. ... ... 117 *n.*
Dembitz, E. 192
Derenbourg, A. 192
Dietrich, E. L. 73
Dillmann, A. 182
Doughty 106

Ebeling, E. 107
Edersheim, A. 42
Eerdmann, B. D. 174
Elbogen, I. 189
Engnell, I. 206
Ephraem Syrus 100
Epstein, I. 32

INDEX

Euripides 114
Falkenstein 114
Fiebig, P. 199
Finkelstein, L. 114
Frazer, Sir J. G. 86, 136 ff., 211

Gadd, C. J. 212
Gaster, M. 143, 152
van Gennep, A. ... 19, 117
Gesenius 99
Ginsburg, L. 183
Gray, G. B. ... 25, 58 ff., 89. 126, 131, 165, 174
Greenup, A. W. 90
Gressmann, H. 208
Gunkel, H. ... 12, 119, 208
Gütesmann 28

Hammurabi ... ... 65 f., 145 f.
Harrison, Miss J. E. ... 9, 21, 55 n.
Hertz, J. H. 178, 189
Hesiod 111
Hirsch, E. G. 14, 191
Hollis, F. J. ... ... 92 ff.
Homer 111
Hooke, S. H. ... 17, 18, 20, 21 f., 59 f., 92 f., 193 f., 196, 206 ff.

Ibn Ezra 100, 126
Isa bar Ali 99
Ishmael b. Jochana b. Beroka 135

Jacobs, J. ... ... 27 n.
Jastrow, M. ... 110, 119, 216
Jevons, F. B. 55
Johns, C. H. W. 66
Johnson, A. R. 218

Kehimkar, H. S. ... 154 ff.
Keil, C. F. 52
Kennett, R. H. ... ... 49 f.
Kennicott, B. 78
King, E. G. ... ... 27 n.
King, L. W. 66
Klauber 105
Knudtzon, J. A. ... 105, 115
Kohler, K. 183
Kruspedai (Rabbi) 165

Lagarde, P. ... ... 102 n.
Langdon, S. 18, 29, 31, 72, 83 f., 99, 104 f., 112, 134, 145 f., 211
Levi, D. 166

Loewe, H. 154
Lofthouse, W. F. 129
Lord, J. H. ... ... 154 ff.

Macalister, R. A. S. 62
Mackay, Cameron 129
Maimonides ... ... 42, 164 f.
Mann, J. 32
Margolis and Merx 141
Martianay, J. 100
McClintock, N. F. 139
Meek, T. J. 55
Meinhold, J. 45, 103
Mitcheson, Naomi 219
Montgomery, J. A. 152
Morgenstern, J. ... 32 n., 34 f.
Mowinckel, S. ... 36 f., 67, 72 f., 111 f., 119, 172, 188, 195 ff., 205 f., 213 ff.
Murray, Sir G. 55

Norris, E. 114

Oesterley, W. O. E. ... 190 ff.
Oesterley and Robinson ... 29
Onqelos 127
Ovid 98

Pallis, S. A. ... 134, 145 ff., 193
Pap, L. I. ... ... 32 ff.
Patai, R. ... ... 55 n.
Philo ... ... 107, 113, 159 f.
Pinches, T. G. 112
Pollard, A. F. 134
Porteous, N. W. ... 36 n., 207
Priestley, J. B. 62

Rabinowitz, L. ... ... 27 n.
Rahabi, David ... 156 ff.
Rashi ... 14 n., 40 n., 41, 102, 123
Rawlinson, H. C. 216
Reade, Charles ... 43 n.
Robertson, E. 143
Robinson, H. W. 69
Robinson, T. H. 172
Rowley, H. H. 47, 55 n., 84

Sa'adiyah 30 f., 81 f., 141, 160 ff.
Sadleir, M. ... ... 43 n.
Salem, A. B. 158
Schick, Sir C. 44
Schmidt, H. 206
Schultz, H. 147

INDEX

Seligmann, C. G.	 169	Trollope, A. ...	... 43 n., 91 n.
Skinner, J.	 129	Tylor, Sir E. ...	 210
Smith, G.	 114		
Smith, J.	 129	Ugolini, D. ...	 199
Smith, W. Robertson...	13, 21		
Snaith, N. H. ... 16, 27 n., 36, 152,		Virolleaud, C.	... 112, 134
	197 ff., 211	Volz, P. ...	66, 72, 89, 206
Solomon ibn Gabriol	... 166		
Spencer, Sir B., and Gillen	10 f.,	Wellhausen, J.	... 13 f., 132
	66	Westermarck, E.	 21
Sträck, H. L. ...	... 97, 217	Wetzstein, J. G.	 117
Strehlow, C. ...	 66	Winckler, H. ...	97, 208, 210
		Wittekindt, W.	 55
Thackeray, St. John ... 27 n., 131,		Wright, A. R. ...	 62
155, 167 ff., 173			
Thureau-Dangin, F. ...	215 f.	Zimmern, H. ...	 210
Toy, C. H. ...	 131	Zunz, L. ...	 167

(e) GENERAL

(See also Table of Contents)

Aaronite priesthood ...	49 f., 152	Coronation Psalms	... 36 f., 195 ff.
Abel's offering	... ... 12 f.	Coronation rites	... 75 ff.
Absalom ...	... 45 f., 80	Counting of the Omer	... 124
Adad-nirari III	 70	Court of Israel	 44
Adonijah	... ... 78 f.	Crown, origin of	 46
Akitu festival ...	... 18, 204-217		
Alexander Jannæus ...	... 88	Dagon's feast ...	... ... 41 f.
All-night festival	... ... 42 f.	Dances of virgins	... 54 f., 70
Amidah ... 182 ff., 186, 190 f.		Day of the Lord	... 71-73
Anthesteria	 21	Dedication feasts	... 41 f., 47 f.
Apotropaic rites	... ... 21 f.	Delayed rains ...	 63
Aqiba	162, 182, 192	Disunion of the kingdoms	49 n.
Aramaic calendar	 146	Divine king ...	 211
Ashkenazi rite ...	118, 197, 201	Douai Version	... 74, 75
Asshur - bani - pal's calendar re-			
forms, 20, 99, 105, 120,		Elephantine ...	... ... 28 f.
134, 212		Elijah on Carmel	66 f., 86, 115
Astronomy, Jewish and Muslim		Enuma elish ...	 213
81 f.		Eucharist ...	 25
Atonement, Day of ... 121, 157,			
165 f., 174, 189		Falashas ...	... 125, 128 f.
Australian aborigines	10, 66, 86	Fast of Ab ...	 118
		Fast of Gedaliah	... 157 f.
Bean king ...	 136	Fast of the New Year	... 157
Bethlehem feast	... 114 f.	First-fruits ...	... ... 16 f.
Cain's offering...	... ... 12 f.		
Catchwords ...	 172	Gates of Temple	... 43 f., 91
Change of Fate	... ... 73 f.	Gezer Calendar	... 62, 183-185
Code of Hammurabi...	... 65 f.	Going-out of year	... ... 58 f.
Coronation Feast	... 186, 195 ff.,	Gregorian calendar	 135
	205 ff.	Gula	... 104, 109 f.

INDEX

Hallowe'en	... ...	139
Harvest moon	52, 88 f.,	93, 99
Hillel	... ...	187 f.
Hogmanay	... ...	139
House of water-pouring		... 88 f.
Hyksos	... ...	28
Ilpirra	... ...	10
Intercalary month	...	31, 147 f.
Intichiuma ceremonies		... 10 f.
Ishtar	... ...	216
Jachin and Boaz	...	... 69
Jephthah's daughter	...	... 54 f.
Jeremiah and Shiloh	...	... 48
Julian calendar	...	... 135
Kai-fung-fu Jews	...	158 f., 178
Karaites	29 f., 32, 118 n.,	125, 140
Karkar	... ...	... 70
Kilt	... ...	139 n.
Kouros and Kore	...	... 55
Maççoth	... ...	... 23
Machzor of Aragon	...	166 f.
Machzor Vitry	...	... 169
Manx dress	... ...	139 n.
Marathi	... ...	156 f.
Marduk	... ...	... 65
Mount of Olives	...	... 93
Nebuchadrezzar's reforms	...	18
New-moon days	...	22, 168 f.
New Year superstitions	...	62
Nippur	... 29, 113,	121, 144 f.
Old Lady Day	... ...	... 134
Orion-Sibzianna	...	... 108
Pantomime	... ...	136
Parsees	... ...	155
Passover	13-18, 23, 25, 26	f., 94 f.
Pentecost		125-126, 155
Phœnician months	... ...	83
Psalms, triennial lectionary		26 n.
Purim	... ...	39, 157
Rape of Persephone	...	... 55
Rape of Shiloh	...	... 54
Ras Shamra	...	193 f., 205 ff.

Rechabites	... ...	38
Rest-days	...	104, 105, 107
Rites de passage	...	... 19
Sabbath	103 f., 106,	111, 118
Sadducees	...	31, 125, 127
Samaritans	...	125, 127, 143
		152 f., 164
Samson	... ...	... 41 f.
Samuel, man of prayer		... 63
Sephardi rite	... ...	... 201
Saturnalia	... ...	... 126
Seven	... ...	110-116
Shabattu	...	20 n., 113 f.
Shalmaneser III	...	... 70
Shammai	... ...	187 f.
Shechem	...	... 39, 69, 77
Shiloh priesthood	...	46-49
Shrines, local	... ...	... 36 f.
Shulamith	... ...	... 55
Solomon's accession	...	... 79
Sumerians	...	31, 144 f., 209
Sun-worship at Jerusalem		90-93
Tammuz-Adonis		19, 54 f., 218
Tell-el-Amarna	...	... 208
Temple courts	...	... 43 f.
Tequphah	... ...	34 f., 53
Teshubath hashShanah		32 ff.
Tiamat	... ...	193, 219 f.
Tiglath-pileser III	...	... 71
Tithes	... ...	... 149
Tribal mark	... ...	12 n.
Twelfth-night	...	136-138
Ur	... ...	18, 145, 214
Uruk	...	113 f., 144 f., 212 f.
Variation of seasons	...	... 52 f.
Vegetation gods	...	... 9
Whitsuntide	... ...	125 f.
Wolf-taboo	... ...	136 f.
Wren	... ...	137 f.
Zadokites	...	47 f., 152 n.
Zagmuk	... ...	134 f.
Zagrean mysteries	...	... 211
Zan	... ...	... 211
Zebach	... ...	... 39 f.

www.ingramcontent.com/pod-product-compliance
Lightning Source LLC
Chambersburg PA
CBHW052339230426
43664CB00041B/2487